PUBLISHED ON THE
KINGSLEY TRUST ASSOCIATION PUBLICATION FUND
ESTABLISHED BY THE
SCROLL AND KEY SOCIETY OF YALE COLLEGE

AUTHOR OF
"THE MAN CHARLES DICKENS"
"JENNY LIND"
"A GUIDE TO BERNARD SHAW"
ETC.

Mark Twain

Mark Twain

THE MAN
AND
HIS WORK

By Edward Wagenknecht

New Haven
YALE UNIVERSITY PRESS
LONDON · HUMPHREY MILFORD · OXFORD UNIVERSITY PRESS
1935

For

DOROTHY

. . . *this book and all besides*

ACKNOWLEDGMENTS

THROUGH the kind offices of Mr. Albert Bigelow Paine, the generosity of Harper & Brothers, publishers, and the courtesy of Mr. Charles T. Lark, attorney for the Mark Twain Estate, I have been permitted to quote freely from Mark Twain's own writings, from Mr. Paine's books about him, and from other volumes on the Harper list. No publishers could have been more generous than the Harpers, and Mr. Paine has been the godfather of my whole enterprise. Without his encouragement in the first place, I should never have undertaken a book about Mark Twain. He has been a fine friend, a discriminating critic, and a tower of strength to me, every step of the way.

Besides Harper & Brothers, the following publishers and copyrightholders have given permission to quote from the sources indicated. To all I offer my warmest thanks.

AMERICAN ACADEMY OF ARTS AND LETTERS, New York. (Joseph H. Twichell's address in the *Report of the Public Meeting under the Auspices of the Academy and the National Institute of Arts and Letters Held at Carnegie Hall, New York, November 3, 1910, in Memory of S. L. Clemens.*)

ATLANTIC MONTHLY PRESS, Boston. (*Memories of a Hostess*, by M. A. DeWolfe Howe.)

THE AMERICAN REVIEW, New York. ("Mark Twain in Clubland," by William H. Rideing, *Bookman*, XXVI; "When They Were Twenty-One," by Bailey Millard, *Bookman*, XXXVII.)

NICHOLAS L. BROWN, New York. (*Abroad with Mark Twain and Eugene Field*, by H. W. Fisher.)

COWARD-MCCANN, INC., New York, and Mr. Arthur Leonard Ross, attorney for the Frank Harris Estate. (*Contemporary Portraits*, Fourth Series, by Frank Harris.)

THOMAS Y. CROWELL CO., New York, and Mrs. Lucy Lockwood Hazard. (*The Frontier in American Literature*, by Lucy Lockwood Hazard.)

CROWELL PUBLISHING CO., New York. ("Painting the Portrait of Mark Twain," by S. J. Woolf, *Collier's*, XLV.)

DOUBLEDAY, DORAN & CO., INC., New York. (*Life in Letters of William Dean Howells*, edited by Mildred Howells; *Midstream*, by Helen Keller; *The Spirit of American Literature,* by John Macy; *Many Celebrities and a Few Others,* by William H. Rideing; *Marse Henry,* by Henry Watterson.)

DUKE UNIVERSITY PRESS, Durham, N. C. ("Mark Twain Juvenilia," by Minnie M. Brashear, *American Literature,* II.)

E. P. DUTTON & Co., INC., New York, and J. M. DENT & SONS, LTD., London. (*The Ordeal of Mark Twain,* by Van Wyck Brooks.)

HARCOURT, BRACE & Co., New York, and the respective authors named. (*A Lifetime with Mark Twain,* by Mary Lawton; *Main Currents in American Thought,* by Vernon Louis Parrington; *American Humour,* by Constance Rourke.)

HENRY HOLT & Co., New York. (*Out of My Life and Thought,* by Albert Schweitzer.)

HOUGHTON MIFFLIN Co., Boston. (*The Education of Henry Adams; Crowding Memories,* by Mrs. Thomas Bailey Aldrich; *Life and Letters of John Burroughs,* by Clara Barrus; *American Portraits, 1875–1900,* by Gamaliel Bradford; "Waiting," a poem, by John Burroughs; *A Golden Age of Authors,* by W. W. Ellsworth; *Life and Letters of Joel Chandler Harris,* by Julia C. Harris.)

HOWELL, JOHN, San Francisco. (*Sketches of the Sixties,* by Bret Harte and Mark Twain.)

IOWA JOURNAL OF HISTORY AND POLITICS, The State Historical Society, Iowa City, Iowa. ("Mark Twain in Iowa," by Fred W. Lorch, *Journal,* XXVII.)

LITTLE, BROWN & Co., Boston, and the respective authors. (*Mark Twain's America,* by Bernard DeVoto; *Remembered Yesterdays,* by Robert Underwood Johnson.)

THE MACMILLAN Co., New York. (*Memories of a Southern Woman of Letters,* by Grace King.)

A. C. McCLURG & Co., Chicago. (*Mark Twain and the Happy Island,* by Elizabeth Wallace.)

MISSOURI HISTORICAL REVIEW, State Historical Society, Columbia, Missouri, and the author. ("The True Character of Mark Twain's Wife," by Cyril Clemens, *Review,* XXIV.)

NORTH AMERICAN REVIEW, New York. ("A Defence of General Funston," by Mark Twain.)

OUTLOOK PUBLISHING Co., New York. ("Mark Twain as a Newspaper Reporter," by Frank M. White, *The Outlook,* XCVI, 1910.)

G. P. PUTNAM'S SONS, New York. (*Talks in a Library,* by Laurence Hutton.)

SATURDAY REVIEW OF LITERATURE, New York. ("Prophet, Pedant, and Pioneer," by Lewis Mumford, *Saturday Review of Literature,* IX.)

CHARLES SCRIBNER'S SONS, New York. (*The Americanization of Edward Bok; A Roving Commission,* by Winston S. Churchill; *The Main Stream,* by Stuart Sherman.)

TENNESSEE HISTORICAL ASSOCIATION, Nashville, Tennessee. ("Mark Twain, Southerner," by A. V. Goodpasture, *Tennessee Historical Magazine,* Ser. II, Vol. I.)

UNIVERSITY OF NORTH CAROLINA PRESS, Chapel Hill, N. C. (*Mark Twain, Son of Missouri,* by Minnie M. Brashear.)

A. P. WATT & SON, London. (*From Sea to Sea, Letters of Travel,* Pt. II, by Rudyard Kipling.)

In addition to the foregoing obligations to publishers, I am indebted as follows.

The Henry E. Huntington Library and Art Gallery, San Marino, California, permitted me to quote from Mark Twain's unpublished letters to Mrs. A. W. Fairbanks and others, in the Huntington Library. These quotations from unpublished sources have also been approved, in behalf of the Mark Twain Estate, by Mr. Paine.

Miss Patricia M. Willson, of Hartford, Connecticut, Mr. Harry Earl Jones, of San Diego, California, and Mr. Harold von Arx, of Flushing, New York, have all looked up material for me in their respective parts of the country. I had no shadow of a claim on any of them, and I am more grateful to them than I can say. Miss Willson was particularly generous of her time and energy; in fact her interest in my book could hardly have been greater if it had been her own.

Three special students of Mark Twain who have been very kind to me are Professor Minnie M. Bashear, of the University of Missouri, Professor Henry A. Pochmann, of Mississippi State College, and Professor Olin H. Moore, of Ohio State University.

My friend, Professor Ottis B. Sperlin, of the University of Washington, read the manuscript at my request and made many helpful suggestions. So did Mr. Eugene A. Davidson, of the Yale University Press.

When I was just beginning my investigations, the following publications carried a letter of mine in which I asked those who had something to contribute to get in touch with me: *The New York Times Book Review, Books, The Boston Evening Transcript, The Saturday Review of Literature,* and *American Literature.* I am grateful to the editors and to my many correspondents. It is impossible to name all of them, but I must not omit Professor Thomas Ollive

Mabbott, Mr. William R. Langfeld, Mr. R. A. Barry, Mr. Russell Lord Tarbox, Mr. Maynard Shipley, Mr. E. W. Evans, Jr., Mrs. S. R. Block, and Mr. Purd B. Wright. My thanks are due also to Mr. Willard S. Morse, of Santa Monica, California.

I regret that *Mark Twain's Notebooks,* edited by Mr. Paine, and the new edition of Merle Johnson's *Bibliography of Mark Twain,* announced for fall publication, are appearing too late to permit me to draw on them for this book.

The portrait of Mark Twain which appears as a frontispiece to this volume is from an etching by Mr. Otto J. Schneider of Chicago, Illinois, and is used here by his kind permission.

E.W.

August 19, 1935.

CONTENTS

I. MARK TWAIN

II. MR. SAMUEL L. CLEMENS

III. THE SAGE OF REDDING

No life is more than half-explicable, even to him who lives it and reflects upon it, and although psychological observation is doubtless one of the oldest amusements of the race, progress in the technique of analysis will probably not remove the risks attendant on it. Those who . . . had rather be safe than sorry may very well let psychological interpretation alone. When they deny the method to others, however, they are smugly attempting to make their own temperament a final criterion.

LEWIS MUMFORD.

I
MARK TWAIN

CHAPTER I

The Matrix

"I put it together out of my own life."

CHARLES RANN KENNEDY: *The Idol Breaker.*

I

MARK TWAIN was an actor who appeared beneath the proscenium arch of the heavens in many different rôles. He was Tom Sawyer (with a touch of Huckleberry Finn); he was Colonel Sellers; he was the Connecticut Yankee; he was Joan of Arc. As Tom Sawyer he spent his youth "drowsing in the sunshine of a summer morning . . . the great Mississippi, the magnificent Mississippi rolling its mile-wide tide along; . . . the dense forest away on the other side"; and many years after, his remembrance of things past made it possible for him to preserve as literature one of the most wonderful aspects of the development of America. As Colonel Sellers, he dreamed mighty dreams of power and glory, dreams of fabulous riches that were to come rolling in upon him, first from the Tennessee land, then from that marvelous typesetting machine of James Paige in which he was to sink a fortune, but always mixing on his palette the colors of fact and the colors of hope until, at last, when old age was upon him, he could remember only the things that had never happened. As the Connecticut Yankee, he first vaunted his Americanism against the old culture and the old corruptions of Europe, attacking with leather-lunged frontier laughter everything that the frontier could not understand; then, widening his scope, he began to think in broadly human terms, assailing selfishness and oppression everywhere, himself gone "grailing" in behalf of a loftier dream than ever King Arthur knew. Finally, as Joan of Arc he became the em-

bodiment of the very chivalry and idealism he had sometimes
been wont to deride.

A mighty figure and an impressive one upon our horizon, a
figure destined for a permanent place in the American mythology—and these were the mighty rôles that he played. I have
called him an actor, and I do not degrade him, for in the larger
sense all creative artists are actors, whatever their special me-
dium may be. Shakespeare creates his characters by the simple
expedient of permitting them to talk themselves alive. Dickens
verifies in his own person the experiences and the emotions of
those whom he brings to us. The prophet Ezekiel is not satisfied merely to declare his message; he must make a drama of it
and act it out. And Jesus of Nazareth himself has been distinguished from other great religious teachers on this very score.
Not merely the herald of his gospel, he was the gospel, and he
reached the supreme height of his self-expression not when he
uttered the words of the Sermon on the Mount but as he hung
on the cross at Golgotha.[1]

In other words, when we speak of a man's art as essentially
histrionic, we intend, or should properly intend, to convey exactly the opposite idea from what the term connotes in the
mind of the average reader. The actor uses himself as the instrument upon which he would play. He is the embodiment of his
own message. He takes upon himself that which he would represent, becomes the incarnation of his own idea. The process is
essentially mystical, creative, and only the mystic can truly understand it. The great characters of fiction are built from the
inside out. Popular demand has not called them into being, nor
do they conform to the types favored by this magazine or by
that publisher. They are so many emanations of the man that
created them; and the life that informs them, as they go about
their business in the world, is his life. Only by life can life be
created. The law holds in biology; it holds also in art.

All these things are true in a peculiarly intimate sense of
Mark Twain. Among the greater writers of the world, I know
of none who is closer to his material or whose success is more

directly dependent upon his ability to assimilate it. This accounts, on the one hand, for his extraordinary vividness when he is at his best; on the other, for the many absurdities he perpetrated when he wandered out of his proper field. To be sure, he is not unique in this. Even the great Sir Walter, king of all British novelists, was completely successful only in books like *The Heart of Midlothian* where he was able to make the fullest possible use of native materials, and as he traveled farther and farther away from home he became less and less convincing. Nevertheless Scott had the ability to "project" himself much farther than Mark Twain ever could. There is an intermediate stage, we may call it, in the creative process that the American seemed never quite able to master. For this reason, there is a special justification, as his centenary approaches, for studying him as he is studied in this book, for using every means at our disposal to achieve an analysis of the man, to penetrate as best we can to the hidden places where he lived his secret life. It is all very well to say that we are not concerned with the life of a man of genius but only with his works. So, essentially, we are. But if his life and his works are one—what then?

II

IT was fortunate for such a writer that he should have lived through a very wide variety of experiences, and we may say of Mark Twain that life groomed him for the business of authorship as she has groomed few Americans. It would be difficult to improve upon his own summary of his qualifications in a letter of 1891:

". . . . I confine myself to life with which I am familiar when pretending to portray life. But I confined myself to the *boy*-life out on the Mississippi because that had a peculiar charm for me, and not because I was not familiar with other phases of life. I was a *soldier* two weeks once in the beginning of the war, and was hunted like a rat the whole time. My splendid Kipling himself hasn't a more burnt-in, hard-baked, and unforgetable

familiarity with that death-on-the-pale-horse-with-hell-follow-
ing-after, which is a raw soldier's first fortnight in the field—
and which, without any doubt, is the most tremendous fortnight and the vividest he is ever going to see.

"Yes, and I have shoveled silver tailings in a quartz-mill a
couple of weeks, and acquired the last possibilities of culture in
that direction. And I've done 'pocket-mining' during three
months in the one little patch of ground in the whole globe
where Nature conceals gold in pockets—or *did* before we
robbed all of those pockets and exhausted, obliterated, annihi-
lated the most curious freak Nature ever indulged in. There are
not thirty men left alive who, being told there was a pocket
hidden on the broad slope of a mountain, would know how to
go and find it, or have even the faintest idea of how to set about
it; but I am one of the possible 20 or 30 who possess the secret,
and I could go and put my hand on that hidden treasure with a
most deadly precision.

"And I've been a prospector, and know pay rock from poor
when I find it—just with a touch of the tongue. And I've been
a *silver* miner and know how to dig and shovel and drill and
put in a blast. And so I know the mines and the miners interi-
orly as well as Bret Harte knows them exteriorly.

"And I was a newspaper reporter four years in cities, and so
saw the inside of many things; and was reporter in a legislature
two sessions and the same in Congress one session, and thus
learned to know personally three sample bodies of the smallest
minds and the selfishest souls and the cowardliest hearts that
God makes.

"And I was some years a Mississippi pilot, and familiarly
knew all the different kinds of steamboatmen—a race apart,
and not like other folk.

"And I was for some years a traveling 'jour' printer, and
wandered from city to city—and so I know *that* sect familiarly.

"And I was a lecturer on the public platform a number of sea-
sons and was a responder to toasts at all the different kinds of
banquets—and so I know a great many secrets about audiences

—secrets not to be got out of books, but only acquirable by experience.

"And I watched over one dear project of mine for years, spent a fortune on it, and failed to make it go—and the history of that would make a large book in which a million men would see themselves as in a mirror; and they would testify and say, Verily, this is not imagination; this fellow has been there—and after would cast dust upon their heads, cursing and blaspheming.

"And I am a publisher, and did pay to one author's widow (General Grant's) the largest copyright checks this world has seen—aggregating more than £80,000 in the first year.

"And I have been an author for 20 years and an ass for 55."

This characteristic statement calls for some comment and amplification.

Samuel Langhorne Clemens was born in the village of Florida, Monroe County, Missouri, on November 30, 1835. When he was four years old, the family removed to Hannibal, in Marion County, on the banks of the Mississippi.

"Circled with bluffs" and "the shining river in the foreground"[2]—the river that was the highway of the nation, the river whose great historian he was to become—Hannibal, on its physical side, became, in *Tom Sawyer* and in *Huckleberry Finn*, a part of the literature of the world. Mark Twain gives us the Missouri countryside also, notably in those magnificent passages in the *Autobiography* where he describes his summers on the farm of his uncle, John Quarles, near Florida. Not even "The Eve of St. Agnes" is richer in sense-impressions than those descriptions. But when we come to deal with immaterialities it is not so easy to know how to describe Hannibal. During recent years, Miss Minnie M. Brashear, the Reverend C. J. Armstrong, and other writers have been making it increasingly clear to us that the place can no longer be thought of in terms of the simple frontier town we once envisaged.[3] A good many families, like Mark Twain's own, had come from the South originally, and they brought something with them in the way of background and tradition. The town seems distinctly to have been interested in culture. Indeed, as Miss Brashear observes, it "had a more distinctly literary atmosphere than towns in Missouri have today." Marion County had 10,000 inhabitants by 1840, including 1,500 slaves. There were twenty-four primary and common schools with a total enrollment of 648. As early as 1835, the year of Mark Twain's birth, Palmyra, the county seat, had a thriving newspaper, a female seminary, a church, and regular stage connections with other towns. Marion College (Presbyterian) had begun as early as 1831. The school got off to a good start, even establishing a branch twelve miles off to the southwest, but its fortunes began to decline with the discovery that its leading spirits were militant abolitionists, and the hard times of 1837–40 put an end to it. Hannibal had only 450 inhabitants when Mark Twain came there in 1839, but it had grown to 3,000 by the time he left, fourteen years later, and was the second city in the state. Carriages, wagons, omnibuses, river boats, and flour were manufactured there. Baptist, Christian, and Episcopal churches existed, and there were two each of the Presbyterian and the Methodist persuasions. The Hannibal Female Academy was open; the Marion Female Academy was housed in the Christian Church; the Reverend Daniel Emerson's English and Classical School held its sessions in the First Presbyterian Church. There were five newspapers, three bookstores, and a public library in which Mark Twain's older brother Orion was a shareholder. Hannibal papers advertised extensively the better British and American magazines, the *Daily Journal,* of March 22, 1853, offering a special rate for a combination subscription to the *London, Edinburgh, Westminster,* and *North British* quarterlies, and to *Blackwood's Magazine.* "Fillers" drew freely upon the classics and the standard English writers, those of the eighteenth century being particular favorites. Mark Twain was not quite the child of the wilderness he has sometimes been represented to have been.

Little sympathy existed at any time between Mark Twain and his father—Virginia born, lawyer by profession and mer-

chant by necessity. The judicial mind could not quite comprehend the nervous imaginative boy. Miss Brashear has argued
convincingly,[4] however, that for this very reason, Mark Twain's
few references to John Marshall Clemens do not mete out to
him the justice that was his due. He was a business failure on
the Missouri frontier, but he possessed unusual qualities in the
way of probity and intelligence. The son's debt may well have
been larger than he ever knew.

With the mother it was a very different matter. Her temperament was Mark Twain's temperament, and her influence can
be seen upon him at every turn. It was not necessarily so nar-
rowing an influence as some writers would have us believe.
Jane Lampton Clemens was Calvinistic, but she did not spend
all her time reading the *Institutes*. She was an intensely social
being—in her youth, a Kentucky belle devoted to dancing. At
one period she had smoked a pipe. From her, Mark Twain inherited many specific tastes and tendencies—his love of the
color red, his tenderness toward all animals, especially cats, his
quick, impulsive emotion, his life-long habit of protecting the
outcast and the unfortunate. She had his curiosity also. In her it
took the special form of investigating strange religions, which
she considered carefully, but without committing herself to
them. She was capable of great indignation and of dauntless
courage. Mark Twain tells us how, on one occasion, when a
burly Corsican pursued his daughter through the streets with a
rope, everybody made haste to get out of his way except Jane
Clemens. Jane opened her door wide to the fugitive, then
planted herself in it, defiant and unashamed, and gave the brute
such a dreadful tongue-lashing that he never ventured to disturb Hannibal's peace again. From his mother Mark Twain inherited his habit of quite innocently mingling fact and fiction.
One of her favorite yarns was the story of how her daughter
Pamela had been captured by Indians, which was an excellent
narrative except that the adventure had never taken place. Like
him, too, she was unconventional, as when she heard two men
arguing about where Mark Twain was born and abruptly broke

in to tell them. "I'm his mother," she said. "I ought to know. I was there." Something of his cryptic gift of phrase was hers also, as shown in her remark, "Never learn to do anything. If you don't learn you'll always find someone else to do it for you."

Fifteen months after his father's death in 1847, Mark Twain started five years of work as a printer in Hannibal; then he set out on his own for eastern parts, spending a year in Washington, Philadelphia, and New York. Afterwards he worked for a time at Orion's printing establishment in Keokuk, Iowa, stayed for a little while in Cincinnati, and then started out for South America. But a meeting, in New Orleans, with Horace Bixby changed his plans, and he apprenticed himself instead to "the stupendous task of learning the twelve hundred miles of the Mississippi River between St. Louis and New Orleans—of knowing it as exactly and as unfailingly, even in the dark, as one knows the way to his own features." Within eighteen months he had become one of the best pilots on the river, and he continued at this trade until the Mississippi was closed to peaceful activities by the outbreak of the Civil War in 1861.

The Mississippi period has a glamor all its own in Mark Twain's life, and it lived always in gorgeous colors in his memory. It was at this time that he really established his independence, proved for himself and for others that he was a man fitted to do a man's work in the world, for the Mississippi pilot was king of all that he surveyed, and he earned what was, for that time, and for a young man with Mark Twain's background, a great deal of money. "When I find a well-drawn character in fiction or biography," he was to write in later years, "I generally take a warm personal interest in him, for the reason that I have known him before—met him on the river." Yet it is likely that he exaggerated the importance of the Mississippi period somewhat, for the more we learn of his Hannibal and Keokuk days, the more deeply do his roots seem to sink into that soil. Nostalgia informs *Life on the Mississippi,* and the pathos of distance hovers around it. The coarser, harsher aspects of steamboat life, in an age of cutthroat competition and easy indulgences, are passed over altogether; a tired man is trying to recapture his lost youth.

Some students of Mark Twain are of the opinion that it was as a pilot that he really found himself, adjusting himself to life, experiencing a satisfaction which not even his later trade of authorship, as he practiced it at least, could ever give him. There are times when Mark Twain himself supports this opinion. "I am a person who would quit authorizing in a minute to go to piloting," he writes Howells in 1874, "if the madam would stand it." But he is writing under the spell of the enthusiasm he has experienced in going back to the river, in his imagination, for his Mississippi articles: it is authorship that has inspired him even while he eagerly disclaims all interest in it! As a matter of fact, we know that he did not return to piloting after the war, even when he had an opportunity to do so. "Do not tell any one that I had any idea of piloting again at present—" he writes his sister from California in 1862, "for it is all a mistake. This country suits me, and—it *shall* suit me, whether or no. . . ." Mining did not suit him really, but when he gave it up, he went on to journalism, not back to steamboating. The truth of the matter is that the pilot's life, though ideally calculated to serve Mark Twain's needs at a critical period in his development, could never have absorbed him permanently. In his old age he used to have nightmares in which he was haunted by the horror of being obliged to go back to the river for bread.

It was during his pilot days, also, that Mark Twain experienced the first great sorrow of his life. In 1858, his adored younger brother, Henry Clemens, drawn to the river by Sam's success, lost his life as the result of injuries sustained in the horrible *Pennsylvania* steamboat disaster. Sam blamed himself, and life was never quite the same again.

In 1861 the Civil War was not taken too seriously in Missouri. Mark Twain's connection with it was of the briefest and most casual description. No doubt "The Private History of a Campaign That Failed" is largely in the burlesque mood. Nevertheless the fact remains that, after a brief period, Lieutenant Clemens mustered himself out of Confederate service, and went to Nevada with his brother Orion, a staunch Union man, whom President Lincoln had newly appointed Secretary of the Territory.

The journey is described in *Roughing It.* Now Mark Twain enters upon his various mining activities, coming in touch with many different aspects of Western life. He had drifted to Aurora, California, and was poor indeed in this world's goods, when the opportunity came, late in the summer of 1862, to take a place on the staff of the Virginia City *Enterprise,* a paper edited by Joe Goodman in an atmosphere of frontier irresponsibility and Bohemian camaraderie, flavored with a good deal in the way of sound literary taste and judgment. Here he first used the name Mark Twain; here he began to build up his West Coast reputation. In those days the journalistic hoax was still his favorite type of humor, and the consequences were not always pleasant. The results of one affair involved a precipitate retreat to San Francisco, where he found a somewhat uncongenial berth on the *Morning Call.* From San Francisco, too, in the course of time, he found it prudent to retreat, but the circumstance, on this occasion, was wholly to his credit. He had been too frank in his criticism of the corrupt San Francisco police department. For three months he lived in Calaveras County where, with Jim Gillis, he tried pocket mining, on Jackass Hill. In 1865, Artemus Ward, whom he had met in Virginia City, wrote to ask for a sketch to be included in a new book of humor. Mark Twain sent a story which he had heard in the California mining camps—a rather stupid story, he thought it— about a jumping frog. Arriving too late to be included in the book, "The Jumping Frog" appeared instead in the *Saturday Press,* November 18, 1865, and "Mark Twain" promptly became a name to conjure with along the Atlantic seaboard.

In 1866 the Sacramento *Union* sent Mark Twain to the Sandwich (or, as we now call them, the Hawaiian) Islands; while there he brought his paper a "scoop" in the form of an exclusive interview with the survivors of the *Hornet* disaster, in which interest was very keen at the time. During the same year he made his initial contribution to *Harper's Magazine* on the same subject. After returning to the Coast, he gave his first lectures. In December, 1866, he went East, as he supposed, for a visit. Unexpectedly he lectured at Cooper Union. Still more unexpectedly, he sailed, in June, 1867, on the *Quaker City* Mediterranean steamboat excursion, writing for the *Alta Californian* the series of travel letters that, very soon, in the form of *The Innocents Abroad,* were to make him the most famous humorist of his time. It was indeed a momentous voyage, for both his personal and his professional future were decided by it. One day, in the Bay of Smyrna, one of his fellow passengers, a wealthy young man of Elmira, New York, named Charles Langdon, showed him a miniature reproduction of the face of his sister Olivia. Mark Twain promptly fell in love with that face, and he never saw another woman as long as he lived. In July, 1869, *The Innocents Abroad* was published, and on February 2, 1870, Samuel L. Clemens and Olivia Langdon were married.

Now begins a new phase in the development of Mark Twain. He has known Hannibal, the Mississippi, the mining camps and the newspaper offices of the Far West; now he is plunged into the world of eastern respectability and convention, a social order in which he feels himself an intruder, which in some of its aspects he scorns, yet which, contradictory as he is, he passionately aspires to fit himself into. His first business venture did not turn out well. Successful as the *Innocents* had been, it did not yet occur to him that he could rely for a livelihood upon authorship alone: he bought an interest in the Buffalo *Express.* The first months of marriage were clouded by sickness and the death of Mrs. Clemens' father; by the end of 1871, Mark Twain had pulled out of the *Express* and moved to Hartford, Connecticut. In Hartford, in 1872, his first child, Langdon—born in Buffalo—died, and in the same year *Roughing It* was published.

The years 1872 and 1873 were spent largely in England, lec-

where he lived after his marriage)

turing, being entertained, and laying the foundations of a later world fame. In ~~1874~~, in Hartford, he built ~~the~~ a big house, overlooking a wooded ravine, that was to be the home of the Clemens family for seventeen happy years. During this period, the summer months were spent at Quarry Farm, ~~near Elmira, the home of Mrs. Clemens' sister,~~ and here, in an open-air hilltop study, much of Mark Twain's best writing was done. During these years, too, he extended his business interests, developing the fatal tendency toward unwise investments that led finally to his business collapse. In 1873 he published, with Charles Dudley Warner, a Hartford neighbor, his first extended piece of fiction, *The Gilded Age*. In 1876 came *The Adventures of Tom Sawyer*. A trip to Europe yielded *A Tramp Abroad* in 1880. *The Prince and the Pauper,* a serious historical juvenile, came out in 1881. In 1883 *Life on the Mississippi* appeared, and was followed a year later by *The Adventures of Huckleberry Finn*. In 1889 came an earnest, extended satire, *A Connecticut Yankee in King Arthur's Court*.

In 1891, sorely harassed by financial difficulties, Mark Twain closed his Hartford house—closed it forever, though he did not know it at the time—and moved with his family to Berlin. The long struggle ended in 1894 with the failure of Charles L. Webster and Company, which left Mark Twain nearly one hundred thousand dollars in debt. Like Sir Walter Scott before him, like D. W. Griffith in our own time, he refused to take advantage of the bankruptcy laws; and in July, 1895, accompanied by Mrs. Clemens and their second daughter, Clara, he set out across the Pacific on a lecture tour of the world. His success was all that he could have hoped for—even in India and Ceylon the response was enthusiastic—but just as the burden of debt had been lifted, Susy, Mark Twain's eldest daughter, whom he so passionately loved, died suddenly in Hartford, and half the reawakening glory of life died with her.

The books continued throughout these years—*The American Claimant,* his worst failure, in 1891, *Tom Sawyer Abroad* and *Pudd'nhead Wilson,* both partial successes, in 1894, then, in

1895 and 1896, a long, serious historical novel, the *Personal Recollections of Joan of Arc,* which was his labor of love, and
which he published anonymously because he feared the public
would never accept such a book over the signature of Mark
Twain. *Following the Equator,* his last full-length book of
travel, and a singularly weary one, came along in 1897 to tell
the tale of the world tour.

The Clemens family remained in Europe until 1900, when
they returned to America, but not to Hartford, for Mrs. Clemens felt she could never bear to see the Hartford house again.
In 1903, when her health broke down, they removed to Florence, and it was here, in an old Italian villa, on June 5, 1904,
that Mrs. Clemens died. Helpless without her, her husband,
with his two remaining daughters, Jean and Clara, returned to
the city of New York.

He was not writing many long pieces these last years of his
life. His "gospel" of determinism, *What is Man?* Mrs. Clemens
would not permit him to publish. It was privately printed, un-
signed, in 1906, but was not added to his collected works until
1917. *The Mysterious Stranger* came out in a special format in
1916. The last books—all brief, all save the second quite unimportant—that Mark Twain himself saw through the press were
Christian Science and *Captain Stormfield's Visit to Heaven,*
both in 1907, and *Is Shakespeare Dead?* in 1909. Yet he was always writing, always when he was not playing billiards, or
cursing the war-lords, or playing with cats and small girls. Col-
lections of short pieces were continually coming out, and some
of them, like *Eve's Diary,* were gems. He filled the magazines
and he filled the public eye. The reporters were after him continually; no public occasion was complete without him. A series
of academic honors was climaxed wonderfully in 1907 when
Oxford draped his venerable whiteness with the scarlet robes of
a Doctor of Letters. In 1908 he moved to his beautiful new
country house, "Stormfield," at Redding, Connecticut. On the
day before Christmas, 1909, life struck at him for the last time,
when his youngest daughter was taken with an epileptic seizure

and died instantly in her bath. When spring came, on April 21, 1910, her father followed her, dying as he had said he would die, while Halley's Comet, which had ushered him into the world seventy-five years before, again illuminated the heavens.[5]

III

THAT was twenty-five years ago, and although a great deal of water has run under our bridges since, we have had nobody to take his place. However much or little of his work shall finally be saved from the wallet of time, whether he shall be judged at last in his personal life a success or a failure, the fact remains that one can no more think of the late nineteenth or the early twentieth century in America without thinking of him than one can think of the years of the Civil War without seeing in imagination the long gaunt figure of Abraham Lincoln. This is a tremendous thing to be able to say of a mere private citizen, of a writer.

To be sure, it was often his personality, rather than his art, by which his contemporaries were enthralled. The man of letters can never achieve such universal acclaim as was given to him in his own proper capacity: there are not enough people in the world who know what literature is. We have had great writers since Mark Twain and we shall have others in the future, but it is not likely, these swiftly moving days, that another will capture the imagination of the public as he captured it and hold it so long. John Galsworthy was a great writer, but the reporters did not get excited when he traveled. To achieve that result, you must be more than an artist, you must be a character.

Today, among famous writers, perhaps only Bernard Shaw comes anywhere within hailing distance of the fame that belonged to Clemens, and even Mr. Shaw is a considerable distance behind him. Still, the man in the street sees Mr. Shaw's name in the papers at very frequent intervals—and, one must immediately add, he knows just about as much concerning what Shaw stands for as he knows about Pope Joan. The addendum carries its own comment as to how much such fame is worth from any serious, critical standpoint, and the artist is perfectly aware of this. For this reason his fear of acclaim, his many eager disclaimers, his insistence that he is indifferent to recognition and interested only in his work have, after all deductions have been made, a perfectly sound instinct behind them. When Edwin Arlington Robinson first heard that Theodore Roosevelt had boomed him in the *Outlook*, he walked the floor in his despair. "I shall never live it down!" he exclaimed. "I shall never live it down!" Even Mark Twain sometimes protests the assumption that he is seeking fame. "Indifferent to nearly everything but work," he writes. "I like that; I enjoy it, and stick to it. I do it without purpose and without ambition; merely for the love of it." But his protests are less numerous than we might have expected, for, as we shall see, he did not take himself very seriously as a man of letters.

Whether he sought fame or not, it came to him, and if he was a lion in America, we shall have to leave the animal kingdom in order to find the proper metaphor under which to present him in his European aspect. Royalty and nobility, brains and character swarmed about him during his foreign residences. In the early days, before the family had got quite accustomed to the wonder of it, Jean expressed the astonishment of them all in the famous remark which her father was never quite sure whether to take as a compliment or not: "Why, papa, if this goes on, pretty soon there won't be anybody left for you to meet except God." Convinced democrat though he was, he could not help being flattered by such attentions, but it is astonishing to see with what easy grace he adapts himself, accepting homage with the graceful ease of one born to the purple, unfailingly courteous, completely free from the brashness of spirit which, among Americans and others, often appears as an attempt to cover up a fundamental, deep-seated uncertainty or embarrassment. He called himself "self-appointed ambassador-at-large of the United States of America—without salary," and he told the simple truth. At home he was called "the belle of New York." With equal propriety, he might have been called the belle of any city he ever lived in, and there are few more delightful anecdotes than the account of how, on a public occasion in Vienna, he was stopped by a guard as he attempted to pass a certain barrier, only to have the officer in charge rush up in great excitement. "Let him pass. *Lieber Gott!* Don't you see it's Herr Mark Twain."

As we look back upon him now, there seems a curious dream quality in his life. Gamaliel Bradford puts it, "During the first decade of the twentieth century he drifted in his white dream garments—as Emily Dickinson did in solitude—through dream clouds who applauded him and looked up to him and loved him." And this impression is firmly rooted in the kind of man that he was. "Mark Twain," says his biographer, "lived curiously apart from the actualities of life." He was tremendously interested in dreams always, and he had a rich, sometimes terrible, dream life of his own. This fantastic quality invades his mundane sphere also, where it serves to explain hundreds of amusing or embarrassing anecdotes concerning his carelessness and his absent-mindedness. Madame Rosika Schwimmer tells of his being entertained in Budapest by the Lipotvaros Club. An enthusiastic speech of welcome was made, and when Mark Twain came to reply to it, he remarked that he only wished he could have understood the language. "But, sir," said the toastmaster, "Mr. X—— has given his toast in English."

When Mrs. Clemens was ill at York Harbor, he went about for all the world like St. Francis himself, pinning up notices on the trees warning the birds not to sing too loudly. "We are such stuff as dreams are made on," wrote Shakespeare at the close of his career, and Mark Twain develops the same conception elaborately in *The Mysterious Stranger*. Sometimes it hardly seemed to him that his own experiences could have taken place. "I dreamed I was born and grew up and was a pilot on the Mississippi and a miner and a journalist in Nevada and a pilgrim in the *Quaker City* and had a wife and children and went to live in a villa at Florence—and this dream goes on and on and sometimes seems so real that I almost believe it is real. I wonder if it is? But there is no way to tell, for if one applies tests they would be part of the dream, too, and so would simply aid the deceit. I wish I knew whether it is a dream or real." Again he sums up the whole human pageant under the same figure in words that are as beautiful as they are sad: "Old Age, white-headed, the temple empty, the idols broken, the worshipers in their graves, nothing left but You, a remnant, a tradition, belated fag-end of a foolish dream, a dream that was so ingeniously dreamed that it seemed real all the time; nothing left but You, center of a snowy desolation, perched on the ice-summit, gazing out over the stages of that long *trek* and asking Yourself, 'Would you do it again if you had the chance?' "

It must be evident that a man who reacts to life in any such fashion as has here been indicated will live inwardly rather than outwardly, and however spectacular his passage across the stage of the world may be, his real life will not lie in the world. If we would understand Mark Twain, as man and as artist, it is time, then, to turn to the world within as he built it up through the various agencies that became available for his use.

CHAPTER II

The World Within

I

FOR æsthetic experiences in general—always in a man of letters so large a part of the inner life—Mark Twain was not well prepared in the sense that he received much in the way of technical training, nor did he come to maturity with any particular critical standards. He had one great advantage, however, in his native, temperamental sensitiveness to beauty, and this appears best of all in his ecstatic response to the beauties of nature, which is one world of glory where no special training is called for. Even in boyhood, he has the genuine romantic passion. "He pitied the dead leaf and the murmuring dried weed of November," writes Mr. Paine, "because their brief lives were ended, and they would never know the summer again or grow glad with another spring." Here the melancholy note predominates, as it does often in Tom Sawyer's meditations, as it did with Byron, Shelley, and Keats; and some of Mark Twain's nature passages in that first heir of his invention, *The Innocents Abroad,* can almost be quoted in the same breath with the outpourings of the romantic poets.

His raptures went deep. "It was heaven and hell and sunset and rainbows and the aurora all fused into one divine harmony," he writes of the autumn splendors, "and you couldn't look at it and keep the tears back." He is "drunk . . . with the autumn foliage." He must shut his eyes when he shaves: "this painted dream distracts my hand and threatens my throat. And I have to stop and write this postscript to quiet my mind and lower my temperature, so that I can go and stand between the windows again and without peril resume." At Stormfield, during his last days, he so loved the glorious New England countryside that he never wished to go to the city again.

Mark Twain's most famous piece of descriptive writing is the picture of the ice storm in *Following the Equator*,[1] which, good as it is, is a little misleading, for it was not the spectacular aspects that attracted him most. Rural England is not spectacular, but he views it with "rapture and ecstasy." Running water always excited him, though he had no love for the ocean, and there is nothing lovelier in his books than his pictures of Hannibal under the shadow of the night, or of dawn breaking over the mighty river in the Mississippi volumes. The experiences of his youth gave him a measuring rod. He watches the sunset in Florence and drinks in its glories, but he declares that it cannot be compared with the sun on the Mississippi River. And neither Como nor Galilee could dim for him his memories of Lake Tahoe.

In the face of the grander aspects of nature, Mark Twain felt —as all sensitive persons must—the pettiness, the insignificance of man and all his fevered, hectic doings. "I said we are situated in a flat, sandy desert," he writes his mother from Carson City in 1861. "True. And surrounded on all sides by such prodigious mountains that when you stand at a distance from Carson and gaze at them awhile,—until, by mentally measuring them, and comparing them with things of smaller size, you begin to conceive of their grandeur, and next to feel their vastness expanding your soul like a balloon, and ultimately find yourself growing, and swelling, and spreading into a colossus, and I say when this point is reached, you look disdainfully down upon the insignificant village of Carson, reposing like a cheap print away yonder at the foot of the big hills, and in that instant you are seized with a burning desire to stretch forth your hand, put the city in your pocket, and walk off with it."[2] At Niagara it seems to him that the tourists and the photographers combine to show what a miserable race human beings are. "Any day, in the hands of these photographers, you may see stately pictures of papa and mamma, Johnny and Bub and Sis, or a couple of country cousins, all smiling hideously, and all disposed in studied and uncomfortable attitudes in their carriage, and all looming up in their grand and awe-inspiring imbecility before the snubbed and diminished presentment of that majestic presence, whose ministering spirits are the rainbows, whose voice is the thunder, whose awful front is veiled in clouds, who was monarch here dead and forgotten ages before this hackful of small reptiles was deemed temporarily necessary to fill a crack in the world's unnoted myriads, and will still be monarch here ages and decades after they shall have gathered themselves to their blood relations, the other worms, and been mingled with the unremembering dust."

But the mood is not always angry. "O Switzerland! the further it recedes into the enriching haze of time, the more intolerably delicious the charm of it and the cheer of it and the glory and majesty and solemnity and pathos of it grow. Those mountains had a soul; they thought; they spoke,—one couldn't hear it with the ears of the body, but what a voice it was!—and how real. Deep down in my memory it is sounding yet. Alp calleth unto Alp!—that stately old Scriptural wording is the right one for God's Alps and God's ocean. How puny we were in that awful presence—and how painless it was to be so; how fitting and right it seemed, and how stingless was the sense of our unspeakable insignificance. And Lord how pervading were the repose and peace and blessedness that poured out of the heart of the invisible Great Spirit of the Mountains."

II

But how much of this enthusiasm can he carry over into his comments on the arts, where special technical training is quite definitely needed for full appreciation?

Concerning sculpture he has comparatively little to say. Architecture he met in many different forms in the course of his travels, and that quick mind of his could not help wondering, generalizing, often on quite insufficient evidence. He distributes praise and blame with an even hand. He is immensely impressed by the ruins at Ephesus, and he is "carried away, infatuated, entranced with the wonders of the Alhambra and the supernatural beauty of the Alcazar. . . ." St. Mark's Cathedral, on the other hand, strikes him as a miracle of ineptitude, and he finds that it has the same fascination for him as hopelessly bad poetry. When he lived in Italy he became considerably interested in the ramshackle construction of the old Italian villas. He was not afraid of new developments. As far back as 1891 he foresaw the American skyscraper. His own house in Hartford was a distinct departure from the "dry goods box style" conventional in the period; the "English violet" design which Edward Potter worked out may be criticized as eccentric, but at least it showed, on his part and on Mark's, an attempt to break through the unimaginative methods of the Gilded Age. Stormfield, designed by John Howells, was, of course, a very beautiful house, but Mark Twain had nothing to do with it; in fact he never set eyes on it until the day he moved in. He had the excellent taste to appreciate it immediately, however, and he took pains to explain to Helen Keller that its architecture "was exactly suited to the natural surroundings: that the dark cedars and pines, which were always green, made a singularly beautiful setting for the white villa." Furthermore, he would have no pictures on the walls. "Pictures in this house would be an impertinence. No artist has ever equaled that landscape."

On the subject of painting, however, there is a great deal more to say, and all readers of Mark Twain will immediately recall his strictures on the old masters in *The Innocents Abroad*. Young Sam Clemens' first contact with the arts of brush and pencil was made in the Mississippi Valley via the media of chromo reproductions of famous paintings, steel engravings of biblical and historical subjects, and landscape daubs by the ambitious young lady of the family. His description in *The Gilded Age* of "the marvelous Historical Paintings" that one must look at in the Capitol at Washington—"and what have you done that you should suffer thus?"—may go back to impressions derived from his first visit to that city at the age of eighteen, though he could not at that time have seen the statue of "Mr. Lincoln as petrified by a young lady artist for ten thousand dollars." His earliest considered piece of art criticism dates, however, from his San Francisco days, and his attitude toward the old masters is already foreshadowed in it. One day, in a saloon, he saw a new picture of Samson and Delilah. He wanted to write about that picture, but his editor—apparently considering art criticism beyond him—was discouraging. Mark was not to be daunted, however, and this is what he turned in: "Now what is the first thing you see in looking at this picture? . . . Is it the gleaming eyes and fine face of Samson, or the muscular Philistine gazing furtively at the lovely Delilah? Or is it the rich drapery or the truth to nature of that pretty foot? No, sir. The first thing that catches the eye is the scissors on the floor at her feet. Them scissors is too modern. There wasn't no scissors like them in them days, by a damned sight!"

This is the kind of criticism that may not unfairly be described as "smart." Purely indifferent to æsthetic problems, or incapable of considering them, the critic fastens his keen, practical mind on some minor fault which happens to lie within the circle of his comprehension—and which is of no importance whatever, artistically speaking—and thereupon closes his eyes to the beauty of the picture. It is precisely on such grounds that Shakespeare has been called a barbarian because he gives Bohemia a seacoast, and because, in *The Merchant of Venice,* the bond story runs three months, while the love story, coming to its highest point of development at the same time, can hardly use more than three days.

As late as 1933, one of Mark Twain's critics assures us that "No one really *saw* the painted works of the old masters till Mark Twain took a look at them." Inasmuch as this gentleman also believes that *Joan of Arc* is an inferior work because the praise bestowed on it by competent critics "was not accompanied by the enjoyment of the uncultured public," and, at the same time, calls *Is Shakespeare Dead?* "the best piece of Shakespearian criticism ever attempted," it does not seem necessary to take his critical judgments very seriously. If we are to base

Mark Twain's claim to affectionate remembrance on his art criticism, I am afraid he will have a very short life.

His strictures on the old masters are so familiar that it is unnecessary to repeat them here in any detail. All the saints and martyrs and madonnas looked alike to him, and all were uninteresting. When he did like a picture, he discovered invariably that it was an unvalued specimen of the painter's art which he had chosen, and he always liked copies better than their originals—their colors were so bright and fresh! Botticelli roused his special antipathy. He went through life thinking up hard things to say about Botticelli; he is as good a critic as Mr. Thomas Craven here. But the Yankee hits savagely at Raphael —especially at his "Miraculous Draught of Fishes," "where he puts in a miracle of his own—puts three men into a canoe which wouldn't have held a dog without upsetting"—and others do not escape by any means scot-free. There are exceptions, to be sure. The Virgin of Murillo takes him off his guard and he quite falls in love with her, and Raphael's "Transfiguration" he calls "wonderfully beautiful."

When he wrote such passages as these, he thought he was engaged in art criticism. He was as careful, as discriminating as he knew how to be, yet it is clear that most of his judgments were determined on non-æsthetic grounds. His democracy and his dislike of Roman Catholicism reinforced each other in this connection: his dislike of the old masters was influenced, probably more than he realized, by his hatred of kings and priests. "Their nauseous adulation of princely patrons was more prominent to me and chained my attention more surely than the charms of color and expression which are claimed to be in the pictures." Unfortunately, too, the princely patrons were, in many cases, unmitigated scoundrels. "Raphael pictured such infernal villains as Catherine and Marie de Medici seated in heaven and conversing familiarly with the Virgin Mary and the angels (to say nothing of higher personages), and yet my friends abuse me because I am a little prejudiced against the old masters—because I fail sometimes to see the beauty that is in their productions. I cannot help but see it, now and then, but I keep on protesting against the groveling spirit that could persuade those masters to prostitute their noble talents to the adulation of such monsters as the French, Venetian, and Florentine princes of two and three hundred years ago, all the same." I have no doubt he was as sincerely shocked by it all as more conventionally minded people ever were by *The Mysterious Stranger* or *Captain Stormfield's Visit to Heaven*. And as a man, if not as a critic, one can hardly avoid feeling some sympathy for him.

How much growth did he experience in his ability to appreciate painting, in the course of the years? When he went back to the old masters on the *Tramp Abroad* tour in the late seventies, he found "a mellow richness, a subdued color" that he had not noticed before, or at least he could believe that these things had once been present, and he takes back his former statement that the copies are better than the originals. He still cannot see beyond the truth or falsity of realistic detail, however—"Paul Veronese's dogs do not resemble dogs; all the horses look like bladders on legs . . ."—and he is still strongly inclined to confuse art and morals and to create a moral issue where none exists—"The most of the picture is a manifest impossibility,—that is to say, a lie; and only rigid cultivation can enable a man to find truth in a lie." He admits the need of standards, he admits his own lack of critical judgment: "As I have had no teaching in art, I cannot decide what is a good picture and what isn't, according to the established standards; I am obliged to depend on my own crude standards." Yet as late as 1899, he condemns the old masters afresh on the old, prejudiced, non-æsthetic grounds: "The office of art seems to be to grovel in the dirt before Emperors and this and that and the other damned breed of priests."

One day, in the Uffizi Gallery in Florence, Robert Underwood Johnson found him absorbed in contemplation before a primitive "in which there appeared a lot of devils together with some monks and bears, the scenery being made up of numerous small mountains all out of perspective." He said: "Here, at last, —at last, I have found a picture worth looking at. In yonder is a whole gallery of pictures, but nothing you can see with pleasure; at last I've got something that is the real thing." I wish I might see that picture, and I wish I could tell whether Mark was taking Mr. Johnson in or whether he was really serious. My guess is that he was indulging his taste for what in poetry he called "hogwash."

Of course there are other painters besides the old masters who are mentioned now and then in Mark Twain's writings. As early as 1860, in St. Louis, he went to see Church's "Heart of the Andes," which, with his sensitiveness to natural beauty, he could hardly fail to enjoy, and he describes at considerable length the profusion of realistic detail contained in it. He enjoyed the New York Academy of Fine Arts, too, in the early days, so much so that the thought of it came back to him as he found himself wandering through the endless corridors of European galleries. In London, in the seventies, he fell in love with the canvases of Sir Edwin Landseer, but when a controversy over Turner was precipitated by the Boston critic who saw in "The Slave Ship" a picture of a yellow cat dying in a platter of tomatoes, Mark Twain was all on the side of the "antis." His remarks on Turner are always amusing and often exasperating; his conversion, in *Tramp Abroad* days, is, therefore, all the more interesting, for when he tried to go through the National Gallery, he was so fascinated by the Turners that he found it impossible to get beyond them. There was always something open-minded about Mark Twain. He had a habit of reaching conclusions on the basis of insufficient evidence, but he was always ready to reconsider as the need arose. When he comes to book illustrators, his judgment is safer. He praises Du Maurier in *Following the Equator,* and he told E. W. Kemble of his admiration for Abbey, Smedley, Frost, Reinhart, and Remington. I am surprised only that he did not mention Howard Pyle. "Abbey had never been equalled, he contended."[3]

III

His musical pilgrimage is more interesting, for here one clearly discerns growth. Music, of course, was a frontier tradition. "Incurably musical," writes Mr. DeVoto, "Americans working westward carried with them fiddles and a folk art. While the frontier was still a boundary of exploration, the wayfarer expected to find a fiddle or a banjo hanging beside the rifle in the shanty when he sought hospitality." In Hannibal Mrs. Holliday had a piano with drum attachment, and young Sam Clemens and Laura Hawkins used to love to go there and thrill to the audible pyrotechnics of "The Battle of Prague." Sam himself had what Howells was later to describe as a fine tenor voice, and he seems to have done some entertaining on the river boats in his pilot days. Later, William R. Gillis tells us, he charmed his cronies in California with his singing and guitar playing.

What he sang we do not know, but we may be sure it was not Mozart. He has no taste, he assures us, rejoices to classify himself among the barbarians, and glories in it. "I suppose it is very low-grade music—I know it *must* be low-grade music—because it so delighted me, it so warmed me, moved me, stirred me, uplifted me, enraptured me, that at times I could have cried, and at others split my throat with shouting. . . . I have never heard enough classic music to be able to enjoy it, and the simple truth is I detest it. Not mildly, but with all my heart."

The very energy of the statement proves that he was not content to have it so—the gentleman doth protest too much—or, as he puts it specifically in connection with the opera, "I dislike the opera because I want to love it and can't." It was true that he had never heard enough classical music to be able to enjoy it, and for years he shied away from it, perhaps because he did not want to prove to himself that his capacity in music was altogether lacking. After his daughter Clara became a singer, however, he could evade the problem no longer. When she sang her first Italian air for him, he was very impatient, he refused to listen even to Schubert; instead he asked for an old Scotch song.

Taken to hear Leschetizky, he was impressed only by the pianist's wonderful memory and the nimbleness of his fingers, and he was willing to have Gabrilowitsch come to dinner only if Clara would promise not to ask him to play. Later, however, upon his daughter's urging, he agreed to have an Orchestrelle installed in his Fifth Avenue home. Using this agency—as, in these latter days, so many have used the radio and the Victrola —he learned to love Beethoven, Schubert, Chopin, and Brahms, loved them so much, indeed, that when the time came to go away for the summer, he could not bear to be separated from them, he must move the Orchestrelle to his summer home. It is not here pretended that Mark Twain ever became, in any sense, a gifted critic of music; nevertheless, under the circumstances, and at his time of life, his achievement was by no means contemptible. Gamaliel Bradford was fond of insisting that music was, in a peculiar sense, the art of ignorance and the art of democracy; Mark Twain's experience seems typical of that of thousands of American men who, afraid of "art" through a large part of their lives, finally learn through music, and through the mechanical reproduction of music, that, after all, the thing they have hated and feared does have some significance for them, and so it enriches their lives at the end.[4]

At the opera, Mark Twain loved the familiar tunes—he always needed to become familiar with a tune before he could enjoy it—and agonized through the recitative. He hated, too, the empty pretension, the affectations and artificialities which appear invariably wherever grand opera becomes a social function. It was inevitable that he should have some interesting experiences with Wagner. "I trust that I know as well as anybody that singing is one of the most entrancing and bewitching and moving and eloquent of all the vehicles invented by man for the conveying of feeling; but it seems to me that the chief virtue in song is melody, air, tune, rhythm, or what you please to call it, and that when this feature is absent what remains is a picture with the color left out." At Mannheim he attended, on one occasion, a performance of *Lohengrin:* "The banging and slamming and booming and crashing were something beyond belief. The racking and pitiless pain of it remains stored up in my memory alongside the memory of the time I had my teeth fixed." Time came, however, when the family made a shrine of Bayreuth, and he simply had to endure it. He became accustomed to the orchestration, but he could not endure the singing; he thought it would be preferable if Wagnerian opera could be performed in pantomime! Yet the "Wedding March" was a lovely thing, certainly, and there was nothing he had ever heard "so solemn and impressive and so divinely beautiful as 'Tannhäuser.' It ought to be used as a religious service." But of all his comments on Bayreuth the most interesting is this in which his strength and his weakness are so curiously commingled, the culture seeker standing beside the realist with his stalwart honesty and his rather naïve village-atheist fear of being fooled: "I feel strongly out of place here. Sometimes I feel like the sane person in a community of the mad; sometimes I feel like the one blind man where all others see; the one groping savage in the college of the learned, and always, during service, I feel like a heretic in heaven."

Fortunately, however, there was one type of music—music of quality, music of dignity and beauty, music utterly free from all pretensions of "art-iness"—that Mark Twain drank in with his mother's milk and which became a part of his very being. I speak, of course, of the Negro Spirituals. When the Jubilee Singers came to Lucerne in 1897, they took him back to his youth, they made him see that the same truth holds in music that he had already learned in literature, that the finest art is not exotic, no hothouse flower, but grows its sturdy stock straight out of the earth, and that common people do not hate it, they love it because it explains them to themselves. "Arduous and painstaking cultivation has not diminished or artificialized their music," he wrote, "but on the contrary—to my surprise— has mightily reinforced its eloquence and beauty. Away back in the beginning—to my mind—their music made all other vocal music cheap; and that early notion is emphasized now. It is utterly beautiful, to me; and it moves me infinitely more than any other music can. I think that in the Jubilees and their songs America has produced the perfectest flower of the ages; and I wish it were a foreign product so that she would worship it and lavish money on it and go properly crazy over it." This is perhaps the loveliest passage in all Mark Twain's criticism; it shows him at his complete best, as he was when he allowed the sensitiveness that was in him to respond unhampered to the finest things with which he came in contact. He himself sang Spirituals to Mrs. Clemens the night that she died. He sang them on other occasions also, one of which has been beautifully described by his servant Katy Leary:

"I heard about one night when there was a company at the Warners' and Mr. Clemens was there, and it was a perfectly lovely night and there was a full moon outside and no lights in the house. They was just settin' there in the music room, looking out at the moonlight. And suddenly Mr. Clemens got right up without any warning and begun to sing one of them negro Spirituals. A lady that was there told me he just stood up with both his eyes shut and begun to sing kind of soft like—a faint sound, just as if there was wind in the trees, she said; and he kept right on singin' kind o' low and sweet, and it was beautiful and made your heart ache somehow. And he kept on singin' and singin' and became kind of lost in it, and he was all lit up—his face was. 'Twas somethin' from another world, she said, and when he got through, he put his two hands up to his head, just as though all the sorrow of them negroes was upon him; and then he begun to sing, 'Nobody Knows the Trouble I Got, Nobody Knows but Jesus.' That was one of them negro spirituals songs, and when he come to the end, to the Glory Halleluiah, he gave a great shout—just like the negroes do—he shouted out the Glory, Glory, Halleluiah! They said it was wonderful and none of them would forget it as long as they lived."

Surely the influence of the Spirituals shows in his never-failing love for the Negro race. There are echoes of them, too, in his loveliest prose.

IV

WE come now, at last, to the art that was Mark Twain's own—literature. Since he did not come out of a distinctively literary environment, it has become the fashion of critics to speak of him, along with Robert Burns, as a quite untutored genius, a breath of fresh air wafted into the overheated drawing rooms of an effete conventionality. In both cases, the popular judgment involves gross misconceptions. Both Burns and Mark Twain drew directly upon life for much of their most precious material, but neither was, from the literary point of view, a young ignoramus, by any means.[5]

Huckleberry Finn tells us some of the books generally available in a mid-Western frontier household: a Bible, a *Pilgrim's Progress, Friendship's Offering,* the Speeches of Henry Clay, and Dr. Gunn's *Family Medicine.* To this list, *Life on the Mississippi* adds, among others, Ossian, *Alonzo and Melissa, Ivanhoe,* and Godey's *Lady's Book.* Young Sam Clemens must have met all these titles at a very early age, and there is evidence, too, that he was familiar with the dreary, pietistic Sunday School books of the period that he was afterwards to ridicule so unmercifully.

But, as I have already pointed out, he was restricted to no such meager diet as this. Few actual data are available as to his reading in Hannibal days, but it seems very likely that his youthful interest in books has been underestimated. The early biography by Will Clemens quotes his mother as saying, "He was always a great boy for history, and could never get tired of that kind of reading; but he hadn't any use for schoolhouses and text-books."[6] At least the reading habit must have been firmly established by the time he made his trip to New York at the age of eighteen. "You ask me where I spend my evenings," he writes home to his sister Pamela. "Where would you suppose with a free printers' library containing more than 4,000 volumes within a quarter of a mile of me, and nobody at home to talk to?" He did not read as a chore; he was likely to neglect the books somebody told him he "ought" to read, but he had not grown very old before he learned to go to books for what Katherine Mansfield calls "the life in the life of them."

We hear a good deal, first and last, of his reading during his Mississippi days, how, for example, he tried to read *The Fortunes of Nigel* behind a barrel on a steamboat, where the master caught him and "read him a lecture upon the ruinous effects of reading." However earnestly he may have declared in later years that piloting was a far more congenial trade than authorship, his contributions to the *Crescent* still exist to prove that he did not altogether lay aside his literary ambitions during this period. He read more in Nevada, and a great deal more in San Francisco, and when he became engaged, he conjured up mental pictures of his wife and himself sitting together through long winter evenings, studying together, reading favorite authors together, and so fixing them upon their minds. There is a significant speech in *Tom Sawyer Abroad,* where Huck Finn is quite out of character: "Tom said we was right in the midst of the *Arabian Nights* now. He said it was right along here that one of the cutest things in that book happened; so we looked down and watched while he told us about it, because there ain't anything that is so interesting to look at as a place that a book has talked about." The unlettered Huck could never have felt that way about it. But Sam Clemens could and did.[7]

Furthermore, the frontier itself existed as literature, literature of pretty poor quality, most of it, but literature nevertheless. Mr. DeVoto has described it clearly—fantasy and realism side by side, burlesque and extravaganza closely connected with satire, and Mr. Meine has illustrated its quality in his *Tall Tales of the Southwest*. DeVoto speaks, too, of Mark Twain's four most important predecessors in the field of frontier humor— Augustus Longstreet, J. J. Hooper, George W. Harris, and William Tappan Thompson, showing clearly that not only *The Jumping Frog* but also *The Innocents Abroad* (in a measure, even *A Connecticut Yankee*) inherited and fulfilled a tradition —they did not establish one.

V

CONCERNING Mark Twain's reading habits in later life we have fuller testimony, and I should like to begin with his own analysis: "I like history, biography, travels, curious facts and strange happenings, and science. And I detest novels, poetry, and theology." He flaunts this nonliterary point of view in the face of Rudyard Kipling: "I never read novels myself, except when the popular persecution forces me to—when people plague me to know what I think of the last book that everyone is reading." And again: "What I like to read about are facts and statistics of any kind. If they are only facts about the raising of radishes, they interest me. Just now, for instance, before you came in— I was reading an article about 'Mathematics.' Perfectly pure mathematics." There is an interesting passage in the *Autobiography* where he explains how he tried three times to read a certain factual narrative in the *Atlantic*, "but was frightened off each time before I could finish. The tale was so vivid and so real that I seemed to be living those adventures myself and sharing their intolerable perils, and the torture of it was so sharp that I was never able to follow the story to the end." This is the most cogent bit of testimony we have concerning Mark Twain's capacity for being absorbed in his reading. It may be not without significance that it is a nonimaginative piece of writing with which we are here concerned.

Mark Twain pays comparatively little attention to the recognized classics, to the giants of letters. He is ignorant of Græco-Roman mythology as well as of the wonder-tales of northern Europe. Dante he mentions twice, but there is no reason for supposing that he read him. In a stray magazine article, he expresses a conventional kind of affection for Chaucer, the only pre-Shakespearean English poet whom he mentions anywhere, as Milton is the earliest among those who came after. No pre-Shakespearean dramatist appears, and of Shakespeare's contemporaries there is only Ben Jonson.

Shakespeare himself fares somewhat better, often as a subject for burlesque. George Ealer read aloud from Shakespeare in river days, and Clemens seems to have enjoyed the readings hugely. Once he speaks of the profound moral lessons to be learned from *Othello* and from *Lear*. He was very fond of *Romeo and Juliet,* and once, under the spell of a glamorous Sothern and Marlowe production of that play, he told Paine that he considered it its author's greatest achievement. Leaving out *Is Shakespeare Dead?*—that curious contribution to the Baconian controversy, a document less learned but no more ridiculous than others that have been called forth by that absurd cause[8]—Pochmann lists twenty allusions to Shakespeare in Mark Twain's writings, nearly twice as many as to any other writer. Yet there is only one, I believe, that shows any information not familiar to all literate persons in the English-speaking world, and this is his reference to Falstaff as Oldcastle in the paper on "Queen Victoria's Jubilee."

There are two or three slighting references to Bunyan (whose theology must have made him *persona non grata* to Mark Twain)—one delightful and penetrating hit in *Huckleberry Finn* where Christian is spoken of as "a man that left his family, it didn't say why"—yet he knew his Bunyan nevertheless and appreciated him, and at one time he anticipated what would today be described as a motion picture production of *The Pilgrim's Progress*. Occasionally he comments on one of the less familiar classics—as Thomas Fuller, whose "pemmican sentences" enthralled him. "Old Fuller . . . boils an elaborate thought down and compresses it into a single crisp and meaty sentence. It is a wonderful faculty."

Among great foreign writers, Voltaire's free thinking might surely be supposed to have attracted him, but I find only one reference, probably intended to be complimentary, in the fantastic sketch called "Sold to Satan." Boccaccio is spoken of twice, both times slightingly, because of his improprieties, and because of his "curt and meagre fashion" of telling his stories. There is one reference to *Gil Blas.*

Of the great English novelists, Dickens was the only one who really existed for him. Meredith, George Eliot, Jane Austen, and Sir Walter Scott he despised, and Mrs. Clemens was once grossly humiliated when obliged to confess that her husband had not read his Thackeray. He misleads us somewhat when he tells us, late in life, that his brother Orion was always trying to get him to read Dickens but he couldn't do it. Of course he couldn't, being Mark Twain, under Orion's prodding; but there is evidence to show that he did nevertheless, though specific references to Dickens in his writings are not numerous. His favorite Dickens novel was *A Tale of Two Cities,* which he read many times. It is interesting to note that the very first time Mark Twain ever went out in the company of Olivia Langdon they attended a Dickens reading at Steinway Hall. Mark Twain had something more important than Dickens on his mind that night, but it is a curious coincidence that the two most successful writers of the nineteenth century—the one beginning his career just as the other was ending it—should, on that occasion, have been sheltered under the same roof.

Stuart Sherman notes the flavor of Dickens in *The Gilded Age,* describing it as the only indication anywhere of an important literary relationship between Mark Twain and an outstanding modern writer. Schönemann, the most important German scholar, doubting indebtedness at this point, finds Mark Twain's own environment sufficient to account for all alleged resemblances, though he admits the possibility that Dickens may have influenced the mode of treatment. In "My Platonic Sweetheart," the delightful scene in "a great plantation house" may have been influenced by Dickens; it may also have been influenced by Lewis Carroll.[9]

If we test Mark Twain by his ability to appreciate poetry— always the final touchstone of literary judgment—he hardly seems a rewarding study. Chaucer and Shakespeare have already been mentioned. Spenser appears once, as "Spencer." In one of his speeches, he declares that nobody has read *Paradise Lost,* and nobody wants to read it or any other classic. He seems to have read it himself, however, and early in life, for an admonitory letter to Orion cites "the Arch-Fiend's terrible energy" as "the grandest thing" in the poem. Burns he speaks of once in passing. He knows Byron's "Prisoner of Chillon" and "The Destruction of Sennacherib." Wordsworth is quoted once in a letter. He appreciated Shelley's "sumptuous imagery." In a talk at Keokuk, Iowa, in 1886, he misquoted "Locksley Hall." He liked to read aloud from William Morris' "Sir Guy of the Dolorous Blast."

Among the Americans, he read Poe in his Keokuk days, but a 1909 letter to Howells declares Poe's prose unreadable. He speaks of "The Bells" in *A Tramp Abroad*. Pochmann thinks the treasure-digging episode in *Tom Sawyer* imitated from *The Gold-Bug,* and finds suggestions of both "The Raven" and "William Watson" in the "Recent Carnival of Crime in Connecticut." Schönemann makes much of the influence of Emerson, but presents little evidence. Personal connections accounted for his enthusiasm for Oliver Wendell Holmes. In general, Mark Twain treats the New England school with more respect than one would have expected from him, but one feels that he respected them as Charles Lamb did the equator. He was, during his early married life, very anxious to be considered "respectable." Pochmann could find no reason to suppose that he had read Holmes's novels, or Hawthorne's, or those of his neighbor, Mrs. Stowe. Among his contemporaries and his juniors, he showed interest, from time to time, in John Hay, Witter Bynner, Angela Morgan, and Willa Cather.

This leaves four poems and poets that really meant something to Mark Twain: "The Burial of Moses," by C. F. Alexander, *The Rubáiyát of Omar Khayyám,* Rudyard Kipling, and Robert Browning. The Alexander poem was discovered at an early date. It is not wholly in the taste of these days, but it is not necessarily any the worse for that, and whatever its limitations, it served Sam Clemens well in that it established for him a standard of taste and dignity, at the same time revealing something of what the harmonies of verbal music can achieve. Omar he was "wild" over from the time FitzGerald's translation first appeared in America; in this instance, the appeal of Omar's philosophy to his mind must have powerfully reinforced the seductive music of the verses. No very cultivated taste is needed for Kipling, and of this he was well aware, but he never tired of those resonant verses. "I am not fond of all poetry, but there's something in Kipling that appeals to me. I guess he's just about my level." In Bermuda days, one who had heard Mark Twain read aloud from Kipling sent him a poem, "When the King Reads Kipling." Mark praised it extravagantly: "That poem does not seem like words—a march of words with interrupting spaces between—it flows like organ music, in blended strains, deep and rich and eloquent. And so moving! I can't read it aloud, my voice breaks. It is noble, stately, beautiful!" As an occasional poem, "When the King Reads Kipling" is extremely good, but Mark Twain's almost unbounded enthusiasm for it shows uncultivated taste or sentimentality or both.

The great surprise in poetry is Browning. One would have expected Mark Twain to hate him, as he hated James and Meredith, but with the perversity so characteristic of him, he decided instead to love him. Perhaps the English poet's enthusiastic robustness was the point of connection. "That man seems to have been to you," he remarked to Howells of Tolstoy, "what Browning was to me." One could hardly say more. The readings he gave from Browning at his Hartford house were famous, and all hearers agreed they were exquisite. "To him there were no obscure passages to be argued over," wrote Grace King, "no guesses at meaning. His slow, deliberate speech and full voice gave each sentence its quota of sound, and sense followed naturally and easily. He understood Browning as did no one else I ever knew."[10]

VI

LIKE most persons of literary bent, Mark Twain enjoyed the theater, though he was not a consistent theater-goer, and the stage was in no sense an abiding passion with him, as it was with Dickens. He speaks of Edwin Forrest and of Adah Isaacs

Menken in early days, later of his friends—William Gillette, Augustin Daly, John Drew, and Ada Rehan—of Edwin Booth, of Irving and Terry, of David Warfield, of Sothern and Marlowe. He had a special tenderness for the old-time minstrel show. His own appearances in amateur theatricals and his attempts to write plays[11] brought him near the outskirts at least of the theater's magic. He was sure that the actor is a public servant to whom society owes a great debt, and he had an unshaken faith in the theater as a teacher of righteousness especially to children. Melodrama, he knew, was always on the side of the angels, and he was particularly enthusiastic about projects like the Jewish children's theater on New York's East Side whose aim was to give the children something better than melodrama. His most detailed criticism of a play is his study of Adolf Wilbrandt's "The Master of Palmyra,"[12] doubtless a work of considerable merit, though Mark Twain's special enthusiasm seems due to the fact that he read his own tragic philosophy of life between Wilbrandt's lines. He once made a very strong plea for an endowed theater. "It would make better citizens, honest citizens. One of the best gifts a millionaire could make would be a theatre here and a theatre there. It would make . . . a real Republic, and bring about an educational level."

VII

Of the books and writers whom Mark Twain particularly disliked, I have already mentioned several. Meredith is berated for his artificialities, especially in characterization. He has no right to be telling us continually how brilliant Diana is without ever having the power to illustrate it! George Eliot, Hawthorne, and Henry James he lumps together, rejecting them for what seems to him their tendency to overanalysis. "If Helen's Babies & Pope's translation of Homer, & Paradise Lost, & Lamb's works had been submitted to me, I would have burned them with a maniacal joy & scalped their authors. See what the world would have lost."[13] When he was an old man, Paine gave him Flaubert's *Salammbo,* hoping that since he enjoyed Suetonius, he might enjoy that great novel of the ancient world. He admitted its art but declared he would never read it again without a salary. Despite all his shafts against exuberant romanticism, there was something in him that rebelled at any suggestion of naturalism.

His four favorite "hates" among writers were the Goldsmith of *The Vicar of Wakefield,* Fenimore Cooper, Scott, and Jane Austen. He attempts no careful analysis of the faults of Goldsmith's lovely story, but he speaks of it always with extreme contempt. Cooper's faults he goes after much more systematically. As early as 1862 he writes his mother from Carson City "a full and correct account of these lovely Indians—not gleaned from Cooper's novels, Madam, but the result of personal observation. . . ." In *Roughing It,* he claims he went West as "a disciple of Cooper and a worshipper of the Red Man," and was cruelly disillusioned when he saw the creature himself. I am inclined to doubt the avowed discipleship. His essay on "Fenimore Cooper's Literary Offences," written at a later date, is one of his most ambitious pieces of literary criticism. In it he accuses Cooper of every conceivable crime against grammar, rhetoric, and common sense. On first consideration, the indictment seems logical enough, but one senses a deep-seated dislike behind it. The writer is not open-minded.

But he does not seem, in his early days, to have disliked Scott. Perhaps this was what he had in mind when he declared in a speech that "you've got to be one of two ages to appreciate Scott. When you're eighteen you can read *Ivanhoe,* and you want to wait until you are ninety to read some of the rest." His letter to Brander Matthews on the subject[14] draws up a careful outline for a study in depreciation. "Lord, it's all so juvenile! so artificial, so shoddy; and such wax figures and skeletons and spectres." In a famous passage in *Life on the Mississippi* he goes so far as to hold Scott responsible for the Civil War, and to contrast *Ivanhoe* and *Don Quixote* as "a curious exemplification of the power of a single book for good or for harm." From Scott's medievalism the South derived her "jejune romanticism," and so she adopted a different social and economic system from that which prevailed in the more advanced and more hardheaded North.[15]

But there is a curious anticlimax in the story of Mark Twain's adventures with Scott. After he had finished *Rob Roy* and *Guy Mannering,* bitterly hating them the while, he got hold of a copy of *Quentin Durward.* "It was like leaving the dead to mingle with the living: it was like withdrawing from the infant class in the College of Journalism to sit under the lectures in English literature in Columbia University. I wonder who wrote Quentin Durward?" I should hate to say anything against a book I love so much as *Quentin Durward,* but certainly there is far more "jejune romanticism" in it, if you want to call it that, than in *Rob Roy* or *Guy Mannering,* or the Scotch books generally. Mark Twain's exception of this particular novel must stand, then, as another example of his many idiosyncrasies of judgment.

But not even against Scott does Mark Twain breathe quite as much fire and brimstone as against Jane Austen. Perhaps Howells had something to do with this special antipathy, for Howells was an extreme Janeite, and his friend, who did not like Miss Austen's kind of fiction, found her perfections held up to him until he seems to have developed a mania on the subject. Any library is a good library that does not include her books. "It seems a great pity that they allowed her to die a natural death." And then, as with music, the old familiar "inferiority complex" raises its head once more: "When I take up one of Jane Austen's books, I feel like a barkeeper entering the kingdom of heaven."

VIII

WE have already observed that Clemens was not classical in his literary tastes. The tendency toward dissent is very strong in him, coupled, as it often is, with a kind of suspicion of everything that orthodox judgment has approved. As Howells puts it, he did not care greatly "for the conventionally accepted masterpieces of literature. He liked to find out good things and great things for himself; sometimes he would discover these in a masterpiece new to him alone, and then, if you brought his ignorance home to him, he enjoyed it, and enjoyed it the more the more you rubbed it in."

Perhaps this kind of literary pioneering works better with contemporary literature than it does with the literature of the past. A good many modern and contemporary books come in for mention—generally commendatory—by Mark Twain. Among American writers mentioned are Booth Tarkington, William Allen White, James Branch Cabell, William Lyon Phelps, Rose Terry Cooke, and the Will Irwin of the *Letters of a Japanese Schoolboy*. British writers include Olive Schreiner, H. G. Wells, Bernard Shaw, Thomas Hardy—whose *Jude* was almost the last continuous reading he did—Flora Annie Steele, Marjorie Bowen, and Elizabeth Robins. There are very few continentals.

Marjorie Bowen had the good fortune to attract his attention at the very beginning of her career; as time went on, he came to think of her almost as a protégé. *An Open Question* by Elizabeth Robins for once won his assent to a straight, strong piece of realistic writing. Occasionally his old taste for superlatives betrayed him, as when he spoke of Miss Steele's *On the Face of the Waters* as "the finest novel ever written by a woman." Nothing surprises me more along this line than his enthusiasm for Cabell's *Chivalry*. If ever there has been a piece of shoddy artificiality in pseudoromantic literature, it is that book. Howard Pyle commented sharply on its limitations. Mark Twain ought to have been the last man to be taken in by it.[16]

Mark Twain's nonclassical bias explains also his interest in literary curiosa—Marjorie Fleming, the Mormon Bible, Pedro Carolino's *New Guide of the Conversation in Portuguese and English,* Watson Wolston's novel, *Love Triumphant, or the Enemy Conquered*. Sometimes he enjoyed such things because they were good, sometimes because they were so surpassingly, so triumphantly, bad. In Australia he amused himself making verses stringing the curious names of a series of Australian towns together. He had one marked characteristic of the artist temperament—his quick response to strong contrasts, or, as he puts it in the *Autobiography,* "A thoroughly beautiful woman and a thoroughly homely woman are creations which I love to gaze upon, and which I cannot tire of gazing upon, for each is perfect in her own line, and it is *perfection,* I think, in many things, and perhaps most things, which is the quality that fascinates us." He found perfection, among other things, in the "hogwash" that so delighted him, and in the precious puerilities of "the Sweet Singer of Michigan."

IX

WEAK as he is in fiction, Mark Twain does not often have a "source" in the sense in which Shakespeare used Plutarch and Holinshed as sources. *A Double-Barrelled Detective Story* was suggested by the Sherlock Holmes stories, and *Captain Stormfield's Visit to Heaven* is a burlesque of Elizabeth Stuart Phelps, in *The Gates Ajar.* Charlotte M. Yonge's *The Prince and the Page* suggested the history of Tom Canty, but Mark Twain's plot is altogether different. The *Joan of Arc,* being at least half biography, was, of course, a special case. The theme of *Tom Sawyer, Detective* was suggested by an actual happening in seventeenth-century Denmark, of which Steen Steensen Blicher had already made a novel. But Mark Twain never read the novel; the narrative came to him from the lips of Lillie de Hegermann-Lindencrone.

A great many books exert literary influences, however, without being, in the narrower sense, describable as "sources." Mark Twain never wrote an essay on "Books That Have Influenced Me"; if he had done so, he must surely have begun with the Bible. He had known it as early as he knew print; he had read it through before he was fifteen years old. Mr. Pochmann counted 124 biblical allusions in his writing—eighty-nine of them, to be sure, in the *Innocents*—far more than to any other

book or writer. But not only does Mark Twain quote the Bible,
he alludes to it, he refers to it, he burlesques it, he takes the
reader's knowledge of it absolutely for granted, and Charles W.
Stoddard has described the thrilling beauty of his reading, one
night in London, from the Book of Ruth. It is not difficult to
agree with Mr. Paine that the limpid beauty and simplicity of
Mark Twain's style at its best owes much to that well of English undefiled.

Next to the Bible, the most important influence was undoubtedly that of Cervantes. Professor Moore has studied this matter
in great detail; I cannot possibly do better than summarize
briefly the results of his investigation. Tom Sawyer is the Don
Quixote to Huckleberry Finn's Sancho Panza. Tom, like the
Don, is an omnivorous reader who seeks to act out romantic
adventures in his own experience, and some of the dialogue between the two boys follows the conversations between Don
Quixote and Sancho Panza very closely. The picnic scene in
Tom Sawyer is clearly indebted to the Don's attack upon the
sheep as well as to his adventures when he tries to halt the funeral procession. In *A Connecticut Yankee* the two types appear
again, Don Quixote as Alisande while the Yankee himself is
Sancho Panza. Professor Moore raises a very interesting question. Was Mark Twain's antiromanticism, his lifelong tendency
to suppress his own romantic tendencies, due, at least in part, to
his admiration for Cervantes plus his dislike of the debilitating
influences of cheap pseudoromantic fiction as he came to know
it in his early days?[17]

Miss Brashear feels very strongly that Mark Twain was influenced much more by the writers of the eighteenth century than
he was by those of his own time. The evangelicalism of the later
period passes him by entirely, nor is he greatly concerned for its
speculative philosophy. His strong social interest expresses itself
in his passion for biography, diaries, and letters—all popular
forms in the age of Queen Anne. This period was greatly interested too in the "character." Miss Brashear finds "Sir Roger
at the Play" in the early Snodgrass letter on "Julius Caesar,"[18]

and points out that the *Spectator* was widely circulated in the Middle West. The essays may show eighteenth-century influence also, though I think she treads on uncertain ground when she tries to develop this thesis in detail in connection with the essays included in the *What Is Man?* volume. There remain fables, moralized legends, and maxims. She can do little with the fables, but there are plenty of maxims. Moralized legends appear in *The Man That Corrupted Hadleyburg, The $30,000 Bequest,* "Was It Heaven or Hell?" *A Dog's Tale,* and *A Horse's Tale,* the last two being "almost sentimental documents to illustrate the XVIII Century doctrine of nature's social union." *Huckleberry Finn* reflects the picaresque romance, another favorite eighteenth-century type, though this influence could not have reached Mark Twain through the essay.

One must not make the eighteenth-century influence go on all fours however. Miss Brashear has done such a very careful piece of work and she is so anxious that no scrap of evidence shall escape her that here and there I think she goes a bit too far. It is no doubt a fact that Pope was very popular in early nineteenth-century America and that many quotations from him appeared in the Hannibal papers, but this much alone can hardly warrant the assumption that Mark Twain may have imitated him "in framing generalizations about the conduct of life with epigrammatic pith and balance." I do not take her remarks on the subject of a possible indebtedness to Smollett and Sterne very seriously, and she herself admits that "not an influence . . . but a mental and emotional trend, must be said to account for the resemblance" between Clemens and Fielding, both of whom were influenced independently by *Don Quixote.*

Of all the writers of the eighteenth century, the one to whom it is most interesting to compare Mark Twain is Jonathan Swift, and here, unfortunately, no direct influence can be traced. There is one vague reference to Swift in *Roughing It,* and H. W. Fisher reports that Mark Twain once denounced him as "a Sadist and a Masochist in one," whom it would be a waste of time to try to explain, but it is evident that he has only the vaguest information concerning Swift: he is not even certain when he lived. Schönemann compares Swift and Mark Twain very interestingly, without actually asserting influence, and finds many parallels.[19] Swift's attitude toward animals, as providing a refuge from the contemptible character of mankind, is interesting in this connection also. Miss Brashear finds humility, chivalry in Mark Twain but not in Swift. "His humor, in fact, was as much a weapon against the ingrowing conscience within himself as against the stupidity of the human race." Swift, she points out further, was not popular reading in America in Mark Twain's youth.

Goldsmith was another matter. The Goldsmith of the *Vicar* was, as we already know, anathema, but the essayist was another story. Mark Twain first came to know him well from George Ealer's readings, and he may well, as Schönemann suggests, have influenced not alone the "colloquial ease" of Mark Twain's style but possibly even his philosophy of history. His most direct imitation of Goldsmith was in the essay, "Goldsmith's Friend Abroad Again," that noble protest against inhumanity toward the Chinese on the Pacific Coast.[20]

X

"MARK TWAIN read not so many books," writes Mr. Paine, "but read a few books often."[21] Among his special favorites, in addition to those already considered, were Pepys, Lecky, Malory, Plutarch, Suetonius, and Saint-Simon. He had a hunger for human fellowship always, and he was more attracted by those books in which he could feel the pulse of "the warm life-blood of a master-spirit" than ever he could have been by anything purely æsthetic or ideational. The particular human specimens which throng the pages of Saint-Simon and Suetonius showed him, generally speaking, the human animal at his worst—a spectacle that always hurt him very much, at the same time that it exercised a deep fascination over him. Malory's appeal was different. He seems to have reverenced the book, first of all, for its style, though he was by no means insensible to the charm of the general atmosphere of romance and adventure and in this instance, for some reason, he did not refuse to follow his natural bent.[22] Schönemann has pointed out several resemblances between Mark Twain and Pepys which may have escaped the general reader. Both were of humble origin. Pepys was careful and conscientious in business, though he compromised sometimes in his own interest, and he was too clear-sighted not to realize his limitations. Like Mark Twain, he was a humorist, fond of "tall tales"; like him, too, he was interested in books and in mathematics, though he is much stronger on the æsthetic side, especially with reference to music. Best of all, he owned a white suit![23]

Mark Twain read many other books of a biographical and semibiographical nature. In his youth, he read the Letters of Horace Walpole; in his own opinion, they exercised a strong and beneficent influence on his style. He read Thomas Hood's Letters also, probably in *Up the Rhine,* but Hood aroused little enthusiasm, for young Sam thought his writing labored in style, distinctly inferior to at least one letter he received from his brother Orion. He read Parkman, Macaulay, Carlyle, Darwin, *Two Years Before the Mast,* the autobiographies of Andrew D. White and Moncure D. Conway, the letters of Madame de Sévigné and of James Russell Lowell. Miss Brashear believes that he did not grow much after he was fifty years old. "He undertook such new tasks as supporting his theories with sources, later in life, but the theories themselves were formed at least before 1885—perhaps earlier. Of the books on his permanent list, the Bible, of course, he knew as early as he could remember, Cervantes probably before 1860, Carlyle from 1871, and Suetonius about the same time, Lecky and Pepys from 1874, Greville from 1875, Casanova from 1880, Saint-Simon from 1883, and the *Morte d'Arthur* from 1884. He died reading Suetonius and Carlyle, who were among his earlier literary passions. He himself . . . seemed to set forty-eight as the crucial age of a man's life. The *Morte d'Arthur* was the only discovery after he passed that mark that became a permanent acquisition."

One great favorite of Mark Twain's remains yet to be considered, and this favorite presents a particular problem—his friend, William Dean Howells. A problem because, even if we discount his expressed dislike of novels in general, Howells always wrote exactly the kind of novels which, when they were written by other people, most emphatically disgusted Mark Twain. In his essay on Howells, he confines himself, for the most part, to praising the novelist's style—"For forty years his English has been to me a continual delight and astonishment" —always one of his great themes in discussing books. But the *Letters* make it abundantly clear that it was not only Howells' style that he admired. "You are really my only author; I am restricted to you, I wouldn't give a damn for the rest." He praises his friend's ability to make all motives and feelings clear "without analyzing the guts out of them, the way George Eliot does." He praises him, too, because he is true to life. "The creatures of God do not act out their natures more unerringly than yours do."

In dealing with a writer whose tastes are as inconsistent as we have observed those of Samuel Clemens to be, we cannot, of course, state positively that he would not have enjoyed Howells' work had he not been friendly with him personally. Though rather extravagant, his criticism is in general sound: he praises Howells for the right things; he is more nearly correct, I believe, than the average critic of 1935 on the same subject. Yet the situation being what it was, it is impossible to believe that the personal element did not enter into it.

Mark Twain admired Howells also because Howells had some gifts that he knew he himself lacked—"can't write a novel, for I lack the faculty"—and Mr. Van Wyck Brooks would make much of this in explaining Mark Twain's attitude toward fiction in general. "Do we ask, then, why Mark Twain 'detested' novels? It was because he had been able to produce only one himself and that a failure." This is an acute observation, but it would be an error to explain the whole situation on this basis. Mark Twain did have a voracious appetite for "facts," for "reality," and I think Mr. Brooks would admit that he was reared in an atmosphere where history and biography were regarded as more worthy the attention of a grown man than imaginative writing could possibly be. Moreover, we can accept his blanket statement only as we make many exceptions: there were many novels which he did enjoy. Even without going in too heavily for æsthetics, his mature judgment told him that the serious novelist was a very important person indeed. "There is only one expert," he declared in his attack on M. Paul Bourget, "who is qualified to examine the souls and the life of a people and make a valuable report—the native novelist."

So it was that he stored the well, and that life stored it for him. It is time now to see what he drew up out of it.

The Divine Amateur

"I am liable, some day, to want to print my opinion on jurisprudence, or
Homeric poetry, or international law, and I shall do it."

MARK TWAIN, 1870.

I

IN 1888, Charles H. Clarke, editor of the Hartford *Courant,*
was chosen to advise Mark Twain that Yale University had
made him a Master of Arts. The humorist declared himself
"mighty proud of that degree," in fact "vain of it." "And," he
added, "why shouldn't I be?—I am the only literary animal of
my particular subspecies who has ever been given a degree by
any College in any age of the world, as far as I know." To
which Clarke immediately replied, "You are 'the only literary
animal of your particular subspecies' in existence and you've no
cause for humility in the fact."

So he was, and so he is still—in the words of William Dean
Howells, "sole, incomparable, the Lincoln of our literature"—
for while he inherited a tradition and exemplified a type, he
alone of the group to which, in a general way, he belonged,
possessed the genius necessary to lift a writer above the common
level, he alone addressed a world audience, and he alone is
widely read and remembered today. At the time of his death
he was certainly the most famous man of letters in America, if
not in the world, yet so far was he from the orthodox notion of
what a literary man ought to be that most readers found it impossible to classify him under this rubric. He was something
different, in some ways perhaps something inferior, but certainly something infinitely more personal and vital. In America
the most distinguished of his immediate contemporaries were
Howells and Henry James—we of these latter days would be
strongly tempted to add Henry Adams. Clemens, however,

could not read James at all—he "would rather be damned to John Bunyan's heaven"—and James cordially returned the compliment, for it seemed to him that Mark Twain's appeal must always be limited to "rudimentary minds." But it is not only when we compare him with extreme, self-conscious artists like James or Meredith that Clemens seems to belong to another order. Compare him with Fielding, compare him with Dickens, compare him even with H. G. Wells, and the contrast is still sufficiently marked. These men can never be accused of living in the ivory tower. They come immediately and directly into contact with a thousand phases of life that the exquisites have never touched; purely æsthetic considerations are never the be-all and the end-all of their concern. Yet they are almost as different from Mark Twain as are James and Meredith themselves.

What is this difference? The answer may be given in a single word: the Frontier. To be sure, Dickens, born near London, quite failed to run the gamut of the school and university life of his day, and we have already seen that young Sam Clemens' opportunities for reading, though in Hannibal, were by no means negligible. Yet these considerations do not, after all, have very much to do with the case. Dickens was born into an old civilization; Mark Twain lived on the edge of the forest. It was not the eddying currents of life in a great city that stimulated his imagination: it was the mighty Mississippi, the Father of Waters, flowing to the sea. He came into daily contact with negro slaves, their minds still full of the imaginings of a primitive race. His was a country whose life was still to come. When Dickens thought about literature, he knew just what he had in mind. He was thinking about Shakespeare and Ben Jonson, about Fielding and Smollett and Sterne. Mark Twain did not think much about literature in this sense, yet he was abnormally sensitive, æsthetic, creative. He was to enter the kingdom by devious paths, yet he had been foreordained to possess it from before the foundation of the world. As we have already seen, he came in time to love books and to use them wisely for whatever they had to give to such a person as himself. But they gave to him always with a difference, and when it came to actual writing on his own account, he never ceased to draw upon the unique reservoir of his own precious experiences. This store served him as long as he lived.

There is, therefore, a distinct folklore element in all the best work of Mark Twain, and Gamaliel Bradford is right when he speaks of him as "the bard . . . the old, epic popular singer, who gathered up in himself, almost unconsciously, the life and spirit of a whole nation and poured it forth, more as a voice, an instrument, than a deliberate artist." Mr. DeVoto, combating Mr. Brooks's view that there was no art on the frontier, adduces the fact that the English and Scottish popular ballads were well known there, but he brings forth no evidence to prove that Mark Twain was familiar with them. The ballads were not native material; he could have derived comparatively little from them in any event. But there was a considerable body of American folklore, notably interpenetrated with negroid elements, that Mark Twain did know and that he assimilated into the very fiber of his being. And there are passages in his own work —Tom Sawyer whitewashing the fence is an example—that have already become a part of American folklore themselves.[1]

He believed that literature of real value—literature which is creative, not derivative—can be produced only by the writer who is willing to give himself, absolutely and unreservedly, to his material. In 1868, his friend Mrs. Fairbanks speaks of his authenticity. "There is nothing," he writes, "that makes me prouder than to be regarded by intelligent people as 'authentic.' A name I have coveted so long—& secured at last! *I* don't care anything about being humorous, or poetical, or eloquent, or anything of that kind—the end & aim of my ambition is to be authentic—is to be considered authentic."[2] Much later in life, he lays down a rule concerning the "native novelist": "This native specialist is not qualified to begin work until he has been absorbing during twenty-five years. How much of his competency is derived from conscious 'observation'? The amount is so slight that it counts for next to nothing in the equipment. Almost the whole capital of the novelist is the slow accumulation of *un*conscious observation—absorption."

Tom Sawyer and *Huckleberry Finn* are the most rewarding of his books to examine from this point of view. Aunt Polly is indebted to Mark Twain's mother and Judge Thatcher to his father; Sid is drawn from his brother Henry, and his sister Pamela furnished the original of Cousin Mary. Huck Finn is Tom Blankenship, the village vagabond; Nigger Jim was derived from Uncle Dan'l, a slave on the plantation owned by John Quarles, Mark Twain's uncle, where the boy spent so many happy days. Tom Blankenship's father was town drunkard in Hannibal, as Huck's father is represented in the book, and Injun Joe was another disreputable local character. The "Duke" was a journeyman printer whom Mark Twain met, at a later date, in Virginia City. According to the Preface, Tom Sawyer too was drawn from life, "but not from an individual— he is a combination of the characteristics of three boys whom I knew." One of them—by far the most important—was named Sam Clemens. He used actual places as well as persons in his stories. John Quarles's farm was moved down to Arkansas both in *Huckleberry Finn* and in *Tom Sawyer, Detective*. "It was all of six hundred miles," said Mark Twain, "but it was no trouble; it was not a very large farm—five hundred acres, perhaps—but I could have done it if it had been twice as large." Yet he never copies blindly; whatever he used was transformed, recharactered, transmuted into art. As he grew older, his memory relinquished its hold on facts, but it retained impressions tenaciously. He may have stretched it a little when he described Tom Sawyer as belonging "to the composite order of architecture," but there are many things in his work that belong to that order. In life, Injun Joe did not die in the cave, though he was lost there on one occasion, and Huck Finn's refusal to surrender Jim is based on a very different kind of circumstance in the life of Tom Blankenship.

Being a folk artist, Mr. Lewisohn has lately remarked, Mark

Twain necessarily lacks aloofness—"there is never a great distance between himself and his subjects"—and he "never stands above the world of illusion which he delineates nor indeed knows it as such." This is description, not disparagement, for as the critic continues: "So in his small and homespun way, Mark Twain, once more like the balladists of Europe, is related to Homer himself who, also, raised into the immortal realm of the imagination the life and conflict of obscure villages among the otherwise forgotten Ionians of the isles and the Asian shore. A poor relation, a late descendant, but of the authentic lineage and blood." You cannot have Homer and Dante combined in the same person; no more can you have Samuel Clemens and James Joyce.

The frontier determined his method as well as his materials.[3] Mr. Brooks, though he speaks disparagingly, is not far off when he calls him "an improvisator . . . who composed extempore." Stuart Sherman's facts are right but his conclusion is wrong when he writes: "He would begin a story . . . on the key of impressive realism, shift to commonplace melodrama, and end with roaring farce; and this amounts to saying that he did not himself steadily take his fiction writing seriously." It "amounts" to nothing of the kind; this is simply the way the "improvisator" works. Sherman comes much closer to understanding Mark Twain in another essay, when he remarks of the General Grant speech: "That was humor befitting the Welsh giants of the Mabinogion"; and it is very interesting to see how the scholar's knowledge of a piece of primitive literature in an alien language here assists Sherman to comprehend an almost contemporary writer who is doing the same sort of thing with native materials. Miss Constance Rourke not only gets her facts correctly but states the case admirably when she writes: "He was primarily a *raconteur,* with an 'unequaled dramatic authority,' as Howells called it. He was never the conscious artist, always the improviser. He had the garrulity and the inconsequence of the earlier comic story-tellers of the stage and tavern; and his comic sense was theirs almost without alteration."

II

THE *raconteur* did not write, he talked; and our folk-ballads and epics were chanted for many years before anyone ever thought of writing them down. To say that Mark Twain was an "improvisator," a *raconteur,* is, therefore, virtually equivalent to saying that he was a talker and not a writer. In 1874, when Howells asked him to look over a manuscript from the point of view of checking the dialect, he replied: "All right, my boy, send proof sheets *here*. I amend dialect stuff by talking and talking and *talking* it till it sounds right." He loved the human voice, even in speech, better than any instrument—"Bob Ingersoll's music will sing through my memory always as the divinest that ever enchanted my ears"—and it was his opinion "that one cannot get out of finely wrought literature all that is in it by reading it mutely." Mr. Paine is the last writer who could be accused of wishing to disparage Mark Twain as a man of letters, yet Mr. Paine has written: "It is the opinion of most people who knew Mark Twain personally that his impromptu utterances, delivered with that ineffable quality of speech, manifested the culmination of his genius."

This being true, it was inevitable that the platform should claim him in many ways. In early days he longed to be a minstrel or a clown. He lectured; he gave readings; he told stories; and when he was not before an audience, he was generally reading aloud to his friends and the family at home. "He was the most perfect reader I have ever known," writes Robert Underwood Johnson. "His voice was peculiarly musical and had its own attraction, while his clear rendering of meanings in the most involved versification was sometimes like the opening of a closed door." I have already spoken of his readings from Browning, but I think I am even more impressed by what happened one night in San Francisco, long before he was a celebrity, when he dropped in at the *Call* office about seven o'clock, just as the boys were getting ready to go to the theater. He sat down and began to reel off stories and reminiscences, and the first time anybody thought to look at his watch it was eleven o'clock.[4]

With acting he had, of course, much less experience. There were amateur theatricals at home—charades, and mimicry of one kind or another—and in 1876 he appeared as Peter Spyle in *Loan of a Lover* when that comedy was presented by a dramatic society in Hartford. He seems to have been good: Mrs. Fields compared him to Joseph Jefferson, and Augustin Daly did his best to bring the play to New York. But here again he was the incurable "improvisator," for, as W. W. Ellsworth tells us, "he would put in lines, which, while very funny to those on the other side of the footlights, were decidedly embarrassing to his fellow actors. At one point I remember he began to tell the audience about the roof which he had just put on an ell of his new house and rambled on for a while, ending up that particular gag by asking Gertrude, much to her embarrassment, if she had ever put a tin roof on *her* house." In an 1881 letter, Mark Twain remarks that he improvised on the stage because to stick to the text was "a thing which would have been impossible with my rickety memory." Whatever the motive, he would, as a professional actor, have experienced the same difficulty in confining himself within the legitimate bounds of drama as he did as a writer trying to keep within the orthodox literary forms. It is no accident that the artist of our own time with whom he is most frequently compared is Will Rogers. Vaudeville and the revue must have been his special field.

He was not very far from either in his platform work, the lecturing and reading that, take it all in all, consumed so large a share of his energies. Platform work would seem to have been even more necessary to him than it was to Dickens. Dickens loved the platform because it satisfied the theatrical side of his nature and brought him into direct, personal contact with his readers, but Mark Twain actually needed it for the full development of his art. Of course both men persuaded themselves that they hated the platform and turned to it only when impelled by direct financial necessity, but we know better than that.

Mark Twain declined some very attractive offers, yet when he had a really good audience he was in heaven, and his wife sized the situation up unerringly when she wrote of the "Equator" tour: "The platform he likes for the two hours that he is on it, but all the rest of the time it grinds him." In other words, he liked lecturing, but he disliked the discomforts which accompany it. As late as 1909, when he was a dying man, he told Miss Wallace he would like to go back to it.

Of the consummate art with which he carried it off there would seem to be no question. Occasionally somebody like H. R. Haweis went to hear him without knowing quite what to expect, and was, as a result, somewhat disappointed in him, yet it is Haweis himself who testifies unmistakably to his spell. The lecturer's appearance was unimpressive, we are told, and he did not seem to be at his ease. He said very little that would have been worth putting in print. Yet when it was over and the disappointed auditor looked at his watch, he was astonished to discover that Mark had been speaking an hour and twenty minutes. "It seemed ten minutes at the outside."

Toward the end of his career, Mark Twain often availed himself of an old man's privilege, and said, on public occasions, whatever happened to come into his head. During his earlier life, however, he made the most careful and elaborate preparation imaginable, always taking great pains that whatever he did should seem to the audience completely casual. He was as particular about his "spot" on the program as the most expensive vaudeville star, and "How To Tell a Story" proves that he had considered the technique of his subject down to the minutest detail. In fact, he virtually writes a treatise on the pause.

III

WHEN it came to the writing of fiction, however, he was quite incapable of thus calculating his effects. Madame Gabrilowitsch, indeed, quotes an interesting letter he once wrote her mother, in which he says: "Yesterday I worked all day on a plan for a story. I got the plan all written down—two pages of note-paper and it was a very satisfactory day's work. I got to work at two in the afternoon and by six-thirty had written 2,500 words, the first chapter and part of the second, and the story already under swift movement." Such things were very unusual, however; generally he starts without a plan and lets the solution come as it will, or refuse to come at all, which, indeed, in a great many cases, it did, and so we get the many abandoned enterprises in the form of great quantities of Mark Twain manuscripts that have never been printed and never will be. "I began with the first red bar," he writes his child friend, Elsie Leslie Lyde, describing the slipper he made for her, "and without ulterior design, or plan of any sort—just as I would begin a Prince and Pauper or any other tale. And mind you it is the easiest and surest way; because if you invent two or three people and turn them loose in your manuscript, something is bound to happen to them—you can't help it; and then it will take you the rest of the book to get them out of the natural consequences of that occurrence, and so, first thing you know, there's your book all finished up and never cost you an idea."

Of course, such an utterance cannot be taken too seriously, but it does not stand alone. Take, for example, the Foreword to *Those Extraordinary Twins*. It, too, is couched in terms of burlesque, yet there is evidence enough to show that he often did work in the manner here described. When he starts to work on a novel, he says, he has no story. "He merely has some people in his mind, and an incident or two, also a locality." Nor is he planning to write a long book: all he has in mind is "a little tale; a very little tale; a six-page tale." As he proceeds, however, not only does his material expand indefinitely, but "the original intention (or motif) is apt to get abolished and find itself superseded by a quite different one." So it was with *Pudd'nhead Wilson,* which began as a farce with one set of characters and ended as a tragedy with a second set of characters. And he describes the difficulties he experienced in taking the twins out of the altered story so that Roxy and her associates might occupy unhin-

dered the foreground of the stage they had usurped for themselves.

Mr. Paine has recorded delightfully how Mark Twain would
make up stories for his children involving various objects of interest in their house. "On one side of the library, along the
book-shelves that joined the mantelpiece were numerous ornaments and pictures. At one end was the head of a girl that they
called 'Emeline,' and at the other was an oil-painting of a cat.
When other subjects failed, the romancer was obliged to build
a story impromptu, and without preparation, beginning with
the cat, working along through the bric-a-brac, and ending
with 'Emeline.'" I should like to have heard those stories, but I
am not sure they afforded the best kind of preparation for the
work he had to do at his desk. "If something beyond or beside
what he was saying occurred to him," writes Howells, "he invited it into his page, and made it as much at home there as the
nature of it would suffer him." There is a good example toward
the end of Chapter XXXV in *Life on the Mississippi:* "Here is
a story which I picked up on board the boat that night. I insert
it in this place merely because it is a good story, not because it
belongs here—for it doesn't." Indeed there are times when
Mark Twain suggests his own yarn about the man who was
never able to finish the story he started out to tell because every
sentence he uttered reminded him of something else, and he
could never resist the temptation to go on and talk about that.

This ragbag structure turns his more discursive books into so
many carryalls, and by the time he comes to write his *Autobiography* he has gone over to a frank glorification of literary anarchy. "Start at no particular time of your life; wander at your
free will all over your life; talk only about the thing which interests you for the moment; drop it the moment its interest
threatens to pale, and turn your talk upon the new and more
interesting thing that has intruded itself into your mind mean-
time." The result was the last kind of autobiography one would
have expected a literary man to write.

Probably no other great writer ever wasted so much of his energy. "Last summer I started 16 things wrong—3 books and 13 mag. articles—and could only make 2 little wee things, 1500 words altogether, succeed:—only that out of piles and stacks of diligently-wrought MS., the labor of 6 weeks' unremitting effort." Once he makes literary capital out of this very failing, in "A Medieval Romance," where he works up a perfectly terrific situation, and then lets us down to work out the solution for ourselves. Even the books he did carry through to completion went along at a distinctly haphazard rate. "It is my habit to keep four or five books in process of erection all the time, and every summer to add a few courses of bricks to two or three of them; but I cannot forecast which of the two or three it is going to be."

None of this, not even the letter to Elsie Lyde, means that Mark Twain was lacking in creative energy; indeed, it would be fairer to say that he had too much creative energy. It is only the literary craftsman who can plan all his effects beforehand.[5] Yet it would certainly be fair to say that his energy was of the wavering variety; it was never more than imperfectly under his own command. The natural result is that hardly any of his books achieve unity of tone or succeed in maintaining anything like a standard of uniform excellence. Hannibal invades Eseldorf in *The Mysterious Stranger,* and in the *Joan of Arc* it breaks through into medieval France. *A Connecticut Yankee* alternates between satire and burlesque; *Tom Sawyer* is both an idyll of remembered childhood experiences and a dime novel. *Huckleberry Finn* starts uncertainly, achieves magnificence in the great days on the river, the feud, the killing of Boggs, and kindred episodes, then "dies" slowly, in the tiresome, long-drawn-out account of the "rescue" of Nigger Jim. On the whole, it seems difficult to avoid accepting Arnold Bennett's judgment on both *Huck* and *Tom,* that while they are "episodically magnificent, as complete works of art they are of quite inferior quality."[6]

Structure, then, was his Waterloo; structure was to him what perspective was to Rossetti's painting. He himself seems to have felt that he was weak also in characterization: "it is a line of characters whose fine shading and artistic development requires an abler hand than mine; so I easily perceived that I must not make the attempt." He was right if by a gift for characterization one understands the faculty of constructing a character as Thackeray and Flaubert and William Dean Howells possessed it, or the ability to portray a complex type against the realized background of a highly involved civilization. On the other hand, his ability to evoke character, as distinct from constructing it, is very great, as many an incident in the odyssey of Huckleberry Finn or in Roxy's adventures with her wayward son, and many a moment even in quite inconsequential sketches, can testify. It is just this touch of genius that, burning fitfully and erratically, glorifies much of even Mark Twain's second-rate work and will always hold the attention of discriminating readers, despite the obvious faults and crudenesses writ large over his achievements.[7]

With such limitations and with such gifts, it was inevitable that Mark Twain's best books should be, as I suggested at the outset, those which permitted him to draw upon the memories of his early life. This is more common among writers than we sometimes realize. Miss Willa Cather, for example, believes that all creative writers assemble their materials, unconsciously, in youth, that during their actual writing careers, they achieve little more than recollecting and reassembling, and she assures us that this has been true in her own case. Mark Twain's sense of the past was always strong in him. He brooded over it, he possessed it, and the curious detachment from the world immediately round about which was natural to his temperament reinforced this inborn tendency. As he grew older, his mind tended more and more to dwell in the past, for the Mississippi world that had produced him was so different from the one in which he spent his maturer years that it took on in memory the iridescent colors of a dream; when he thought about it, it always seemed as if he were reliving a previous existence. That lovely land he held fast and made his own, safe against change, safe from the vicissitudes of actual experience. He operated on it; he turned it into the stuff of art. I have already remarked that Hannibal intrudes upon both the *Joan of Arc* and *The Mysterious Stranger*. Mr. West has pointed out in some detail the elements of Mississippi folklore that have been permitted to enter into the history of the Maid of Orleans, and Parrington is right when he says that *"The Mysterious Stranger* is only *Tom Sawyer* retold in the midnight of his disillusion."* Mr. Brooks touches the same aspect of his mind when he marks the difference in *The Innocents Abroad* between his poetic treatment of Palestine and his "hard-boiled" attitude toward Europe. "His attention had been fixed in his childhood upon the civilization of the Biblical lands, and that is why they seemed to him so full of poetry and dignity; his attention had never been fixed upon the civilization of Europe, and that is why it seemed to him so empty and stupid." As he grew older, his writing became more and more personal:[8] it is no accident then that, like Doctor Johnson on the other side of the water, he should seem to loom more impressively in American literature as a personality than he does as a writer. Once he himself touches upon this matter: "If Byron—" he says, "if any man—draws 50 characters, they are all himself—50 shades, 50 moods, of his own character." This theory alone might lead one to draw the conclusion that no man's writing can possibly have any interest or any appeal except for the writer himself, in other words, to give up the idea that art involves the communication of life-experience altogether. To this ridiculous position some of the "advanced" artists of these latter days seem very nearly to have come. Mark Twain does nothing so silly. For he immediately adds: "And when the man draws them well why do they stir my admiration? Because they are me—I recognize myself." It is this fundamental, underlying community of human experience upon which all art must finally depend.

IV

Mark Twain began scribbling before he had left Hannibal, and even during his years on the river he did not wholly lay his pen aside. Yet his approach to the writer's career was slow, hesitant, and indirect. As has already been pointed out, even after the phenomenal success of *The Innocents Abroad,* he thought of himself as a journalist rather than as an author, and even when he was firmly established as a man of letters, he could still permit other interests to deflect him from his work. During the happy Hartford days, social and domestic obligations were so pressing in the winter season that he came practically to confine his writing to the summer months at Quarry Farm. At a later date, nearly all his energies went into his publishing business, the Paige typesetter, and other promotional enterprises of various kinds. During the whole of the year 1885, when he was in the plenitude of his powers, he produced virtually nothing save "The Private History of a Campaign That Failed." He even talked of giving up literature altogether. "It's my swan-song," he writes Howells of the *Yankee,* "my retirement from literature permanently, and I wish to pass to the cemetery unclodded." Susy's clear mind understood the reason for all this: "Mama and I have both been very much troubled of late because papa, since he had been publishing General Grant's books, has seemed to forget his own."

His attitude toward himself as a man of letters is, in general, depreciating. When he tells Howells that he expects to appear in the encyclopedias of the future as "Mark Twain; history and occupation unknown—but he was personally acquainted with Howells," he is paying a graceful compliment—indeed he played a variation upon it in praising Ada Rehan and Augustin Daly—but the statement reflects his admiration for an art he felt he could never rival in kind. "The papers have found at last the courage to pull me down off my pedestal & cast slurs at me—" he writes Mrs. Fairbanks in 1871, "& that is simply a popular author's death rattle. Though he wrote an *inspired*

book after that, it would not save him."[9] Five years later, he
views the future no less unhopefully: "Two or three years more
will see the end of my ability to do acceptable work, & then I
shall have a great long compulsory holiday in which to drift
around & annoy people with over-liberal visits."[10] To "make"
the *Atlantic* seemed quite beyond him, and he was astonished
when Howells asked him to contribute. "I do not know that I
have any printable stuff just now . . . but I shall have by and
by. It is very gratifying to hear that it is wanted by anybody. I
stand always prepared to hear the reverse, and am constantly
surprised that it is delayed so long." When he was on his death-
bed, he told his daughter that he was doubtful that the sale of
his books would continue for more than a brief period following his death.

As time went on and he progressed steadily toward world
fame, Mark Twain naturally gained some confidence in himself
as a writer, though he never reached the point where he could
rely unaided upon his own judgment. "I will mail the book to
you and get you to examine it and see if it is good or if it is bad.
I think it is good, and I thought the Claimant bad, when I saw
it in print; but as for real judgment, I think I am destitute of
it." Mr. Paine has described in some detail the numerous abortive projects, entered upon enthusiastically and without plan,
some of them so eccentric that literature could not possibly have
been mined out of them, no matter how carefully they had been
wrought. The blindfold novelettes, *Simon Wheeler, Detective,
The Autobiography of a Damn Fool,* the history of the microbes—such projects awakened his wildest enthusiasm while
Huckleberry Finn lay about the house for years, unfinished and
unregarded. It is this capacity for absorption in even the most
trumpery projects that explains such fiascos in his career as the
Whittier birthday speech, where he is so carried away by the
idea he plans to develop that he utterly fails to consider the effect that his burlesque must have in the particular setting where
he plans to present it. After he has delivered the address he is
immersed in Stygian gloom: it seems to him that he has dis-

graced himself completely, both as a writer and as a man. Thirty years later he re-reads it: "I find it gross, coarse. . . . I don't like any part of it from the beginning to the end." But, almost immediately, he re-reads once more—and reverses his opinion entirely! "I have read it twice, and unless I am an idiot it hasn't a single defect in it, from the first word to the last. It is just as good as good can be. It is smart; it is saturated with humor. There isn't a suggestion of coarseness or vulgarity in it anywhere." Once he came late to dinner at the home of Carl Schurz. "I am very sorry, Miss Schurz; I was absorbed in reading the proofs of a new edition of my collected works and I had not noticed the time." He added: "I found myself discouraged in going over the pages, because I could find in them nothing or little that struck me as humorous." Toward the end of his life, he praises *Eve's Diary,* heartily but not, I think, too highly; on the other hand, he quite overestimates *A Horse's Tale.* Six weeks before he died, he re-read *A Connecticut Yankee* for the first time in thirty years. "I am prodigiously pleased with it—" he writes Clara, "a most gratifying surprise."

I have already spoken of his failure to realize the value of *Huckleberry Finn.* "I have written nearly 400 pages on it—" he writes Howells in 1876, "therefore it is very nearly half done. . . . I like it only tolerably well, as far as I have got, and may possibly pigeonhole or burn the MS when it is done." Undoubtedly Mrs. Clemens had some influence here. *Huckleberry Finn* was not the kind of literature that she appreciated, and it suffered in her eyes in comparison with *The Prince and the Pauper,* which was completed about the same time. He himself was greatly pleased with this latter book, partly, no doubt, because of the family's enthusiasm for it, but partly also because it represented a nearer approach than anything he had done before to being a sustained piece of creative writing, of what the late nineteenth century understood by a work of art. It was something to have proved, to himself and to others, that he was more than a frontier humorist!

By the time *Huck* was published, however, Mark Twain

seems to have thought more highly of him. At least he writes
Joel Chandler Harris, in November, 1885, to thank him "for the
good word about Huck, that abused child of mine, who has had
so much mud flung at him. Somehow I can't help believing in
him, and it's a great refreshment to my faith to have a man
back me up who has been where such boys live, and knows
what he is talking about." After all, it is not surprising that
Mark Twain should have been somewhat slow to appreciate
the full merit of either *Huck* or *Tom*. They were something
new in literature; he was too close to them to judge their material dispassionately. In 1887, he senses the true idyllic quality of
Tom Sawyer: Tom Sawyer, he says, "is simply a hymn, put into
prose form to give it a worldly air." In 1904 William Lyon
Phelps asked him which of his books he valued most. He threw
the question back upon his interlocutor, and Phelps chose
Huckleberry Finn. After a pause, Mark said, "That is undoubtedly my best book." This was not his own settled opinion, however: in his biography, he goes on record officially as being
of the opinion that *Joan of Arc* is worth all the rest of his out-
put together.

V

ALONGSIDE his modesty, however, Mark Twain has faith in the
value of his work, his best work in any event. Theoretically he
is quite clear that the pursuit of fame is futile. "There is no satisfaction in the world's praise anyhow, and it has no worth to
me save in the way of business." You may prate all you like of
the pleasure there is to be found in the praise of discriminating
readers; the trouble with discriminating readers is that they do
not discriminate. The critics are the worst of all. "I'm not writing for those parties who miscall themselves critics, and I don't
care to have them paw the book at all." No, whatever reward
there is in creative work must be derived from the work itself.
"Dear Clara, I am very, very glad you are profoundly absorbed
in your labors, and care for no other pleasures, no other dissipa-
tions. It is as I used to be with the pen long ago, and it is life,

life, LIFE—there is no life comparable to it for a moment. Genius lives in a world of its own. . . . Everybody lives, but only Genius lives richly, sumptuously, imperially." He knew.

While he was still in Nevada he had come to realize that some of his things were good enough to deserve a wider audience than he habitually addressed. "But sometimes I throw off a pearl (there is no self-conceit about that, I beg you to observe) which ought for the eternal welfare of my race to have a more extensive circulation than is afforded by a local daily paper." When *The Jumping Frog* is widely reprinted and makes his name known on the East Coast, he is indignant to think that a sketch has been selected for Eastern circulation which does not represent him at his best. "To think that, after writing many an article a man might be excused for thinking tolerably good, those New York people should single out a villainous backwoods sketch to compliment me on!" He might despise the reviewers, but he would manipulate them just the same: he would send his books first to Howells, and Howells could set the tone for the rest. "I knew he would say the truth about the book—I also knew that he would find more merit than demerit in it, because I already knew that that was the condition of the book." He hated the British pirate, John C. Hotten, most of all, for adding drivel of his own to his books in order that he might get copyright on them in England. "My books are bad enough just as they are written, but what must they be after Mr. John Camden Hotten has composed half-a-dozen chapters and added the same to them?" And he is almost equally offended by inaccuracies in a newspaper article. "They put words into my mouth. I'd rather they had put street sweepings."[11]

Perhaps it is in connection with his *Autobiography* that we get from Mark Twain the frankest expressions of his faith in the interest of posterity. As his dictations absorbed him, his enthusiasm grew, and he told Paine he intended to go on until he had dictated a library, some of which would not be printed for a thousand years. "The edition of A. D. 2006 will make a stir when it comes out. I shall be hovering around taking notice, along with other dead pals." We must discount here, for he was always enthusiastic over a new enterprise, yet I think there can be no doubt that he lived a good deal in the thought of those who were to come after. Miss Wallace noticed that he seldom refused anyone permission to photograph him, and that he always faced the camera with a serious expression. "I think a photograph is a most important document, and there is nothing more damning to go down to posterity than a silly foolish smile caught and fixed forever."

He loved praise at all times, and was charmingly, almost naïvely grateful for it when it came. When Grace King told him how her father, in the agonies of Reconstruction, had turned for solace to *The Innocents Abroad,* how it was the first book, after Shakespeare, that he found money to buy, Mark's eyes filled with tears. "We shook hands," she writes, "and there was no need to say it, we felt we were friends for life." And if he was touched by the praise of an individual, how much more thankful, how proud he was when recognition came, as it were, officially, from a great university like Yale or Oxford. "Although I wouldn't cross an ocean again for the price of the ship that carried me, I am glad to do it for an Oxford degree." There was something pathetic about his gratitude. It was almost as though he needed to be reassured of his value.

He was not always true to his chaste mistress, but when disasters came upon him—when Susy died and the comforts of money crumbled—then he learned how much he had loved her. "Indifferent to nearly everything but work. I like that; I enjoy it, and stick to it. I do it without purpose and without ambition; merely for the love of it." It was his solace, his comfort, his refuge from tears. His old friend Joe Goodman had set him the example of self-denying absorption in an intellectual task. "You think you get 'poor pay,' for your twenty years? No, oh no. You have lived in a paradise of the intellect whose lightest joys were beyond the reach of the longest purse in Christendom." If only he himself had never left his own particular paradise! Now he was back, back from "following false images of good," and his heart would never wander again. "I work all the days, and trouble vanishes away when I use that magic. This book will not long stand between it and me, now; but that is no matter. I have many unwritten books to fly to for my preservation; the interval between the finishing of this one and the beginning of the next will not be more than an hour, at most." Mark Twain's biographer tells us that in his old age he was inaccurate on all subjects except those connected with his books. Mr. Brooks is surely right in his interpretation of this circumstance: "We can see from this that although his conscious life had been overwhelmingly occupied with non-artistic and anti-artistic interests, his 'heart,' as we say, had always been, not in them, but in literature."

VI

MARK TWAIN began his writing on the frontier, and the only kind of literary man that the frontier understood or encouraged or made possible was the humorist; therefore Mark Twain became a humorist. Mr. Brooks sees this circumstance as the first of a series of sins that life committed against Mark Twain, finds here a potentially great satirist, a true artist, warped in his growth, condemned and confined to an inferior type of work. Brooks has justly emphasized the elements of frontier violence that Mark Twain recoiled against; he has exhibited the crudenesses that, had Clemens been born in Boston, might never have disfigured his work. And if we object that he did come East at a comparatively early date, and might then have changed his type, Mr. Brooks is ready with two answers, both of which happen to be of considerable interest. The first is that by this time Mark Twain had established his reputation as a humorist; people expected him to be funny. And the second is that once more fate was unkind to him, for he was set down in the midst of the Gilded Age, and the Gilded Age hated art, asked of him indeed virtually the same self-suppression of his deeper instincts and emotions that the frontier itself had required.

That there is nothing here of any value to one who would

understand Mark Twain, I think only a very one-sided criticism could maintain, though I must add immediately that I think Mr. Brooks pushes his theory too eagerly and too far. It is true that Mark Twain's early humor is "of a singular ferocity," but so is that of all the other frontier humorists: they cannot, every one, have been kicking against the pricks, longing passionately to be Rabelais or Shelley. When Mark Twain complains of "the d—n San Francisco style of wearing out life," I attach no special significance to the circumstance: the praise of ease is a very common theme in his writings. When he fails to mention literature in his letters to his family, he is not necessarily ashamed of what he is writing. His business in the West is to build up a fortune, and he writes the folks back home about the kind of thing he thinks will interest them most. Finally, with regard to his reluctance to join the staff of the *Enterprise*. I cannot believe with Mr. Brooks that it means he feels he is betraying his genius in becoming a humorist. Rather, I think he is reluctant to give up the mining enterprise and own himself beaten in practical life.

A more fundamental objection to this particular phase of Mr. Brooks's theory would be that while undoubtedly Mark Twain was molded by the influences of the frontier, his humor was so intimately interwoven with the very quality of his mind that it is difficult to think he could ever have escaped the humorist's rôle, no matter what the surroundings of his early days might have been. His appearance was humorous, his speech was humorous—Hamlin Garland found that his drawl "and a curious aloofness of glance (as though he spoke through a mask) made it difficult . . . to take his serious statements at their face value." He was a "character," an "original," he saw things differently from the conventional person, he expressed them differently, as his mother had done before him. He could not anywhere have lived like the conventional person, not if the salvation of his soul had depended on it. After all, a man who will issue a public statement that the report of his death has been somewhat exaggerated, who will telephone the newspapers that it is not true that he is dying, for he would not do such a thing at his time of life, has no right to complain if he finds himself regarded more or less as a professional humorist. To Mr. Brooks all these things simply go to prove the point: the jester is wearing the mask to which he has condemned himself. Yet Mr. Brooks argues also that Mark Twain was subservient to his wife. He was not playing to the gallery when he enacted the funny man in the family circle, for such antics distressed her unspeakably. Despite his profound love, he could not avoid distressing her, for he could not avoid being himself.

No, he was a humorist, but even from the beginning he was more than a humorist, and he disliked it intensely when people failed to see that "more." He fears lest his platform work is degrading him, making him "a mere buffoon"; he stipulates that "no humorous pictures" must be used to illustrate one of his stories; he likes the *Atlantic* audience, "for the simple reason that it doesn't require a 'humorist' to paint himself striped and stand on his head every fifteen minutes." As early as 1870 he declares in his department in *The Galaxy,* that "These *Memoranda* are not a 'humorous' department. I would not conduct an exclusively and professedly humorous department for any one. I would always prefer to have the privilege of printing a serious and sensible remark, in case one occurred to me, without the reader's feeling obliged to consider himself outraged." "I like you, Trent," he told Professor W. P. Trent, when he crossed the ocean with him. "You are the only man on this ship who hasn't asked me to tell him a funny story."[12] On his first meeting with Helen Keller, he went out of his way to tell her that Mark Twain was a good name for him, because "he was sometimes light and on the surface, and sometimes—'Deep,' interrupted the child." Later, when she was older, and he could talk to her heart to heart, he confided that he wished he had been able to accomplish more. She protested. "Ah, Helen, you have a honeyed tongue; but you don't understand. I have only amused people. Their laughter has submerged me."

The facts are unquestionable, yet it still does not seem to me necessary to assume that Mark Twain was a writer forced out of the normal course of his life's development. Any self-respecting writer would become impatient of being considered merely a funmaker; it would inevitably be annoying to have to publish what you considered your best work anonymously, as Mark Twain published his *Joan of Arc,* because only on that basis could you hope to gain a fair hearing for it. A month to the day before he died, he wrote a little girl who had praised *The Prince and the Pauper* that he liked himself best when he was serious. I think we must allow something for sheer human perversity in this connection—a writer always tends to respect most highly the things that he cannot do himself—and I suspect we come pretty close to the heart of Mark Twain's objection in an 1881 letter in which he declares that he likes the *Prince* better than *Tom Sawyer* because "I haven't put any fun in it. I think that is why I liked it best. You know a body always enjoys seeing himself attempting something out of his line."

Yet when he stopped to reason the matter out, he knew that humor itself was a serious business. "Everything human is pathetic," says Pudd'nhead Wilson. "The secret source of Humor itself is not joy but sorrow. There is no humor in heaven." But here, on this earth, humor is the salt of society. "The minute it crops up all our hardnesses yield, all our irritations and resentments flit away, and a sunny spirit takes their place." Even, as the Mysterious Stranger points out, humor is of the highest value as a means of controlling social behavior. "For your race, in its poverty, has unquestionably one really effective weapon—laughter. Power, money, persuasion, supplication, persecution—these can lift a colossal humbug—push it a little— weaken it a little, century by century; but only laughter can blow it to rags and atoms at a blast. Against the assault of laughter nothing can stand."

Even aside from the problem of humor, however, Mark Twain would always have been impatient toward some aspects of his reputation and his work, for he was a writer always definitely conscious of the need for improvement. As soon as the

Innocents contract is signed, he sees himself moving onward to better things. "I shall write to the Enterprise and Alta every week, as usual, I guess, and to the Herald twice a week—occasionally to the Tribune and the Magazines . . . but I am not going to write to this, that and the other paper any more." The instinct of the journalist is strong in him, but he is not willing to permit the public to set his tone for him. He promises himself that after he is married, he will be done with "literature to please the general public." Emancipation did not come so soon. In 1899, he writes Howells of *The Mysterious Stranger:* "For several years I have been intending to stop writing for print as soon as I could afford it. At last I can afford it, and have put the potboiler pen away. What I have been wanting is a chance to write a book without reserves—a book which should take account of no one's feelings, and no one's prejudices, opinions, beliefs, hopes, illusions, delusions; a book which should say my say, right out of my heart, in the plainest language and without a limitation of any sort. I judged that that would be an unimaginable luxury, heaven on earth."

VII

MARK TWAIN never developed anything so elaborate as a critical theory in judging literature. Take modern French fiction, for example. Save that he dislikes *Salammbo,* he never comments upon it, except to sneer that the French novelists "know only one plan, and when that is expurgated there is nothing left of the book." He did not know French fiction well enough to justify any generalization concerning it, but even if he had, the detachment, the "artistic" point of view characteristic of modern French writers would not have endeared them to him. His own emotions are intimately involved in those of the characters he creates; he has all the authority of Anglo-Saxon tradition behind him when he declares that it is incumbent upon an author "that he shall make the reader love the good people in his tale and hate the bad ones." He insisted on truth, was impatient of anything savoring of humbug, either in literature or in life, yet, as we have already observed, he would have nothing to do with naturalism. "In the very last weeks of his life," writes Howells, "he burst forth, and, though too weak himself to write, he dictated his rage with me for recommending to him a certain author whose truthfulness he could not deny, but whom he hated for his truthfulness to sordid and ugly conditions."[13] When it came to constructing a literary theory, indeed, Mark Twain never got much further than his letter to Andrew Lang, written when he was disgusted over the English critics who had condemned *A Connecticut Yankee:* "I have never tried in even one single instance, to help cultivate the cultivated classes. I was not equipped for it, either by native gifts or training. And I never had any ambition in that direction but always hunted for bigger game—the masses. I have seldom deliberately tried to instruct them, but have done my best to entertain them. To simply amuse them would have satisfied my dearest ambition at any time. . . ."

On the technical aspects of style, he is much more precise and detailed. He prided himself on his skill in dialect, and an explanatory note at the beginning of *Huckleberry Finn* identifies the particular shadings employed because he did not want his readers to suppose "that all these characters were trying to talk alike and not succeeding." A grammarian would find his own English far from perfect. Split infinitives are common, and it is not unusual to come across such expressions as "I and my agents" and "it don't fit." On the whole, however, he gives the impression not so much of carelessness as of deliberate colloquial ease. "No one in the world speaks blemishless grammar . . .; therefore it would not be fair to exact grammatical perfection from the peoples of the Valley; but they and all other peoples may justly be required to refrain from *knowingly* and *purposely* debauching their grammar." There is an essay "Concerning the American Language," and in *Life on the Mississippi* there is a careful analysis of the speech of the South. Sometimes, when he is talking about a book he happens to dislike,

dialect

his comments on grammar become almost pernickety. And he was very sensitive about his punctuation: "Let the printers follow my punctuation—it is the one thing I am inflexibly particular about. For corrections turning 'sprang' into 'sprung' I am thankful; also for corrections of grammar, for grammar is a science that was always too many for yours truly; but I like to have my punctuation respected. I learned it in a hundred printing-offices when I was a journeyman printer; so it's got more real variety about it than any other accomplishment I possess, and I reverence it accordingly."

Style is the aspect he considers most frequently in the writers on whom he seeks to pass judgment, as when he condemns Cooper and Scott, Prescott, Lew Wallace, Bret Harte, or Charles Francis Adams. Dowden's biography of Shelley, which he detests for its treatment of Harriet, is "a literary cake-walk." He comments at some length on the clichés of Southern journalism, and his book on Christian Science attacks Mrs. Eddy for the barbarities of her style almost as heartily as for her cupidity.

When he approves, style is quite as important a factor. We have already seen this in connection with Howells. He reads one of Ingersoll's speeches to a group of girls in Hartford and tells them "to remember that it was doubtful if its superior existed in our language." He looks out for style even in informational writings which make no claim to be considered as literature, as when, in *Roughing It,* he quotes a sentence from Thomas J. Dimsdale's book on *The Vigilantes of Montana,* and comments: "For compactness, simplicity, and vigor of expression, I will 'back' that sentence against anything in literature." He is sensitive, too, to the fine qualities of style in the writing of his daughter Susy, which was certainly worthy of all the praise he bestowed on it: "I have been delighted to note your easy facility with your pen and proud to note also your literary superiorities of one kind and another—clearness of statement, directness, felicity of expression, photographic ability in setting forth an incident—style—good style—no barnacles on it in the way of unnecessary, retarding words."

On this basis, it should not be difficult to decide what he considered good style to be, a matter fully covered in the "nineteen rules governing literary art" which he draws up in his paper on Fenimore Cooper. "As to the Adjective:" says Pudd'nhead Wilson, "when in doubt, strike it out." Quotations from foreign languages impressed him as an unnecessary affectation. In his appreciation of Howells, he lays considerable stress on the novelist's ability always to be "able to find that elusive and shifty grain of gold, the right word."[14]

Feeling the importance of style so strongly as he did, Mark Twain surely could not have held up his own head as a self-respecting writer if he had not considered his own work at least competent along this line. He did so consider it. No other compliment ever pleases him quite so much as praise of his style. "At this moment, by good fortune, there chanced to fall into my hands a biographical sketch of me of so just and laudatory a character—particularly as concerned one detail—that it gave my spirit great contentment; and also set my head to swelling—I will not deny it. For it contained praises of the very thing which I most loved to hear praised—*the good quality of my English;* moreover, they were uttered by four English and American literary experts of high authority." Even more to the point is a remark in the book on Christian Science: "No one can write perfect English and keep it up through a stretch of ten chapters. It has never been done. It was approached in the 'well of English undefiled'; it has been approached in Mrs. Eddy's Annex to that Book; it has been approached in several English grammars; I have even approached it myself; but none of us has made port."

VIII

IT is interesting to cast a passing glance at Mark Twain as poet and dramatist. No man with his structural deficiencies could ever have hoped for success as a dramatist, yet he tried it, as he tried everything else, and the play made from *The Gilded Age* was, when acted by John T. Raymond, a great success. In 1874, he wrote a five-act play with only one character in it, the interest of the audience being centered on two other persons who never appear at all.[15] Theoretically, Mark Twain quite recognized his disqualifications as a dramatist: "I mean to have the modesty to serve a decent apprenticeship," he told Augustin Daly, "before I make such a lofty venture." Early in his career he collaborated with Bret Harte in a play called *Ah Sin,* and in 1877 he became greatly interested in an impossible drama about a detective. In 1883 he and Howells got together in an abortive attempt to revive Colonel Sellers. Howells rejected Mark's preliminary scenario on the ground that it was "as nearly nothing as chaos could be," and Mark "agreed hilariously . . . and was willing to let it stand in proof of his entire dramatic inability." Yet he went on with other dramatic plans and enthusiasms, he actually did dramatize *Tom Sawyer* and *The Prince and the Pauper,* and on one occasion, he attempted to collaborate with a Viennese dramatist in preparing plays in German for the Burg Theater! "I don't know that I can write a play that will play," he writes Howells in 1908, "but no matter, I'll write half a dozen that won't anyway." So he did, and we may take leave of his dramatic experiments with a letter to H. H. Rogers: "Put 'Is He Dead?' in the fire. God will bless you. I too. I started to convince myself that I could write a play, or couldn't. I'm convinced. Nothing can disturb that conviction."

As a poet, Mark Twain reminds one of Doctor Johnson's remark about the lady who had written a book. You would hardly raise the question whether or not he did it well; the wonderful thing was that he should have been able to do it at all. Miss Brashear thinks he wrote more doggerel and humorous verse during his Hannibal period than can now be identified. "The Aged Pilot-Man," in *Roughing It,* crude as it is, has a kind of ballad quality and manifests an elementary capacity for meter and rime. "The Derelict," the song of the fairy tree at the beginning of *Joan of Arc,* and the poem written in memory of his daughter Susy are much better, and these are Mark Twain's best pieces of verse.

IX

HE seems to have demanded no special concessions in the way of working conditions. When Mrs. Clemens arranged his desk for him neatly, he would be obliged to upset everything before he could get to work. Sometimes he would hire a room away from the family where he might have uninterrupted concentration, but when he was really interested he could write under conditions that many of us would consider absolutely prohibitive. "I am here in Twichell's house at work, with the noise of the children and an army of carpenters to help. Of course they don't help, but neither do they hinder. It's like a boiler factory for racket, and in nailing a wooden ceiling on to the room under me the hammering tickles my feet amazingly, sometimes jars my table a good deal, but I never am conscious of the racket at all, and I move my feet into positions of relief without knowing when I do it."

His habits as an author were irregular: he could never have confined himself to a Trollopean schedule. Once he waits weeks for a "call" before starting to work. There are occasions, on the other hand, when the subject takes "full charge"; the words "leap out" before he knows what is coming. Katy Leary says that when the spirit came upon him, he would sometimes jump out of bed in the middle of the night and sit down to write for hours at a stretch. In his old age, he remembered having written the bulk of *The Innocents Abroad* in sixty days. "I worked every night from eleven or twelve until broad day in the morning, and as I did 200,000 words in the sixty days the average was more than 3,000 words a day." When he was at work on *Roughing It,* he turned out between thirty and sixty-five manuscript pages a day: "I find myself so thoroughly interested in my work now (a thing I have not experienced for months) that I can't bear to lose a single moment of the inspiration." In 1894, he speaks of having added 1,500 words to *Joan of Arc* in a single day, "which was a proper enough day's work though not a full one." During the next two days he wrote 6,000 words, "and that was a very large mistake. My head hasn't been worth a cent since." *Joan* was, in general, easy for him—probably because of his own overwhelming interest in the subject—"a tale which tells itself"; he calls it, "I merely have to hold the pen."

You would not expect a man who took such a common-sense attitude toward the business of writing to be especially intractable in his dealings with editors, illustrators, and publishers, and Mark Twain was not. As editor of the *Atlantic* Howells testified that "with all his wilfulness there never was a more biddable man in things you could show him a reason for." Though he was at one time very much upset over what he considered unfair dealing on the part of Bliss and the American Publishing Company, such disagreements are not common in his life, and with Harpers, at the end, all went smoothly. When Dan Beard was chosen to illustrate the *Yankee,* Mark Twain remarked sarcastically that he hoped the artist would read the book before drawing his pictures, adding that he believed this was not the usual custom among book illustrators. The request was eminently a fair one, and both Beard and Hitchcock have testified to the warmth of his approbation and his eagerness to appreciate good work. When Hitchcock was working on *A Horse's Tale,* Mark Twain was much more specific than was his custom, for he was eager to have Susy appear in the pictures as the heroine, yet even here he acknowledged, "I find the artist knows more about what will make a good picture than I do. What I thought a good subject for a picture isn't worth a hang, and something I should not have thought of at all makes a very good one, so I will leave all that with you." The most famous set of illustrations ever prepared for a Mark Twain opus was, if we may trust the memory of the artist, inspired by Mark Twain himself. In a copy of *Life,* he saw a drawing by E. W. Kemble which resembled his conception of Huckleberry, and the choice was accordingly made.

John Drinkwater once expressed his impatience with those persons who are forever "suggesting" subjects to creative writers, the point being that if the writer undertakes what he must, he cannot accept commissions that have been imposed upon him, and if he is capable of handling the theme in question, he will be led to it sooner or later in the natural course of events. So it is or should be with every writer who evolves from within; so was it not with Mark Twain. He saw *The Innocents Abroad* only as a series of travel letters; it was Bliss who suggested the book, as later he suggested *Roughing It* also. *The Gilded Age* began with a half-serious challenge thrown out by Mrs. Clemens and Mrs. Warner. Even the Mississippi book, which Mark Twain wrote out of his own experience if he ever wrote anything, might never have seen the light if it had not been for Twichell's enthusiasm over his oral reminiscences. "What a virgin subject to hurl into a magazine!"[16] Here is the most striking illustration we have of the essentially undirected quality of his literary career.

II

MR. SAMUEL L. CLEMENS

CHAPTER I

Paradoxes

Do I contradict myself?
Very well then I contradict myself.
(I am large, I contain multitudes).

WALT WHITMAN: A Song of Myself.

I

CHAUCER writes of his "Doctour of Phisik":

He knew the cause of everich maladye—
Were it of hoot, or cold, or moyste, or drye—
And where they engendred, and of what humour.

We no longer believe, with medieval medical science, that
our particular "complexion," or temperament, is determined by
the balance of "humours" that make up our being, but the ideal
of a well-rounded life still rules us, and lucky is the man who is
able to carry sufficient spiritual ballast about with him to keep
his ship comfortably upright and afloat amid the eddying currents. As we turn now from Mark Twain the artist to Samuel
L. Clemens the man, there is nothing more important for us at
the outset than to determine, as best we can, the fundamental
basis of his temperament, to see him as he stands or fails to
stand in the midst of the varied influences and stimuli that life
brings to bear upon him.

Let us begin with the most external, the most obvious thing—
his appearance. It might seem that the best way to discover how
he looked would be to glance at a photograph. Language,
which is supremely fitted for narration, is much less apt when it
comes to description. This is true, yet a description involves a
larger element of interpretation than a photograph can give,
and we are not without interest to observe how Mark Twain
impressed various types of persons with whom he came in contact.

It may be well to begin with Bret Harte:

"His head was striking. He had the curly hair, the aquiline nose, and even the aquiline *eye*—an eye so eagle-like that a second lid would not have surprised me—of an unusual and dominant nature. His eyebrows were very thick and bushy. His dress was careless, and his general manner one of supreme indifference to surroundings and circumstances."

Let us hear Senator William M. Stewart, of Nevada, one of the few men who cordially disliked Mark Twain:

"I was seated at my window one morning when a very disreputable looking person slouched into the room. He was arrayed in a seedy suit, which hung upon his loose frame in bunches with no style worth mentioning. A sheaf of scraggy black hair leaked out of a battered old slouch hat, like stuffing from an ancient Colonial sofa, and an evil-smelling cigar butt, very much frazzled, protruded from the corner of his mouth. He had a very sinister appearance. He was a man I had known around the Nevada mining camps several years before, and his name was Samuel L. Clemens."

Mrs. James T. Fields took this snapshot at a later period:

"I want to stop here to give a little idea of the appearance of our host. He is forty years old, with some color in his cheeks and a heavy light-colored moustache, and overhanging light eyebrows. His eyes are grey and piercing, yet soft, and his whole face expresses great sensitiveness. He is exquisitely neat also, though careless, and his hands are small, not without delicacy. He is a small man, but his mass of hair seems the one rugged-looking thing about him."

Susy sees him with the eyes of love:

"Papa's appearance has been described many times, but very incorrectly. He has beautiful gray hair, not any too thick or any too long, but just right; a Roman nose, which greatly improves the beauty of his features; kind blue eyes and a small mustache. He has a wonderfully shaped head and profile. He has a very good figure—in short, he is an extraordinarily fine looking man."

William Dean Howells' picture has been painted with care: "Clemens was then hard upon fifty, and he had kept, as he did to the end, the slender figure of his youth, but the ashes of the burnt-out years were beginning to gray the fires of that splendid shock of red hair which he held to the height of a stature apparently greater than it was, and tilted from side to side in his undulating walk. He glimmered at you from the narrow slits of fine blue-greenish eyes, under branching brows, which with age grew more and more like a sort of plumage, and he was apt to smile into your face with a subtle but amiable perception, and yet with a sort of remote absence; you were all there for him, but he was not all there for you."

Joseph H. Twichell, on the other hand, gives us a rapid pen-and-ink sketch of Clemens on a special occasion, his meeting with the Prince of Wales at Hamburg, in 1892. The two men walked along the promenade together, "presenting in their person a striking and even comical contrast—the Prince, solid, erect, stepping with a firm and soldier-like tread; Mark moving along in that shambling gait of his, in full tide of talk, brandishing, as an instrument of gesture, an umbrella of the most scandalous description. . . ."

Finally, we have S. J. Woolf, the artist who painted him in 1906:

"Instead of the weather-beaten face which I had expected, I saw one softer and calmer, but no less strong, while the delicacy and refinement of his features were most noticeable. His hair, too, which I had always thought wiry, was glossy and silken. Never have I seen a head where it seemed more an integral part—its ivory-like tones melting imperceptibly into the lighter hues of the skin, so that the line of juncture was almost entirely lost. Even his hands betrayed a more actively nervous man than one would be led to imagine a former river-pilot could be."

So far, the balance of sweetness and strength would seem to be well maintained.

The delicacy of his features was not always appreciated by those who came into mere casual touch with him, however, for, in the early days especially, the aroma of the frontier still clung to him. Twichell speaks of his slouch hat pulled down in front, a lighted cigar tilted up almost to the brim. Bliss, too, was disappointed on his first sight of him. "Mark Twain's traveling costume was neither new nor neat, and he was smoking steadily a pipe of power."

People were impressed by his eyes; they were impressed also by his voice. "It was not a laughing voice," writes W. H. Rideing, "or a light-hearted voice, but deep and earnest like that of one of the graver musical instruments, rich and solemn, and in emotion vibrant and swelling with its own passionate feeling." He told Rideing he had discovered that the Jumping Frog story was two thousand years old. "Two thousand years never seemed so long to me, nor could they have seemed longer to anybody than they did in his enunciation of them which seemed to make visible and tangible all the mystery, all the remoteness and all the awe of that chilling stretch of time. His way of uttering them and his application of them often gave the simplest words which he habitually used a pictorial vividness, a richness of suggestion, a fulness of meaning with which genius alone could endue them." A part of his charm and his power was in the famous drawl he inherited from his mother, and that art played quite as large a part in it as accident, we may safely infer from his daughter's observation that he often lost it in private life.

During his early lecture days, Mark Twain was sometimes described by the newspapers as a curiosity rather than a beauty, and in his *Autobiography* he pretends to be greatly hurt by this. "I was never ugly in my life! Forty years ago I was not so good-looking. A looking glass then lasted me three months. Now I can wear it out in two days." He does seem to have been seriously concerned about his hair, however, for he had Katy Leary massage his head every morning, which, he had an idea, would prevent his ever growing bald.

Persons who found Mark Twain a phenomenon in his personal appearance were generally strongly influenced by their impression of his clothes. The first time Thomas Bailey Aldrich brought him home, one dark winter's night, his astonished wife saw "a most unusual guest, clothed in a coat of sealskin, the fur worn outward; a sealskin cap well down over his ears; the cap half revealing and half concealing the mass of reddish hair underneath; the heavy mustache having the same red tint. The trousers came well below the coat, and were of a yellowish-brown color; stockings of the same tawny hue, which the low black shoes emphasized. May and December intermixed, producing strange confusion in one's preconceived ideas."

He had always been rather interested in clothes. He was the glass of fashion in his pilot days, "given to patent leathers, blue serge, white duck, and fancy striped shirts," and there is a photograph of him, in his days of glory in Carson City, "in a long broadcloth cloak, a starched shirt, and polished boots." When he was thrown into the mining camps, such things were, of course, out of the question, and he went to the other extreme, taking the same pains to make himself a picturesque roughneck that he had once taken to appear as a picturesque dandy. Some of this he brought with him to the East, though he later outgrew it entirely, and Katy Leary tells how he would spend all morning dressing for the opera at Bayreuth. The careful attention he gives to the matter of proper attire for our diplomatic representatives abroad in his paper, "Diplomatic Pay and Clothes," is more like what one would expect from a woman than from a man.

Toward the end of his life, Mark Twain came before the world as a clothes-reformer, when he laid aside the conventional dark men's suit—he had always hated it—and, save for formal evening occasions, arrayed himself thereafter exclusively in white. He had always been sensitive to color combinations, in house furnishings as well as in clothes; he had often drawn the contrast between the graceful splendor of oriental garments and the stiff, cold awkwardness of the West. "I should like to dress in a loose and flowing costume made all of silks and velvets resplendent with stunning dyes, and so would every man I have ever known; but none of us dares to venture it." He could do the next best; he could wear white, which was at least cheerful, even if it did fall a long way behind oriental splendors. "He used to go," says Katy Leary, "in the beginning of the summer, and sit on the steps at 21 Fifth Avenue for a little while, in his clean white suit, white shoes, and everything spotless, and he'd have a nice straw hat on his head, too. Then when he'd see one of the busses coming along, he'd just run out and stop it and climb on top and ride to the end of the route to get the fresh air. Everybody used to look at him, on top of the bus, but he didn't mind that." Katy knew. Hadn't she, long years before, got him to put on warm, long nightgowns by the simple expedient of decorating them with red, and had he not cast aside his old, plain, short ones forevermore?

Mark Twain lives in the American imagination in those white clothes, but there was one garment that came his way before the end which he prized even more highly, and this was the scarlet gown he acquired when Oxford gave him the doctor's degree. He was utterly, disarmingly simple and childlike and charming about it. "I like the degree well enough, but I'm crazy about the clothes! I wish I could wear 'em all day and all night. Think of the gloomy garb I have to walk the streets in at home, when my whole soul cries out for gold braid, yellow and scarlet sashes, jewels and a turban!" He could not wear it all the time, but he did wear it at Clara's wedding, and it was not the only unusual garb that Stormfield ever saw him in. Once, when he entertained Miss Wallace, he had a girl's pink hair ribbon nodding waggishly in his white locks all evening.

II

MARK TWAIN's health is hardly a profitable subject to talk about, not because, as in the famous case of the snakes in Ireland, he didn't have any, but rather because he had too much. He was, it is true, a delicate child—seven months' children generally are—but when he was nine years old the change came, and he was always a remarkably well man. To be sure, we hear, now and again, of rheumatism, of gout, of lumbago; he was subject to bronchial colds; and with his superb disregard of diet, it was inevitable that he should suffer at times from indigestion. But he states categorically that he never had a headache or a toothache in his life. It was sometimes difficult for him to get to sleep, but, as Howells says, the trouble here was not so much sleeplessness as a "reluctant sleepiness," and he seems to have needed less sleep than most men. Even in his old age, he wore out his billiard partners. "Don't you ever get tired?" H. H. Rogers asked him. And he replied, "I don't know what it is to get tired. I wish I did."

The question changes its aspect somewhat when we turn from his physical to his nervous health. The imaginative temperament is never to be particularly recommended in this connection, and the scenes of violence and terror he witnessed in his youth—plus the stimulus of African magic—did not tend to improve the situation. When he was twelve years old, a terrible epidemic of measles raged in Hannibal, and the children died off like flies. "At some time or other every day and every night a sudden shiver shook me to the marrow, and I said to myself, 'There, I've got it! and I shall die.'" So nervous did he become that he felt it quite impossible any longer to endure his uncertainty, with the result that he deliberately exposed himself to the disease, contracted it, and for days hovered on the brink of death.[1]

It was always in the nighttime that he suffered most. A somnambulist in childhood, he recovered from this tendency in later years, but the night was always full of fearful dreams and horrible imaginings. We may call this a sign of his perpetual adolescence if we like, but if we are to be as honest as he was, we shall probably have to admit that not very many of us are as comfortable in the night watches as we are in the light of the blessed sun. Little things always fretted him terribly, and many of his outbursts of temper must be excused on the basis of his abnormally sensitive nature, for he was always calm and courageous in the face of a great calamity.

His nervousness appears also in his sensitiveness to sound. The ticking of a clock, the gnawing of a mouse, the rustling of paper, the monotonous whirr of a spinning wheel—these things were agony unspeakable to him. "Clocks . . . were a very serious aversion with my father," writes Madame Gabrilowitsch, "and he could not bear even the ticking of a watch. I do not believe that he ever carried a watch himself, and I am sure that at home we virtually lived without clocks." There is the picturesque story—sometimes made even more picturesque in the telling—of the time when he stayed at the house of Thomas Nast, and even though he had an early train to make in the morning, he could not get to sleep until he had stopped every clock in the house. He was terribly annoyed by late comers at his lectures, and he devised a special form of program, printed on stiff cord paper, which could neither rustle nor be used as a fan. One night, in a blinding fog, he went out in his nightgown to silence a barking dog. Clara's silk umbrella in his hand, he chased that dog two miles along the road, until the animal took to the fields, and Mark came home in the dawn, soaking wet and covered with mud.

Mark Twain, too, as we have seen, found one of life's richest satisfactions in the sound of the human voice, and only those who are similarly constituted can realize how much this meant to him, but alas! the penalty one must pay for this kind of enjoyment is that of, too often, being tormented by unpleasant voices. In the West, there was a little Swede who sang away continuously at one tune, "and it seemed to me, at last, that I would be content to die, in order to be rid of the torture." Even as a child, he was markedly sensitive in this regard. There was a slave boy in Hannibal, who was "the noisiest creature that ever was, perhaps." One day, Sam went raging to his mother, "and said Sandy had been singing for an hour without a single break, and I couldn't stand it, and *wouldn't* she please shut him up." The tears came into Jane Clemens' eyes, and she said, "Poor thing, when he sings it shows that he is not remembering . . . but when he is still I am afraid he is thinking. . . . He will never see his mother again; if he can sing, I must not hinder it, but be thankful for it." Sam's nerves were not very strong, but his humanity was, and Sandy's singing did not trouble him any more.

III

WITH regard to his diet, Mark Twain's only rule was to eat whatever he liked and as much as he liked. For breakfast he enjoyed beefsteak and coffee—much coffee—and his food was more likely to receive his undivided attention at this time than would be the case later in the day, when, especially if there were guests, he might very well prefer to give up eating, and march about the room, using his napkin as a flag, and deliver himself the while of a variety of well- or ill-considered opinions on all sorts of subjects. Lunch he rarely ate, though when Katy Leary laid a trap for him by ordering milk and huckleberry pie, he generally obliged her by disposing of half the pie. Pond found him extremely irregular in his eating habits, and Katy complains of his fads: "Sometimes he would just leave off eating everything except one thing, and would live on that all the time. Then there was a certain kind of bread he would have to have; and he took it into his head once to live just on breakfast food, and ran all about with it. Why, he would even go to dinners and parties and carry that old breakfast food with him." The breakfast food may have been wholesome enough, but some of his notions would have spelled suicide to any but a man with a cast-iron stomach. "I take only one meal a day just now. . . . It consists of four boiled eggs and coffee. I stir in a *lot* of salt and then keep on dusting and stirring in black pepper till the eggs look dirty—then they're booming with fire and energy and you can taste them all the way down and even after they get there." Once, at the home of Thomas Nast, he disposed of five plates of oysters, and his daughter prints one letter with the comment that "on lecture tours he seemed to have an appetite of magnificent proportions, quite unlike his usual one." The letter reads as follows: "I ate a hearty breakfast at nine this morning. On the hotel car at 1 P.M. I took a sirloin steak and mushrooms, sweet potatoes, Irish ditto, plate of trout, bowl of tomato soup, three cups of coffee, four pieces of apple-pie (or one complete pie), two plates of ice-cream and one orange. But I stopped then on account of the expense, although still hungry." He did not add, with Chaucer's eagle,

> Tak it in ernest or in game.

I prefer to take it "in game."

And he liked his food washed down by good liquor. When he first left home, his mother made him promise neither to drink nor to play cards, and he seems to have kept this promise faithfully until, on his becoming a pilot, she released him from it. Mr. Paine found him extremely temperate during the years of their intimacy, but is clear that spirituous refreshment is definitely a part of his life. He went in for high living occasionally during his San Francisco days, when he was associated with the bohemian newspaper crowd, though he seems to have cared little for it, and Henry Watterson is a good deal preoccupied with drinking in his recollections of the good times he and Mark shared together. Mark drank through the night, too, with C. W. Stoddard, following his lectures in London, after which he foresaw the end of his popularity and prophesied the poorhouse for himself and his family. At one time he got it into his head that he needed hot Scotch or ale or beer—the nostrum varied from time to time—to put him to sleep. Drunkenness appears frequently as a source of humor in the early Californian sketches, but not very often at a later date, and H. W. Fisher quotes him as saying, "I love a drink, but I never encourage drunkenness by harping on its alleged funny side." Mr. DeVoto reports on "private but unimpeachable information" that Mark Twain was once jailed for drunkenness, which is a little like asking us to credit an anonymous letter. But Mark himself writes Howells of an 1882 dinner in Boston: "Osgood, full, Boyle O'Reilly, full, Fairchild responsibly loaded, and Aldrich and myself possessing the floor, and properly fortified." He says

little about the temperance movement, save to rejoice in one letter that the churches of Hartford have never indulged in any
"rot," though he does wholeheartedly defend the women temperance crusaders, even when they use means that are outside
the law. In a country where "every ignorant whisky-drinking
foreign-born savage . . . may hold office, help to make the
laws," while these same rights are denied to them, he can see
no reason why women need be overscrupulous in the means
they choose "to protect their sons from destruction by intem-
perance."

But his particular indulgence, as all the world knows, was
smoking. He began to smoke as a small boy, and he lived thereafter until the day of his death in a cloud of tobacco. During his
mature life, he smoked almost incessantly—"Me, who never
learned to smoke, but always smoked; me, who came into the
world asking for a light"—and in his Seventieth Birthday
speech, he tells us that he made only two rules concerning it—
never to smoke more than one cigar at a time, and never to
smoke while sleeping or to refrain while awake. Howells and
Pond were alike appalled by his excesses. "I do not know,"
wrote the novelist, who detested tobacco, "how much a man
may smoke and live, but apparently he smoked as much as a
man could, for he smoked incessantly." He insisted he was master of the habit, not the habit master of him, for after their
marriage he did deprive himself of tobacco for a time to please
his wife—"not that I believed there was the faintest *reason* in
the matter, but just as I would deprive myself of sugar in my
coffee if she wished it, or quit wearing socks if she thought
them immoral"—but he considered it a good habit nevertheless,
and if you tried to tell him he was shortening his life, you made
no impression whatever. "Why, my old boy, when they used to
tell me I would shorten my life ten years by smoking, they little
knew the devotee they were wasting their puerile words upon;
they little knew how trivial and valueless I would regard a
decade that had no smoking in it!" Probably he did shorten his
life by it; he died of angina pectoris.

He would not smoke a "good" cigar, he had to have horrible, vile cheap cigars that nobody else would smoke, and a pipe was no good to him until someone else had broken it in. "I get a cheap man—a man who doesn't amount to much, anyhow: who would be as well, or better, dead—and pay him a dollar to break in the pipe for me. I get him to smoke the pipe for a couple of weeks, then put in a new stem, and continue operations as long as the pipe holds together." That this is literally true I very much doubt, but there can be no question that this is what he would have liked to do. Coulson Kernahan tells how in England Mark Twain went about with a pocketful of stemless bowls of corncob pipes and another pocket full of stems. He gave one pipe to Kernahan, who tried to smoke it, but the result was a dry tongue and a sore throat.

Yet every Napoleon meets his Waterloo sooner or later: otherwise human pride would become insufferable, and the gods would blot us from the earth. Mark Twain, accomplished smoker, met his in the "narghili" of the Orient. "I took one blast at it, and it was sufficient; the smoke went in a great volume down into my stomach, my lungs, even into the uttermost parts of my frame. I exploded one mighty cough, and it was as if Vesuvius had let go."

Smoking by women he ran across only in Europe, but he seems to have approved. If he had lived a little longer, he might have become more familiar with this exquisite contemporary symbol of refinement and sophistication.

IV

Mrs. Clemens called her husband "Youth," and never was there a more appropriate nickname. He was always young. He skipped lightly up and down the stairs as long as he lived, and because he liked the carved wooden Cupids on the headboard of his bed so much, he would lie at the foot always, in order that he might have the pleasure of looking at them. Youth was "the only thing that was worth giving to the race"; old age was an insult. For himself, he feared it; he held it off; he insisted that he did not feel old, whatever the calendar might say. Like Dickens, he hates leave-takings. "To part is to die a little," he will not say good-by to anybody if he can possibly avoid it. They throw his picture on the screen; it is made from a negative fifteen years old, without a single grey hair showing in his head, and a great feeling of sadness comes over him. When he dies at seventy-five, Katy Leary says, "It was a terrible, cruel thing to have him die, really, because he was too young—that is, he *felt* young, you know, and that made him young; and he could have said a good deal more."

When youth goes in fact, he clings to it in memory. He loved to talk about the past. When S. J. Woolf comes to paint his portrait, he walks up and down the room recalling the scenes of bygone days for some time before he can settle down to the sitting. This done, he shows the artist his mementoes, "and how his eyes glistened as he showed the various little keepsakes which brought back the memories of dead years." In his dreams he can still be a boy—thank God!—and when he returns to Hannibal for a visit and is received like a king, his feelings are very nearly too much for him.

He is youthful in his eagerness and intensity: he will get up at six o'clock in the morning to make the 4:00 P.M. train. His extreme reactions of glory and despair are youthful, his proneness to fall into moods, his extravagant praise and condemnation. His interest in curiosa, his taste for freaks is youthful. Youthful, too, are his fads, his "rages," and he is eminently youthful in his attitude toward money. Once he "discovered" that the use of spectacles was unnecessary, and not only did he lay aside his own, he persuaded the other members of his family to do likewise, with the result that they nearly all wrecked their eyesight before the enthusiasm wore off. "Plasmon" was another discovery, the wonderful food-medicine that was going to cure the human race of all its ills. He was always discovering something—generally something that the rest of the world had discovered long before, quite frequently something that the rest of the world had long since discovered was of no value.

His pranks, his eccentricities, his love of playing tricks on
other people combined with his utter inability to appreciate
them when they were played on himself, his love of the outré
and the unusual, his passion for shocking people—all these
things were youthful. The first time Mrs. Aldrich saw him, she
thought he was drunk, and if you think Mrs. Aldrich was
merely a prim, fussy New England woman, I give you Calvin
H. Higbie, Mark's partner in Western mining activities, who
was nothing of the sort. Higbie mistook him for a lunatic! In
toys and games of all kinds he had precisely the interest of a
child. Once a friend brought in a mechanical leapfrog. "Mark
was more amused," writes Moncure D. Conway, "than I had
ever seen him. He got down on his hands and knees and followed the leaping automaton all about the room."

He is youthful, too, in his restlessness. "A life of don't-care-a-
damn in a boarding house is what I have asked for in many a
secret prayer." His body roams up and down the world—he
crossed the Atlantic fourteen times within three and a half
years—and his mind ranges through the heights and depths of
speculation, yet he never stays anywhere long enough to feel
really at home. Partly it was because, as we shall see, he was always looking for something; he never arrived. But partly, too,
it was because there were so many, many wonderful things to
challenge his attention, so many objects luring him on, and he
could no more resist them than a kitten can—or a child. Helen
Keller tells how when she dined at his house, he became restless
during the meal and got up to walk around the table, talking,
bringing flowers to her to see if she could identify them. When
she could, he would hold forth on the undeveloped powers of
human beings. Then he would start the organ to discover
whether she could feel the vibrations, and when he had satisfied
himself on that score, he would think of something else.

His love of pageantry and his love of color mark the boy in
him also. He loved parades. When he was a child, he joined the
Sons of Temperance, not because he accepted their principles,
but because he loved the brilliant red sash they were permitted

to wear. Always he must have the most brilliant colors possible: his billiard table itself must be red, not the conventional green. White he never cared for greatly, save in his own white suits. He thought the brown-skinned races much more handsome than the Caucasians, and when he had occasion to point out to his daughter Jean that white was not God's favorite color, he told her that "Andrea del Sarto's pink-and-lily Madonnas revolt Him. . . . That is, they *would,* but He never looks at them."

Finally, he is youthful in his inability to stand alone, his life-long tendency to cast his burdens upon others. The most striking illustration is the way he rallies after H. H. Rogers takes over his financial affairs and orders him to stop walking the floor. Everything is all right now, and there is no need for him to worry any more. The same tendency appears all through his life. Without it, Mrs. Clemens would never have obtained the supremacy she established over his literary work.

V

So much has been written about Mark Twain's temper that one is inclined to pass over the subject lightly, yet I do not know in what connection his self-contradictory nature could be more clearly or more picturesquely set forth. "You observe that under a cheerful exterior I have got a spirit that is angry with me and gives me freely its contempt." He explains that this is the reason why he cannot write good satire. "I *hate* travel, and I *hate* hotels, and I *hate* the opera, and I *hate* the old masters. In truth, I don't ever seem to be in a good-enough humor with anything to satirize it. No, I want to stand up before it and curse it and foam at the mouth, or to take a club and pound it to rags and pulp." Serious crises, as we know, he met with fortitude and courage, but he was never able to control himself in little things. Perhaps he did not try, for his was a very intense, very nervous nature, and he may have felt that the satisfaction he derived from "blowing off steam" more than compensated him for the effort involved. In any case, let him misplace his matches, let the waiter fail to bring in his bacon grilled as he liked it, let a new suit of clothes arrive which he imagined did not fit him properly, let an autograph hunter forget to inclose a self-addressed envelope—and there was a veritable battle of the frogs and mice. It would not be fair to leave the impression that he never controlled himself. There was, for example, the time when he alone, among a group of listeners, kept his seat throughout the reading of an interminable and impossible poem. "Well, that young man thought he had a divine message to deliver," he remarked afterward, "and I thought he was entitled to at least one auditor, so I stayed with him." But this was rather exceptional. When he was full of malice, he once declared, he felt nearer to the Lord than ever before. "I feel as He feels of a Saturday night when the weekly report is in and He has had a satisfactory clean-up of the human race."

The terror he inspired on such occasions seems to have varied considerably. "When anger moved him," writes W. H. Rideing, "you could see his lean figure contract and his eyes ominously screw themselves into their sockets. Every fibre in him quivered, and for the moment his voice became acid and sibilant and out of tune—almost a whine. Then he would let himself out in a break, like that of a dam unable to hold the flood, in language as candid and unshrinking as the vernacular of the Eliza-bethans." Katy Leary, who, being Irish, loved a "scrap," was much less impressed, and so were his children. "We used to call Father the 'spitting gray kitten,' " writes Madame Gabri-lowitsch, "because in many of his spurts of irritation he kept a soft, fuzzy quality in his demeanor that reminded us of a little kitten with its fur all ruffled. We enjoyed this spectacle, and were inclined to inspire it whenever we could. When his performance was ended, we could exclaim, 'Oh, you bad, spitting gray kitten!' and he would laugh a gay little laugh and shake his leonine head of gray curls."[2]

The billiards to which Mark Twain devoted almost the lion's share of his attention in later years were not exactly calculated to minimize the probability of such outbursts as these to which

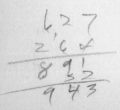

he was subject, and Mr. Paine describes the results with uncommon vividness:

"He was not an even-tempered player. When his game was going badly his language sometimes became violent and he was likely to become critical of his opponent. Then reaction would set in, and remorse. He would become gentle and kindly, hurrying the length of the table to set up the balls as I knocked them into the pockets, as if to show in every way except by actual confession in words that he was sorry for what no doubt seemed to him an unworthy display of temper.

"Once, when luck seemed to have quite deserted him and he was unable to make any of his favorite shots, the air became fairly charged, the lightning fierce and picturesque. Finally with a regular thunder blast he seized the cue with both hands and literally mowed the balls across the table, landing some of them on the floor. I do not recall his remarks during that performance—I was chiefly concerned in getting out of the way. Then I gathered up the balls and we went on playing as if nothing had happened, only he was very gentle and sweet, like a sunny meadow after a storm had passed by. After a little he said:

"'This is a most—amusing game. When you play—badly, it —amuses *me*. And when I play badly, and lose my temper, it certainly *must*—amuse—*you*.'"

One of his most admirable characteristics is illustrated here— his eagerness to make amends when he feels that he has done wrong. He did not always pour out his wrath upon others. He was quite as likely as not to treat the object of his anger with careful politeness and then go off by himself to blow steam to the four walls of his bedroom, which were not in the least disturbed by the performance. A lady betrays him into a sharp expression. "I am sorry," he writes; "for she didn't know anything about the subject, and I did; and one should be gentle with the ignorant, for they are the chosen of God." He goes to visit his mother and sister in Fredonia; while he is there, he has a clash with a man whom he despises, and he comes away "ashamed of myself;—almost too much humiliated to hold up my head and say good-bye. . . . I would have gone to that detestably oyster-brained bore and apologized for my inexcusable rudeness to him, but that I was satisfied he was of too small a calibre to know how to receive an apology with magnanimity. . . . I came away feeling that in return for your constant and tireless efforts to secure our bodily comfort and make our visit enjoyable, I had basely repaid you by making you sad and sore-hearted and leaving you so." At Victoria, B.C., he upbraids a captain for keeping a passenger boat waiting while he loads on freight. After thinking it over, he sends Pond to go see the captain, "to apologize for his unmanly abuse, and see if any possible restitution could be made." Before the voyage is over, he and the captain are the best of friends. He writes a sharp letter to William D. McCrackan, with whom he is having a controversy over Christian Science, then makes up his mind not to send it, but finds that it has already gone into the mail. With rare fineness of spirit, McCrackan returns the letter: the writer, he is sure, does not really mean the things he has written in it. Mark Twain recognizes this kind of spirit when he finds it—whether in Christian Scientists or others—and he and McCrackan are thereafter firm friends. He makes the acquaintance of Thomas Bailey Aldrich by writing him, rather sharply, demanding that he correct a misstatement in the paper he is editing, and before Aldrich has time to reply, he writes again. "I hear a good deal about doing things on the 'spur of the moment'—I invariably regret things I do on the spur of the moment. That disclaimer of mine was a case in point. I am ashamed every time I think of my bursting out before an unconcerned public with that bombastic pow-wow about burning publishers' letters and all that sort of imbecility, and about my not being an imitator, etc. Who would find out that I am a natural fool if I kept always cool and never let nature come to the surface? Nobody."

The most striking element in Mark Twain's rages was undoubtedly that furnished by his profanity, and however much some of us may have gained by being born in the latter days, we have all, I think, suffered one great loss: we have never heard Mark Twain swear. There can be no doubt that his profanity was one of his great gifts, that here his wonderful gift of phrase, his magnificent descriptive power were seen at their best. We have in print some lovely specimens of his invective. There is his epitaph for Leopold of Belgium, for example: "Here under this gilded tomb lies rotting the body of one the smell of whose name may still offend the nostrils of men ages upon ages after all the Caesars and Washingtons and Napoleons shall have ceased to be praised or blamed and been forgotten—Leopold of Belgium." Or, again, take the description he made, during one of his Christian Science rages, of the *Manual of the First Church of Christ, Scientist*—"that deceptively innocent-looking little book, that cunning little devilish book, that slumbering little brown volcano, with hell in its bowels." But it is a melancholy thing to be obliged to confine ourselves to mere descriptions of his actual performance. "To hear him denounce a thing," writes Mr. Paine, "was to give one the fierce, searching delight of galvanic waves. Every characterization seemed the most perfect fit possible until he applied the next. . . . His selection of epithet was always dignified and stately, from whatever source—and it might be from the Bible or the gutter." It was the cool deliberation with which he turned himself loose that was so unusual, and this comes out clearly in the description of Miss Elizabeth Wallace, who heard him occasionally in the billiard room. "Gently, slowly, with no profane inflexions of voice, but irresistibly as though they had the head-waters of the Mississippi for their source, came this stream of unholy adjectives and choice expletives. I don't mean to imply that he indulged himself thus before promiscuous audiences. It was only when some member of the inner circle of his friends was present that he showed him this mark of confidence, for he meant it in the nature of a compliment."

Of those who have recorded their opinions concerning Mark Twain's habit of swearing, only Robertson Nicoll seems to have been greatly shocked—"his habitual, incessant, and disgusting profanity"—and it is very likely that the fact that Nicoll, an Englishman, met him when he was raging over the Boer War may have had something to do with the intensity of his reaction. The usual view is that of Katy Leary who insists that it "never seemed really bad" to her. "It was sort of funny, and a part of him, somehow. Sort of amusing it was—and gay—not like real swearing, 'cause he swore like an angel." And she tells, further, the story of how Baby Jean was shocked one day when she heard a rough man swear in the streets, and how, when she was reminded that she had often heard her father swear, she replied earnestly, "Oh, no Katy! You're mistaken. That wasn't swearing. That was only one of papa's *jokes!*" It is out of the mouths of babes that the truth may come, and Mark Twain himself has stated the principle: "For it is not the word that is the sin, it is the spirit back of the word. When an irritated lady says 'oh!' the spirit back of it is 'damn!' and that is the way it is going to be recorded against her. It always makes me sorry when I hear a lady swear like that. But if she says 'damn,' and says it in an amiable, nice way, it isn't going to be recorded at all." When Mark Twain was introduced to Charles Major, his greeting was "I'm *damned* glad to meet you," and Major felt a warm, human friendliness behind the words and was not offended at all.[3]

It is said of him that he cherished resentments, that he made an art of hatred. Pond speaks of his "fierce spirit of retaliation" toward those who had injured him, and Howells refers guardedly to two men "of whom he used to talk terrifyingly, even after they were out of the world. He went farther than Heine, who said that he forgave his enemies, but not till they were dead. Clemens did not forgive his dead enemies; their death seemed to deepen their crimes, like a base evasion, or a cowardly attempt to escape; he pursued them to the grave; he would like to dig them up and take vengeance upon their clay." Probably one of these men was Paige, Paige of the typesetting machine. "Paige and I always meet on effusively affectionate terms, and yet he knows perfectly well that if I had him in a steel trap I would shut out all human succor and watch that trap until he died."[4]

Even a comparatively slight injury might call forth such expressions of undying hatred. The president of Vassar is not courteous to him when he gives a lecture there. "I did not see him any more, but I detest his memory." He was rudely treated, too, or thinks he was, in Buffalo; therefore, prima donna like, he will never lecture there again. Redpath has made a booking, but he must break it. "Otherwise I'll have no recourse left but to get sick. . . ." In 1876, he writes to Howells, "Carlton insulted me in Feb. 1867, and so when the day arrives that sees me doing him a civility I shall feel that I am ready for Paradise, since my list of possible and impossible forgivenesses will then be complete."

When he was an old man, Mark Twain remembered that he had once bought a revolver and traveled twelve hundred miles with it for the express purpose of killing a man. "He was away. With nothing else to do, I *had* to stop and think—and did. Within an hour—within half of it—I was ashamed of myself— and felt unspeakably ridiculous." Nothing further is known of this event. It may have occurred; it may have occurred exactly as related. But I would not place implicit confidence in it, for it may be only another example of Mark Twain remembering the thing that didn't happen.[5]

There is no particular reason why I should seek to whitewash Mark Twain, but I am not greatly shocked by the wickedness he displays in the foregoing quotations, nor do I feel that those who would accept them at face value, or even anything approximating face value, have sufficiently allowed for the volatile quality, the easy surface excitability of the man with whom we have to deal. There is a type of human being who when he says "You're crazy" means simply to indicate a mild sort of dissent from the opinion you have expressed, and who, when he threatens to kill you, intends simply to express a normal displeasure. It was to this type that Mark Twain belonged. His loves were real, but there was a fantastic quality in his hates, and when he really did insult a man, he was more than likely to grieve over it for years to come.[6] On Jackass Hill, he tried, one day, to play with a goat, and the goat did not care to be played with. Mark was very angry; he wanted to buy the goat in order that he might have him killed; such an animal was a menace to the lives of all the children on Jackass Hill—and much more to the same effect. Already he had learned to dramatize, to rationalize his dislikes, to identify his own passing whims with the common weal. But he did not immediately obtain possession of the goat, his anger passed away, and he ultimately so far forgot his anger as to become quite friendly with the beast—who killed no children. As he treated that goat, so he would have treated men, and Howells adds to the passage I have just quoted, "So he said, but no doubt he would not have hurt them if he had had them living before him."

When Tom Sawyer finds the corpse of Injun Joe in the cave, he "was touched, for he knew by his own experience how this wretch had suffered." But I will let the last word go to that great philosopher, Huckleberry Finn. When Huck finds himself stranded on the raft with the murderers, he can feel only terror and horror. These emotions, however, are soon succeeded by others. "I begun to think how dreadful it was, even for murderers, to be in such a fix. I says to myself, there ain't no telling but I might come to be a murderer myself yet, and then how would I like it?"

What a triumph of Christian humility! What a triumph of understanding and imagination! It is Mark Twain's version of the generally misquoted and misattributed utterance of old John Bradford, on seeing some criminals on the way to execution: "But for the grace of God there goes John Bradford."

VI

MARK TWAIN always considered himself a lazy man: when he found in his Suetonius a reference to one Flavius Clemens, a man widely known "for his want of energy," he wrote in the margin, "I guess this is where our line starts." "I do not like work," he says, "even when another person does it," and his best-known piece of writing tells how Tom Sawyer persuaded the other boys to do his work for him by the simple expedient of being "smart." "I am not as lazy as I was—" he writes Mrs. Fairbanks, "but I am lazy enough yet, for two people. But I am improving all the time. I always make it a point, now, every day, to resolve deliberately to do something the next day. It is a powerful incentive to industry—I wish I had adopted it sooner."[7] Those associated with Mark Twain, in his early days, have borne no unambiguous testimony to his extreme reluctance to engage in physical labor of any kind.

But a man may dislike physical labor and still be anything but lazy in the ordinary sense of the term: indeed it is the very excess of nervous and mental energy in some men that makes the drain and drag of an unvarying imposed routine impossible. Mark Twain is clearly of this type. We have his own glorification of energy in an early letter to Orion: "What is a government without energy? And what is *a man* without energy? Nothing—nothing at all. What is the grandest thing in 'Paradise Lost'—the Arch-Fiend's terrible energy! . . . And to-day, if I were a heathen, I would rear a statue to energy, and fall down and worship it!" In the first flush of his success as a river pilot, he condescends to advise his older brother, a rôle he was never afterwards wholly to relinquish. "I want a man to—I want *you* to—take up a line of action, and *follow* it out, in spite of the very devil."

His practice did not fall far short of his precepts. Like Dickens, like Theodore Roosevelt, he lived in a storm. Not outwardly, exteriorly, as these men lived—he moved, he talked like a lord of the manor always—but inwardly. It was said of Roswell Smith that he used to come down to the office every morning with three new ideas. It would take his colleagues until eleven o'clock to prove to him that two of them were not good, and the rest of the day to carry out the third. It might have been said with equal propriety of Mark Twain. In literature

and out of literature, there was the same vast fertility; he had
it in youth, and he had it in age. While he was working on
Roughing It, "he discussed a scheme with Goodman for a six-
hundred-page work which they were to do jointly; he planned
and wrote one or two scenes from a Western play . . .; he per-
fected one of his several inventions—an automatically adjusting
vest-strap; he wrote a number of sketches, made an occasional
business trip to New York and Hartford; prospected the latter
place for a new home."[8]

His resources were so abundant that he did not need to husband them. When he imagines Whitelaw Reid has been con-
ducting a campaign against him, he sets to work on a grand
scale to counteract that sinister influence. He works day and
night himself, he employs agents both in London and in New
York to work for him, and the mountain falls in labor to bring
forth a mouse, until it occurs to Mrs. Clemens that it might be
well to check the rumors first, to make sure that there has been
a campaign against him, and he discovers that there has been
nothing of the kind, and all his time and energy are thrown
away. It makes no difference, nor is he in the least distressed
about it. He generates power like a dynamo; he has far more
than any man can use; it was quite as well to be engaged in
elaborate plans to blast Whitelaw Reid as it would have been to
be writing ream after ream of unmailable letters or to retire to
his bedroom and swear until the air was blue.

The average author hates to write letters. Writing is his day's
work, and once he has laid the pen down, he is extremely reluctant to take it up again. Not so Mark. When he called on
Henry Watterson in London, he chanced to find him living
next door to the workhouse. His pen was tickle o' the sere; that
was quite enough to set it off. He sat down and wrote Watterson a long letter. "He had loved me, but he had always feared
that I would end by disgracing the family—being hanged, or
something—but the 'work'us,' that was beyond him; he had not
thought it would come to that. And so on through pages of
horseplay; his relief on ascertaining the truth and learning his

mistake—his regret at not finding me at home—closing with a dinner invitation." It must have taken as much out of him as a short story.

Think of the work he did on the history game. Think of the strength that went into his social engagements—in New York, in 1894—when he was nearly sixty—when he was, moreover, facing bankruptcy. "By half past 4 I had danced all those people down—and yet was not tired; merely breathless. I was in bed at 5, and asleep in ten minutes. Up at 9 and presently at work on this letter to you. I think I wrote until 2 or half-past. Then I walked leisurely out to Mr. Rogers's (it is called 3 miles but it is short of it) arriving at 3:30, but he was out—to return at 5.30—(and a person was *in,* whom I don't particularly like)—so I didn't stay, but dropped over and chatted with the Howellses until 6." Can you think of another famous author who, in the midst of a busy career, would actually sit down and, with his own hands, fantastically "embroider" a slipper for a little girl, as Mark Twain did for Elsie Leslie Lyde? Even while his business world is crashing around him, he plans a new magazine. And less than a week before the passage of the copyright law of 1909 he comes to Robert Underwood Johnson with a new plan which is ever so much better than the one they had all previously sponsored!

He lived intensely:

> No-where so bisy a man as he ther nas.

Yet there is a sense in which the next line applies to him also, though in a very different sense from that in which Chaucer applied it to the Sergeant of the Law,

> And yet he semed bisier than he was.

For it is the very fury of his energy that indicates Mark Twain's weakness. The eagerness of his response to varied stimuli betrays an undisciplined imagination; this is why so much of his work is occasional in character, why there are so few works that call for and get a sustained, continued power of imagination.

Plato said that the unexamined life was not worth living, and the extremely busy man is often the man who is running away from himself.

> Serene, I fold my hands and wait,
>   Nor care for wind, nor tide, nor sea;
> I rave no more 'gainst Time or Fate,
>   For lo! my own shall come to me.[9]

Such a mood was impossible for Mark Twain, and the very impossibility indicates his weakness, both as an artist and as a man.

VII

BUT we have not yet done with the paradoxes connected with this energy-laziness matter. Young Sam Clemens, setting out to find his place in the world, would not seem, on first consideration, to have been a very ambitious youngster. In 1863, when he is working on the *Enterprise,* his mother tells him that if he works hard, he may well look forward to holding a place, some day, on a big San Francisco paper. In his reply, he assures her that he could have such a place at any time, but he does not want it. "No paper in the United States can afford to pay me what my place on the 'Enterprise' is worth. If I were not naturally a lazy, idle, good-for-nothing vagabond, I could make it pay me $20,000 a year. But I don't suppose I shall ever be any account. I lead an easy life, though, and I don't care a cent whether school keeps or not. Everybody knows me, and I fare like a prince wherever I go, be it on this side of the mountains or the other. And I am proud to say I am the most conceited ass in the Territory."

An appalling picture, no doubt, and it must have given any woman save Jane Clemens a bad moment. Jane, however, had probably already learned the truth of the principle she once enunciated, that one must discount her son's sayings about ninety per cent and learn to strike a proper average: the remaining ten per cent was pure gold. She remembered how early he had risen above the Hannibal horizon, how he shook the dust of the town from his feet and set out to bustle his way in the world, how he had made good, first as a printer, then as a pilot, and now as a newspaper man. . . .

The piloting business may well have given her pause, and it may well halt us. More than a little has already been said in these pages about Mark Twain's unreliable memory. So we get the famous story of the visitor whom he mistook for a picture agent and treated accordingly, because his own pictures, which he did not recognize, had been removed from the walls and were lying at the stranger's feet when Mark Twain entered the drawing room; and the even more curious anecdote of how he went out, one day, to invite a neighbor to come over to play billiards, and when he reached the street, was quite unable to recognize the house in which his friend lived, so that he was obliged to come back for the butler to have it pointed out to him. "More than once," writes Mr. Paine, "I have known him to relate an occurrence of the day before with a reality of circumstance that carried absolute conviction, when the details themselves were precisely reversed." If he remembered anything about his life, one might suppose he would surely remember his speech at the Whittier Birthday Dinner, which cost him, first and last, so much agony, yet in 1910 we find him asking his secretary to call up Howells to ask "what occasion it was in Boston when he *raised Hell* about Emerson and Longfellow." And this was the man who learned the course of the mighty Mississippi, memorized the physical features of twelve hundred miles of shifting, ever-changing current so perfectly that he could steer a boat through its tortuous recesses by day or by night!

The creative artist in Mark Twain doubtless assisted him in jumbling facts and fiction: he was like the too-imaginative child who is so interested in his daydreams that he loses the power to differentiate between what actually happened and what he has only dreamed. No doubt the quality of attention entered into it largely also. He learned the river because he gave his whole mind to it. His piloting days behind him, there was no need for giving such close attention to anything else, and the natural bent of his taste and temperament inclined him to live, more and more, within himself. "It is all a matter of ability to observe things," he once declared. "I never observe anything now. I gave up the habit years ago. You should keep a habit up if you want to become proficient in it." Yet on the visual side at least, there would seem to have been some constitutional defect, for he lacked the power to recall to his mind at will the features even of the members of his own family, and this idiosyncrasy became nothing short of a calamity in the days after Mrs. Clemens died.

In early days, Mark Twain's ambition was impelled, no doubt, by the thought of the business incompetency of his father and his elder brother. Orion was grossly libeled when James O'Donnell Bennett called him a Village Idiot. Reacting against such unfair treatment, his admirers now show a tendency to rush to the other extreme, to glorify Orion as a man whose only fault was that he was too sensitive to cope with the brutal exigencies of a capitalistic civilization, and to censure Mark Twain himself for his patronizing attitude toward his brother. I do not think it necessary to hold a brief for capitalism in order to perceive that it was not wholly the fault of others that Orion was unsuccessful. It would be difficult to devise any kind of economic system in which a man who scattered his energies as fearfully as Orion did—and who changed his convictions almost literally as often as he changed his coat—could have achieved success. Yet Mark Twain was like his brother in many, many ways. "One of his characteristics," we read of Orion in the *Autobiography*, "was eagerness. He woke with an eagerness about some matter or other every morning; it consumed him all day; it perished in the night and he was on fire with a fresh new interest next morning before he could get his clothes on. He exploited in this way three hundred and sixty-five red-hot new eagernesses every year of his life—until he died sitting at a table with a pen in his hand, in the early morning, jotting down the conflagration for that day and preparing to enjoy the fire and smoke of it until night should extinguish it.

He was then seventy-two years old. But I am forgetting another
characteristic, a very pronounced one. That was his deep
glooms, his despondencies, his despairs; these had their place in
each and every day along with the eagernesses. Thus his day
was divided—no, not divided, mottled—from sunrise to midnight with alternating brilliant sunshine and black cloud. Every
day he was the most joyous and hopeful man that ever was, I
think, and also every day he was the most miserable man that
ever was." Does it not read like a perfect description of Mark
Twain himself? And how infinitely suggestive is Mr. Paine's
comment, "Clemens proposed almost as many things to Howells as his brother Orion proposed to him."

There is a large fortuitous element in success; full many a
flower is born to blush unseen; and Mark Twain knew it well.
He dramatized it in "Luck," in "Edward Mills and George
Benton," in the early fables of the Good and the Bad Little
Boys. Unless he had happened to possess genius, would he have
been another Orion? Not quite, I think, for he did have a practical energy, a determination to get somewhere that Orion
lacked. But undoubtedly he would have come a good deal
closer to Orion than he did. In some respects, indeed, he came
alarmingly close as it was.

If there were times when Mark Twain refused to emulate the
Horatio Alger hero, it was not so much laziness that impelled
him as his love of freedom, of personal independence. The
standardization of life and thought, which has proceeded to
such appalling lengths in our own time, was already beginning
in his, and with the tradition of the Old South behind him, he
resisted it with all his might. It was not only that he was born
different, he could not be pushed into a mold; he would not if
he could, he resisted on principle. For example, he was naturally a good speller, but he felt no pride in his capacity. "Before
the spelling-book came with its arbitrary forms, men unconsciously revealed shades of their characters, and also added en-
lightening shades of expression to what they wrote by their
spelling, and so it is possible that the spelling-book has been a

doubtful benevolence to us." If a rule did not seem reasonable to him, he would break it whether or no, and if you told him he must not do a thing he would be sure to do it, as when in Washington, he discussed the precise aspect of the copyright question he had been warned to avoid. Relations were very amicable between him and his wealthy father-in-law, and he immensely appreciated Mr. Langdon's broad-minded liberality in receiving him—rough son of the West that he was—into his family, but he would accept no favors that impinged upon his individual freedom, he must retain control of his individual actions and of his family every step of the way. This is why he was unhappy in San Francisco, not because he had to work harder than he had worked on the *Enterprise,* but because he was hedged in with restrictions; he was not an independent human being; he was a cog in the machine. Yes, he had the Old South behind him, and the industrial North ahead of him; in the true sense, he was an apostle of "rugged individualism," however appalled he was by the results of "ruthless individualism" as he saw them increasingly in industry and in trade. There is some penetrating social criticism in the last chapter of *Tom Sawyer,* where Huck finds his money and his new position in life an appalling burden and only wishes he could throw it all off and go back to the days of comfortable poverty when he had nothing to do except to be himself. I think it has not been sufficiently recognized how close Huck is, in these pages, to the point of view of that young saint of Italy who chose My Lady Poverty as his bride.

VIII

For all that he had hated going to school, no man ever had more faith in education than Mark Twain. He had educated himself, largely, through miscellaneous reading, and he believed in this method: indeed, when he learned that the passage of the copyright law might make the classics more expensive for persons in humble circumstances, he began to wonder seriously whether he had not made a mistake in supporting it. But reading alone was not enough, for he did not, like so many "self-made men," glorify his limitations. "The self-made man," he says, "seldom knows anything accurately, and he does not know a tenth as much as he could have known if he had worked under teachers; and, besides, he brags, and is the means of fooling other thoughtless people into going and doing as he himself has done." Wherever he goes, he is interested in the schools, he rejoices when he finds them prosperous, for, unlike some of our own respected contemporaries, he realizes that the welfare of the nation is bound up with their prosperity. It is true his comments are sometimes a bit naïve, as when he remarks of the graduate of the German gymnasium that he has "an education . . . so extensive and complete, that the most a university can do for it is to perfect some of its profounder specialties." But there are suggestions of penetration also.

He is impressed, he is even oppressed by the vast scope and variety of what there is to be learned. When he is brought into association with learned men on terms of equality, he is vastly flattered. "I was at breakfast lately," he writes in 1894, "where people of seven separate nationalities sat and the seven languages were going all the time. At my side sat a charming gentleman who was a delightful and active talker, and interesting. He talked glibly to those folks in all those seven languages —and still had a language to spare! I wanted to kill him, for very envy." It was a lovely sort of envy. Indeed those of us who feel that it is not only the Kingdom of God that one must enter as a little child—for intellectual humility is quite as necessary in the Kingdom of Wisdom—find much of Mark Twain's charm in his complete freedom from all pride of intellect, his delightful readiness to be impressed by the achievements of others. Mrs. Fields has a priceless phrase when she speaks of him as "this growing man of forty." But he did not stop at forty; even on the "Equator" tour, we find him reading scientific books, "to improve the mind." He even tends, rather romantically I fear, to identify learning with virtue. "Learning goes usually with uprightness, broad views, and humanity."

What of his own learning?

We may begin with history, in which field much of his most absorbed reading was done. It was history that had first awakened his intellectual curiosity; perhaps he had some dim prescience of what the future held for him that day when the wind brought a stray sheet from the life of Joan of Arc across his path.

His actual knowledge of history—its extent and its accuracy—must always remain speculative. Mr. Paine was impressed by it—in Roman, French, and English history particularly, and regretted "that he had not devoted some of his public effort to work of this sort." He had an unusually strong sense of the romance of the past: "Here is a crumbling wall that was old when Columbus discovered America; was old when Peter the Hermit roused the knightly men of the Middle Ages to arm for the first Crusade; was old when Charlemagne and his paladins beleaguered enchanted castles and battled with giants and genii in the fabled days of the olden time; was old when Christ and his disciples walked the earth; stood where it stands to-day when the lips of Memnon were vocal, and men bought and sold in the streets of ancient Thebes!" The first time he ever saw a Jewish boy, in childhood, he was awe-struck: "To my fancy they [the Jews] were clothed invisibly in the damp and cobwebby mold of antiquity. They carried me back to Egypt, and in imagination I moved among the Pharaohs and all the shadowy celebrities of that remote age." He knew very well what it was that gave the past its charm for him: it was "a haunting sense of the myriads of human lives that had blossomed, and withered, and perished here, repeating and repeating and repeating, century after century, and age after age, the barren and meaningless process. . . ." Even India, whose past he knew so little about, cast this spell upon him. On the other hand, "The deserts of Australia and the ice-barrens of Greenland have no speech, for they have no venerable history; with nothing to tell of man and his vanities, his fleeting glories and his miseries, they have nothing wherewith to spiritualize their ugliness and veil it with a charm."

This is a poet's response to the past, or a mystic's, not a scholar's. Mark Twain loved to spin romances out of the glories of vanished ages; he was comparatively indifferent to the question whether the vision in his heart corresponded or not to any objective reality that had ever existed on the earth. Like Dickens, he judges the past always by the standards of the present; whatever does not square with his notion of the fitness of things in the twentieth century is summarily condemned. Consider his argument in the closing pages of *Is Shakespeare Dead?* where he tries to prove that if Shakespeare wrote the plays attributed to him, he must have been much better known in his own time, specifically his death must have attracted more attention, than we have any reason to suppose was the case. In establishing this conclusion, he relies on a comparison between Shakespeare and himself, entirely disregarding all the differences between his own America and seventeenth-century England, between the craft of authorship in the two periods and the attitude of the public toward authors. Mr. Brooks speaks of Mark Twain quite rightly, in this connection, as a man in whom the continuity of racial experience has been sharply cut.

In science, his interest is distinctly of the amateur variety. The stars began to fascinate him in his pilot days, and in later years the immense distances suggested by the studies of the more advanced astronomers stimulated his imagination. He tried to compute the astronomical light year, and he makes considerable imaginative use of astronomy in *Captain Stormfield's Visit to Heaven*. He loves collecting geological specimens and mulling over geologic problems; in his old age he tells Miss Wallace he is trying to enlarge his knowledge of geology. Zoölogy I think he touches only in connection with the ant. There are some interesting speculations concerning radium in one of his sketches. But it is the sensational aspects of science— perhaps I ought to say of pseudo-science—that almost necessarily appeal most strongly to so imaginative a man. I have already mentioned *Captain Stormfield;* among his unfinished projects was a vast book about microbes. The catalogue of his library shows few entries in the scientific field.

On mathematics, he is a bit contradictory. He assures us that he detests it, yet few things give him more pleasure than to manipulate statistics. The "light-year" calculation already referred to was his most spectacular achievement in this field and about as practical as most of them. It is interesting to know that, on one occasion, when he applied this gift to the study of his household expenses, he was utterly betrayed. "When I came down in the morning a gray and aged wreck, and went over the figures again, I found that in some unaccountable way . . . I had multiplied the totals by 2. By God I dropped 75 years on the floor where I stood."

Mark Twain's weakness as a critic of literature has already been indicated. Language study was another matter. If, under any set of circumstances, we can think of Mark Twain as having made himself a scholar in any field, certainly it must have been philology that he would have chosen. Syntax and grammar, word order and structure—he finds such things very fascinating. The connotations, the overtones of words stimulate his imagination, and there is one passage on the technical aspects of style which indicates that he might have been greatly interested in Miss Edith Rickert's recent attempt to analyze the sources of our reactions to various types of rhythm and structure.[10]

His language gift appears, also, in his study of foreign languages. French he began as far back as his pilot days, and his two essays on Italian show both keenness and imagination. But German was, after English, the language to which he devoted most of his attention, and in spite of all his denunciations of its awkward immobility, German was still the foreign language that he knew and loved best of all. He made at least one speech in German; he translated a good deal of material from German into English, and one story, at least, from English into German. The translation of "Die Lorelei" in the first chapter of *A*

Tramp Abroad is a very good one. The amateur spirit appears clearly in his proposals for reforming the German language, but his suggestions have a good deal of cogency about them.

Mark Twain had considerable conscience, too, in the matter of documentation. He could burlesque citation of authorities when he chose to do so; he could make an elaborate parade of mock learning, but he knew how to take pains to get things right, and when he departed from historic fact, he liked to indicate the fact and to explain his reasons, as he did in *The Prince and the Pauper*. There is a good deal of documentation in this book, especially when one remembers that it was intended largely for children; and there are footnotes, corrections, citations, and their like, all through the book on Christian Science. In *The Gilded Age,* he states precisely that he would not venture to depart from the language of actual conversation in "a book which professes to deal with social possibilities"; and in *Joan of Arc,* he explains carefully in advance just how he proposes to use the records of the trial. Even in *Tom Sawyer* you will find a note: "The pretended 'compositions' quoted in this chapter are taken without alteration from a volume entitled 'Prose and Poetry, by a Western Lady'—but they are exactly and precisely after the school-girl pattern, and hence are much happier than any mere imitations could be."

What, finally, can we say of Mark Twain's thinking? Gamaliel Bradford reminds us that we must remember the "late dawning of his speculative turn" in estimating its value. "It accounts for the singular gaps in his information about simple matters, for the impression of terrific but not very well-guided energy which comes from his intellectual effort. It accounts for the sense of surprise and novelty in his spiritual attitude, which Howells so justly pointed out. He seems always like a man discovering things which are perfectly well known to trained thinkers, and this gives an extraordinary freshness and spirit to his pronouncements on all speculative topics."

In other words, we might say of Mark Twain's thinking what he himself said of Macfarlane's: "Of course his thinking and reasoning and philosophizings were those of a but partly taught and wholly untrained mind, yet he hit by accident upon some curious and striking things." This kind of thinking has its drawbacks: one generalizes from insufficient data; one is often carried away by emotion; one fails sometimes to look up the necessary information and consequently must retrace steps. It was said of George Moore that he conducted his literary education in public. Was there any phase of his education in any field that Mark Twain did not conduct in public?

There was another drawback also—the danger that an idea might occur to you which, so far as you knew, was completely original, and you might work yourself into a sweat about it, as Huckleberry Finn would say, only to discover that it had been used, time and again, before you. "The ancients stole our best thoughts," said Dr. Johnson, and Mark Twain had more than one corroborating experience. "I was summering somewhere away from home," he writes, "and one day I had a new idea— a *motif* for a drama. I was enchanted with the felicity of the conception—I might say intoxicated with it. It seemed to me that no idea was ever so exquisite, so beautiful, so freighted with wonderful possibilities. I believed that when I should get it fittingly dressed out in the right dramatic clothes it would not only delight the world, but astonish it. Then came a stealthy, searching, disagreeable little chill; what if the idea was not new, after all?" So he asked his friend James Hammond Trumbull about it. "His answer covered six pages. . . . The theft of my idea had been consummated two hundred and sixty-eight times. The latest instance mentioned was English, and not yet three years old; the earliest had electrified China eight hundred years before Christ." And he adds: "I did not write the play."

That was the kind of disadvantage under which he labored— or was it, perhaps, not a disadvantage? Suppose he had never asked Trumbull about it; suppose Trumbull had not known so confounded much. Might he not have written a very good play? And would it necessarily have been any the worse because

there had been two hundred and sixty-eight others before it?
There had been revenge plays before Shakespeare, but that fact
did not deter Shakespeare from writing *Hamlet,* and it did not
prevent him from making *Hamlet* the greatest revenge play
that has ever been written. We hear a great deal about the
power of knowledge; let us not forget that ignorance is a great
power also. Look at the Daughters of the American Revolution.
Look at the American Legion. Look at Hitler. Look at Hearst.
Where would they be—any of them—without ignorance? And
if ignorance is a tremendous power for evil, it is sometimes,
also, a power for good. We should probably none of us ever
attack any considerable undertaking did we first stop to consider how utterly insignificant our power is, or what a ridiculous figure we must be cutting in the eyes of those who are
wiser than ourselves. Hamlet himself did not think too precisely on the event, for all his self-accusation and self-upbraid-
ing along this line; the notion of a weak, procrastinating Hamlet is one of the fictions of recent romantic criticism. Many
others have done so, however, for the ideal of the scholar is to
balance evidence against evidence, doing full justice to all con-
cepts involved. The man of action, on the other hand, must assume the truth of a single hypothesis, staking everything upon
it, right or wrong.

The creative artist in literature is, from this point of view,
closer to the man of action than he is to the scholar. Lack of information does not often get in the way of the free operation of
creative genius, but too much information often does. After all,
Mark Twain did think out that idea for himself; he was just as
original as he would have been, had nobody else ever done it
before him. And there are many instances in his thinking of
which exactly the same thing might be said. He delighted in
the use of his mind. It was not a great mind; the minds of creative artists seldom are. But within the limitations that circum-
scribed him, he loved to think things through. "What is it that
confers the noblest delight?" he asks. "What is that which
swells a man's breast with pride above that which any other ex-

perience can bring to him? Discovery! To know that you are walking where none others have walked; that you are beholding what human eye has not seen before; that you are breathing a virgin atmosphere." In a world as old as this one, it is difficult to achieve such an ideal, but at least one may strive toward it. Mark Twain's conclusions on many subjects had little absolute value, but they did have a value for him, or, as he puts it in connection with one theme that long interested him, "I am not playing with Christian Science and its founder, I am examining them; and I am doing it because of the interest I feel in the inquiry. My results may seem inadequate to the reader, but they have for me clarified a muddle and brought a sort of order out of a chaos, and so I value them." After all, can the great scholar say much more?

IX

WHEN William Dean Howells introduced Mark Twain at the Whittier Birthday Dinner, on December 17, 1877, he laid special stress on the fact that he was "a humorist who never left you hanging your head for having enjoyed his joke." This is, in general, true. Mark Twain must have seen sex naked in his frontier days, for the frontier is notably blatant and unashamed about such things. What was his reaction to it, we do not know; there is no anecdote, no suggestion anywhere to indicate that he was not, in the conventional sense, a moral man. Harlots swarmed on the river boats, but you would never guess it from *Life on the Mississippi,* where the old life is swathed in all the romantic iridescence of a purple land where youth was king.

When the dark flower of passion raises its head, he can generally be counted on for the "correct" reaction toward it. This seems all the more significant because he is so likely to be anything but "correct" in other matters. When he witnesses the cancan he places his hands before his face, "for very shame"; he is almost equally shocked by the hula-hula. When he speaks of Boccaccio in his *Autobiography,* he cannot refrain from taking a fling at his "improper tales," and the Yankee is much im-

pressed, too, by the improprieties of Elizabethan and of eighteenth-century literature. Toward Lancelot and Guinevere,
toward Petrarch's devotion to Laura, toward Abélard and Hé-
loise, he takes distinctly a Philistine attitude; in the last-named
instance, he is, indeed, almost hysterical, though at the last minute his chivalry comes to his aid, and he will not be too severe
on the lady! In *Life on the Mississippi,* he uses the pious formula "they sinned" to indicate sexual intercourse outside of
marriage. His Fenimore Cooper paper accepts, as one of the
canons of criticism, the obligation resting upon the author to
discourage vice and inculcate virtue. In an early essay, he speaks
of the Byron scandal as not susceptible of burlesque, "because
the central feature of it, incest, was a 'situation' so tremendous
and so imposing that the happiest available resources of burlesque seemed tame and cheap in its presence. Burlesque could
invent nothing to transcend incest, except by enlisting two
crimes, neither of which is ever mentioned among women and
children, and one of which is only mentioned in rare books of
the law, and there as 'the crime without a name'—a term with
a shudder in it." Finally, all the world has heard how, for all
his interest in the Russian revolution, Mark Twain joined in
repudiating Gorky, when that gentleman had the bad judgment to come to New York in company with a lady who was
not his wife.

As a child, I read Mark Twain's description of Titian's
Venus in the last chapter of *A Tramp Abroad,* read and marveled at the wickedness of the world. It was not until years
afterward, when I first saw the original, that I realized how
narrow he was in this particular, and how unfair were his
charges, an unfairness I find it the more difficult to understand
because of his sane and healthy attitude toward nakedness elsewhere.

Mark Twain's strictness in this connection cannot be entirely
explained on the basis of his Puritanical training. Part of it was
due to his native sensitiveness and fineness. "He was in some external respects emphatically a 'man with the bark on,'" wrote

Twichell, "yet there was no more exquisite refinement of taste and sentiment. I have seldom known any one so easily moved to tears." And Laura Hawkins, his childhood sweetheart, remembered in after years that he had always been different from the other boys. "I didn't know then . . . what it was that made him different, but afterward . . . I realized that it was his natural refinement. He played hookey from school, he cared nothing at all for his books, and he was guilty of all sorts of mischievous pranks, just as *Tom Sawyer* is in the book, but I never heard a coarse word from him in all our childhood acquaintance."

Yet we have "1601"—the most famous piece of pornography in American literature. We have "The Doleful Ballad of the Rejected Lover," which he and Steve Gillis sang in the streets of San Francisco. We have the famous speech before the Stomach Club in Paris, which has attained a universal celebrity, though not even its title can be mentioned in print. We have the testimony of Howells, Robert Underwood Johnson, and others concerning the Rabelaisianism of his letters and his conversation. We have, finally, his own explicit statement: "Delicacy—a sad, sad false delicacy—robs literature of the best two things among its belongings. Family circle narrative and obscene stories."

On "1601" alone, I should be reluctant to base any conclusive argument. It is dirty enough, certainly; it has too much gusto to be dismissed as a mere literary exercise; but it cannot be denied that it is literature. Yet it is not mere smut for smut's sake; it has a point of view—that of illustrating the difference between the Elizabethan sense of propriety and our own. It has a little, a very little, of the flavor of Swift's obscenity: the writer will show the human race what filthy creatures they are. These considerations do not completely cover the case, however, nor can they reasonably be held to have applied to all his bawdry, to the letters, for example, of which Howells speaks: "He had the Southwestern, the Lincolnian, the Elizabethan breadth of parlance, which I suppose one ought not to call coarse without calling one's self prudish; and I was often hiding away in discreet holes and corners the letters in which he had loosed his bold fancy to stoop on rank suggestion; I could not bear to burn them, and I could not, after the first reading, quite bear to look at them."

H. W. Fisher tells an amusing story of the time when he and Mark Twain found in the Berlin Royal Library some indecent verses written by Voltaire to Frederick the Great. After having a few of them translated to him, Mark said, "Too much is enough. I would blush to remember any of these stanzas except to tell Krafft-Ebing about them when I get to Vienna." Fisher copied one verse down for him, however, and he put it in his pocket saying, "Livy is so busy mispronouncing German these days she can't even attempt to get at this."[11]

Mr. Brooks works Mark Twain's bawdry into his general interpretation of him as a suppressed genius: "Mark Twain's verbal Rabelaisianism was obviously the expression of that vital sap which, not having been permitted to inform his work had been driven inward and left there to ferment." It is not necessary to accept this statement at face value; neither, I believe, is it necessary altogether to reject it. That such things as "1601" do manifest vitality—vitality and imagination—nobody who has read them can deny. Probably there are few men of immense vitality who can live in civilization, in its present stage of development, without being obliged, through a large part of their lives, to suppress some part of their natural inclinations. It is this circumstance that weakens the gospel of the expressionists, that lends force—shall we say—to such a point of view as that championed by the late Irving Babbitt; and the fact that the will of the man in question may itself be altogether enlisted in the suppression, as I think Mark Twain's generally was, does not alter the facts. "The Southwestern, the Lincolnian, the Elizabethan breadth of parlance"—to quote Howells again—explains much, especially as to the particular forms of obscene humor employed, though the native tendency might still have been there had Clemens never seen the frontier. And again I cannot help thinking of Chaucer. If ever there was a sophisticated littérateur it was Chaucer—and the suggestion that he ever suppressed his gifts or refused to exercise the endowment the gods had given him would be quite beside the mark—yet Chaucer has a taste for bawdry even stronger than Mark Twain's. In the face of almost certain criticism, he included a generous array of ribald tales in the work he must have regarded as his literary masterpiece, and it is futile to attempt to explain them away on the hypothesis that fourteenth-century readers would not be shocked by them—the very terms of Chaucer's apology for them preclude this view altogether. They prove that he had a coarse streak in him, if you choose, yet it would be quite as accurate to say that they prove the sensitiveness, the delicacy of his perceptions, for the artist, by his very nature, reaches out, antennæ-like, in all directions, and the first question he asks of a proffered stimulus is not whether it is "good" but whether it is "strong." This is the glory of the artistic temperament; it is also its peril; and Mark Twain did not altogether escape it.

I would connect his bawdry with more than his sensitiveness, however; I would connect it also with his antiromanticism. I shall enlarge my field of discussion in a moment to speak in more general terms of the conflict of these two elements in his temperament—the tendency to bow down and worship, the tendency to tear the idol from its throne, to grind it to powder, to dance upon its dust. He has been called—or, if he has not, let me name him now—the first of the "muckrakers"; he was also the first of the "debunkers." There are times when he seems to rejoice to tear the mask from the face of life, to show her up, when he reduces human conduct to its lowest common denominator, and leaves no stone unturned to show how bad it all really is. This is, I believe, at the bottom of many of the ugly passages in his humor, his use of offensive smells, of vomiting and nausea, of violence and death. It is a temper which has grown in America during the years since he left us; the character of those years has encouraged its growth; we ought, therefore, to be in a better position to understand its significance than Mark Twain's contemporaries were. Despite my own lack of sympathy with it either in him or in his successors, it would be unfair not to notice that it was bound up not only with his weakness but also with his strength.

X

Lewis Mumford accuses Mark Twain of being afraid of his imagination. He was afraid of romance at any rate. Romance was a specious gilding, a false light thrown over life, an attempt to live by illusions instead of facing the truth. The Yankee sees himself as "the champion of hard unsentimental common-sense and reason," and Mark Twain himself had the same ambition. It is not only that the romantic fritters away his energy in fruit-less maunderings, that he lives with shadows and unfits himself for playing a part in real life. It is even worse than that. Ro-mance is vicious. Romance paints black white, and upsets men's moral judgments. Romance casts a deceptive haze over Abé-lard's criminal passion, the world at large is led to revere what it ought to detest, and many an error by the same example shall rush into the state. In "A Curious Experience," we have a case-study of a boy who has fed his imagination on the cheap ro-manticism of dime novels until the real world and the world of the imagination have become hopelessly confused. Daydream-ing utterly ruins the moral backbone of the hero and heroine of *The $30,000 Bequest* also, and there is hope that Sally Sellers may become a happy and useful young woman only when she has put her dreams forever behind her. Romanticism is a moral question, then, but it is more than a question of individual morality. Social progress is impossible until the cobwebs of musty sentimentality have been rudely dispersed, until men's eyes are strong enough to see things as they are. Even Tom Sawyer is confused. The healthy, unimaginative, Sancho Panza barbarism of Huckleberry Finn does not represent the ideal, but at least Huckleberry sees the Crusades for the vulgar free-booting expeditions that they were; he is more promising stuff

for citizenship in the age of the robber barons than the romantic Tom.

So Mark Twain comes out an aggressive modernist; he is
completely convinced that the age in which he himself is living
is far and away the greatest that the world has ever known.
"The valuable part . . . of what we call civilization" did not,
in his opinion, exist when Queen Victoria was born. Gutenberg,
Watt, Arkwright, Whitney, Morse, Stephenson, and Bell are
"the creators of the world—after God." There was no knowledge in the past: Tom Sawyer abroad laments that he is obliged
to consort with "a passel of low-down animals that don't know
no more than the head boss of a university did three or four
hundred years ago." There were, even, no gentlemen in Europe
earlier than the nineteenth century. Speaking at Keokuk, Iowa,
in 1886, Mark Twain declared: "A poet has said, 'Better fifty
years of England than all the cycles of Cathay.' But I say better
one decade of this period than the 900 years of Methuselah.
There is more done now in a year than he ever saw in all his
life."[12] When he praises the civilization of ancient Egypt, it is
simply because he believes Egypt anticipated certain modern
discoveries.

This rejoicing necessarily often took the form of a glorying
in material progress. New inventions stimulate his imagination
as one might expect the imagination of a young engineer,
rather than that of a literary man, to be stimulated. To borrow
the language of Dickens and of Wordsworth, he felt that he
was living "in the summer-dawn of time."

> Bliss was it in that dawn to be alive,
> But to be young was very Heaven!

In Mark Twain, it was telephones and typesetters and writing-
machines that induced this ecstatic mood. He was the first man
in the history of the world to install a telephone in his private
residence, he was one of the first to use the fountain pen. He
was the first author of distinction to employ the typewriter.
Notice the pioneering enthusiasm in this sentence from a letter

to Orion, written January 5, 1889: "At 12:20 this afternoon a line of movable types was spaced and justified by machinery, for the first time in the history of the world! And I was there to see."

It was not enough to keep up with the present; he must anticipate the future. He made fingerprinting an element in *Pudd'nhead Wilson,* at a time when fingerprinting was a new thing—"virgin ground—absolutely *fresh,*" he calls it.[13] As early as the late seventies, he himself made a balloon ascension, and *Tom Sawyer Abroad* prophesies modern developments in aviation. He develops the idea of the long-distance telephone too, the radio, and the motion picture. In fact, he is ahead of us still, for he foresaw television also.[14]

Here is ammunition, indeed, for those who believe that, for all his specific revolts, Mark Twain was a "go-getter" at heart, that he shared the myopia of the dollar-chasing Americans of his time. When he goes to Italy he damns the masterpieces and lavishes his praise on the railroads: "These things win me more than Italy's hundred galleries of priceless art treasures, because I can understand the one and am not competent to appreciate the other." Could anything be more stupid than to fail to find any knowledge, any civilization in the Middle Ages, anything of value that is lacking from our lives today? Could anything be more insensitive than his absurd assessment of French culture at the beginning of his essay on Paul Bourget? And could anything be more amazing, more incomprehensible than the letter he wrote Walt Whitman on his seventieth birthday? The Whittier fiasco was nothing compared to that barbarous letter; if Mark Twain had deliberately set out to burlesque himself, he could have written nothing else. As Mr. Brooks puts it: "He congratulated the poet for having lived in an age that had witnessed, among other benefactions, 'the amazing, infinitely varied and innumerable products of coal-tar'; he neglected to congratulate the age for having produced Walt Whitman."[15]

But here again we meet a paradox. No man could have denounced romanticism as Mark Twain denounced it without having felt something of its power in his own life. As we have already observed, Mark Twain is, on one side, Colonel Sellers, and though he dreamed in terms of typesetting machines and other mechanical contrivances, as his father had dreamed of the Tennessee land before him, it was never as a practical man that he approached these things. "The castle-building habit," he writes in *The $30,000 Bequest,* and writes feelingly, "the day-dreaming habit—how it grows! what a luxury it becomes; how we fly to its enchantments at every idle moment, how we revel in them, steep our souls in them, intoxicate ourselves with their beguiling fantasies—oh yes, and how soon and how easily our dream-life and our material life become so intermingled and so fused together that we can't quite tell which is which, any more." And there is an observation in *The Gilded Age* that has much force in this connection: "One never ceases to make a hero of one's self (in private), during life, but only alters the style of his heroism from time to time as the drifting years be-little certain gods of his admiration and raise up others in their stead that seem greater."

There is a partial justification for his antiromanticism, then, in Mark Twain's consciousness of his own weakness: when he fights romance, he is fighting the Sellers-side of himself and of his family. There is partial justification also in the kind of romantic literature in vogue, especially in the South, during his own early life, in the juvenile literature of the time, in the sort of travel books he himself burlesqued in *The Innocents Abroad*.[16]

One notes a strong resemblance, at this point, between Mark Twain and Bernard Shaw, who reacted similarly against romance, because he saw it as a cloak for error and oppression, and who, of course, went at the whole thing in a much more thoroughgoing, more doctrinaire fashion than Mark Twain.[17] He would be a brave man, however, who could dare assert that either of these writers succeeded in killing the romancer in himself, and the world's literature would be poorer if they had. Certainly Mark did not, and the superb rhetoric in his descriptions of Palestine brooding in sackcloth and ashes, of distant lands under the spell of the darkness of night are still fresh in our minds. His love of legends is familiar to readers of *A Tramp Abroad,* and though he was not an Irishman, he was quite capable of imagining, not too seriously, that he had seen the little people scampering away through the forest. For if romance can corrupt, he knew too that romance can ennoble. The effect of Tom Canty's reading on his own mind, at the beginning of *The Prince and the Pauper,* is a perfect illustration of Oscar Wilde's saying that art does not imitate life any more than life imitates art, and it will be remembered that Mark Twain always fully appreciated the power of the theater's romance to transfigure the lives of children, "the power," as Miss Jane Addams puts it, "of even a mimic stage to afford to the young a magic space in which lives may be lived in efflorescence, where manners may be courtly and elaborate without exciting ridicule, where the sequence of events is impressive and comprehensible." There is considerable verisimilitude, to be sure, in *The $30,000 Bequest,* in *The Man That Corrupted Hadleyburg,* even in *The Prince and the Pauper* itself, but, in each case, even as in Shakespeare's own romances, the situation rests upon an initial, inherent improbability or even absurdity which is the element of "given," and which must simply be accepted. Howells believed his friend fundamentally romantic, and Mr. DeVoto speaks of the *Joan of Arc* as "his capitulation to romance." *Joan of Arc* is a book which some of Mark Twain's hardboiled admirers will never forgive his having written, yet Mr. DeVoto himself is quite as romantic in his own remarks concerning Tom and Huck and the things that they represent as ever Mark himself was toward Joan; indeed, he is romantic in his whole conception of the frontier. But we need not, in the present contingency, decide the question of the relative merit of *Joan of Arc* in comparison with Mark Twain's other books, for, as both Schönemann and Miss Brashear have been at some pains to point out, even that supreme expression of his disillusion and despair, *The Mysterious Stranger,* is drenched in romanticism.

Harper and Brothers have often been berated for giving this book to the world in a fairy-tale format; it seems curious that none of their critics has perceived that Mark Twain himself was fundamentally responsible for the incongruity.

The letter to Walt Whitman was written in 1889. Let us look now at another letter, this one to Twichell, written in 1905:

"Well, the 19th century made progress—the first progress after 'ages and ages'—colossal progress. In what? Materialities. Prodigious acquisitions were made in those things which add to the comfort of many and make life harder for as many more. But the addition to righteousness? Is it discoverable? I think not. The materialities were not invented in the interest of righteousness; that there is more righteousness in the world because of them than there was before, is hardly demonstrable, I think. In Europe and America there is a vast change (due to them) in ideals—do you admire it? All Europe and all America are feverishly scrambling for money. Money is the supreme ideal—all others take tenth place with the great bulk of the nations named. Money-lust has always existed, but not in the history of the world was it ever a craze, a madness until your time and mine. This lust has rotted these nations; it has made them hard, sordid, ungentle, dishonest, oppressive."

So he learned after all then. Learned that science, too, is a false god, learned what some of us had to wait for the war to find out, that he had been leaning on a broken reed, that materialities cannot solve the problem of human life. The typesetters were working perfectly now, and men had wings at last. For what? For this?—this that men had in 1905? Poor Mark Twain! He who had believed so passionately. And yet they twit him for his pessimism!

CHAPTER II

God's Fool

"Ah, well, I am a great and sublime fool. But then I am God's fool, and all His works must be contemplated with respect."

MARK TWAIN, 1877.

I

MARK TWAIN uses self-vaunting and self-depreciation with fine impartiality as elements in his humor. On the one hand, he is not satisfied with mere ignorance —he must claim idiocy, utter selfishness, and complete savagery; on the other hand, he advertises for obituaries, compares himself to the Czar and the Pacific Ocean, and when a new planet appears in the skies, he is sure it is going to be named for him. As a Mississippi pilot, the opportunity came to him to establish his right to be considered a person with some business in the world under circumstances that appealed powerfully to his always dramatic temperament, for the pilot was, in the river towns as well as on the boat itself, the cock o' the walk. It is clear that Mark took advantage of his opportunity to swagger a bit before those who had manifested a tendency to patronize him hitherto, and the fact that at the same time he became the principal support of his family naturally tended to strengthen his conviction that he was a pretty good fellow. From then on, he always occupied the center of a steadily widening stage, and he always felt perfectly at home on it, no matter how many spotlights played on him. When he went to Washington, at the time of the copyright hearings, Paine tried to take him into the dining room at the Willard Hotel in an inconspicuous, roundabout way, but he would have none of that: they must go back and travel the full length of Peacock Alley, making the most spectacular, the most ostentatious entrance possible. He definitely plans a record for posterity, wonders who may be reading his letters and looking at his photographs in the years to come. When S. J. Woolf comes to paint him, he wants the picture to be as handsome as possible, explains how he wears his hair, keeps the artist waiting while he goes upstairs to brush it, so that it may look just right. He was a celebrity; he knew he was a celebrity; he could see no point in pretending that he was not. "I am afraid my talking bothers you," he tells Woolf. "I guess you are one of the few people who would be willing to pay me to keep quiet." In 1905, apparently in reply to a request for his autograph, he sends an old letter, a long one, to a correspondent: "Just as I was about to comply with your request in the formal and customary fashion, this old letter fell out of an old book, and I though maybe you might prefer it." And when the newspapers accuse him of having quoted from George Greenwood's book on Shakespeare without making the proper acknowledgments, he is not in the least disturbed, for the fact that he has been caught stealing from it will, he knows, give the book far more notoriety than it could otherwise possibly have had.

There is nothing offensive about all this; it is too natural, too unself-conscious. Take his love of compliments, his basking in the light of praise. He quotes the kind things that people have said about him, he repeats them, he rolls them with his tongue. "I can live for two months on a good compliment." And it is not only the great whose praise can please him, as he himself takes pains to point out. "We despise no source that can pay us a pleasing attention—there is no source that is humble enough for that." He compels a boor in a railway carriage to remove his package from the seat beside him in order that a lady may sit down. The lady thanks him, saying, "It is not often one has so distinguished a defender." And Mark is delighted. "She knew me, she knew me!" he exclaims to his companion.[1] And more precious than praise, of the ordinary variety, is straight human affection. "Praise is well, compliment is well, but affection—that is the last and final and most precious reward that any man can win, whether by character or achievement, and I am very grateful to have that reward." Or, as he puts it more directly and touchingly, when his neighbors welcome him at Storm-field, "I wonder why they all go to so much trouble for me. I never go to any trouble for anybody."

For, in the last analysis—the Czar and the Pacific Ocean not-withstanding—Mark Twain did not think of himself more highly than he ought to think. He had a man's proper pride, a man's self-respect. He resents a slur or a libel; he dislikes being dependent or beholden; he will form his own judgments, wisely or unwisely, will not accept opinions ready-made, not even from those who are wiser than he. Twice, in Berlin, he is mistaken for the historian Mommsen. "We have the same hair," he says, "but on examination it was found the brains were different." When he was a very young man, he met Anson Burlingame and was encouraged by him. "You have great ability," said Burlingame; "I believe you have genius. What you need now is the refinement of association. Seek companionship among men of superior intellect and character. Refine yourself and your work. Never affiliate with inferiors; always climb." He accepted the advice and followed it, and Burlingame himself had ever after a place all his own in his heart.

He was modest concerning his art; he was modest concerning his knowledge; he was modest concerning his character. The newspapers might attack him. What of it? "I have never seen an opinion of me in print which was as low down as my private opinion of myself. Of course that is something of an exaggeration, but there is a great big element of fact in it, neverthe-less."[2] Men praise him, and he loves it, but it is not enough. "We can secure other people's approval, if we do right and try hard; but our own is worth a hundred of it, and no way has been found out of securing that." He could never be sure of himself. "I am *bound* to wander out of the straight path & do outrageous things occasionally, & believe I have a genuinely bad heart anyhow—but in the course of time I will get some of the badness out of it or break it."[3]

The publishers want to use his picture as a frontispiece for *The Innocents Abroad,* but he will not hear of it: he hates "the effrontery of shoving the pictures of nobodies under people's

noses that way, after the fashion of quacks & negro minstrels."
He tells them to use a picture of the *Quaker City* instead.[4] He
would like to speak to General Pope, when he sees him at the
Grand Army reunion in Chicago, but he lacks the courage,
"thinking it might be presumptuous to tackle a man so high up
in military history." Charles Eliot Norton learns that Darwin is
in the habit of reading himself to sleep with Mark Twain's
books every night, and he passes the word on with some diffi-
dence, not quite sure whether Clemens will take it as a compliment or not. But he does. "I do regard it as a very great compliment and a very high honor that that great mind, laboring
for the whole human race, should rest itself on my books. I am
proud that he should rest himself to sleep with them." His
friends wish to name a day for him at the St. Louis fair, but he
will not hear of it: such honors are not for the living. "So long
as we remain alive we are not safe from doing things which
. . . can wreck our repute and extinguish our friendships."

Some men are modest toward the outside world who still
vaunt themselves in very unseemly fashion toward those who
are obliged to live with them from day to day. Not so Mark
Twain. When he compares himself with his wife, with Susy,
he is nothing, he is less than nothing. He is sure that he never
appreciated Susy, he could not, "for she was above my duller
comprehension. I merely knew that she was my superior in
fineness of mind, in the delicacy and subtlety of her intellect,
but to fully measure her I was not competent." He is sure, too,
that he never treated Mrs. Clemens as she deserved. "I have
known few meaner men than I am." And one thinks of the
words of Beatrice to Dante:

> But when from one's own cheeks comes bursting forth
> The accusal of the sin, in our tribunal
> Against the edge the wheel doth turn itself.

II

NONE of this means, however, that Mark Twain was not the
king-figure in the group in which he moved, or that he did not

relish that position and in later years accept it as a matter of course. He was called "the King" at the end, and he behaved like a king, as is abundantly clear from many passages in Paine's account. He had acquired the habits of kingship early; they clung to him; naturally they did not tend to fall away with age and fame. He knew it. "By long habit," he writes in *Life on the Mississippi,* "pilots came to put all their wishes in the form of commands. It 'gravels' me, to this day, to put my will in the weak shape of a request, instead of launching it in the crisp language of an order." He did not have to with Paine, his most intimate associate at the end, for Paine stood to him in a subordinate position; as his biographer, he had much at stake; he loved Mark Twain and respected him too much ever to take offense, even when he might legitimately have done so. "It is hardly necessary to say," he writes in one place, "that no one ever undertook to contradict any statements of this sort from him." This is not the best way for a human being to be treated, and Mark Twain would have had to be something more than human to escape all the disadvantages. Perhaps the note of royalty is strongest in Helen Keller's account of the time he read *Eve's Diary* for her and a small company. At the end, she was weeping openly, and the others were trying to choke back their tears. Mark Twain sat enthroned, monarch of his little world. He put on his Oxford robes for Helen Keller also. "He seemed pleased that I was impressed. He drew me towards him and kissed me on the brow, as a cardinal or pope or a feudal monarch might have kissed a little child."

We have all been told that Mark Twain was a great conversationalist, but he seems to have preferred monologues to conversations. "With no more inspiration than a 'yes' or a 'no' from one of us to prove he had our attention," writes Madame Gabrilowitsch, "Father could lead, fill, and finish the conversation all by himself," though she never felt this as a fault in him, for she tells us elsewhere that he was always so natural and unaffected that it was difficult to remember he was a great man. Susy is more penetrating when she writes, "He doesn't like to go to church at all, why I never understood, until just now, he told us the other day that he couldn't bear to hear anyone talk but himself, but that he could listen to himself talk for hours without getting tired, of course he said this in joke, but I've no doubt it was founded on truth." Robert Underwood Johnson reports of a meeting with Mark Twain in Venice, Mrs. Fields, Miss Jewett, and himself being present, that "the great humorist did most of the talking, the others only putting in a few words now and then by way of keeping him going." And he himself once declared that he made it a rule to do all the talking in his own house. Nobody could enjoy a dinner, he said, when he had to be thinking up something to say.

But all this indicates not so much the egoist as the eager, enthusiastic spirit. He had such capacity for self-absorption, such ability to put his whole soul into what he was doing that, with the best will in the world, he could not avoid seeming to dominate wherever he chanced to be. This appears, as already noted, in the improvised passages he added to the play in which he appeared; it appears in Calvin Higbie's delightful account of the Aurora dance;[5] it appears in his extensive preoccupation, both in his writings and his letters, with the things that had happened to him. These things were real to him; they were vital; they were intimately present in his consciousness; he was hardly more self-conscious in speaking of them than a child is when it babbles on about the concerns of its own little world. Mark Twain's was a highly personalized world; abstract matters did not enter, or, if they did, he infused personal emotion into them.

If he is to blame here in any important particular, the charge must probably proceed along this line, that sometimes he became so deeply interested in his own ideas—and especially in the pessimistic philosophy of his later years—that he developed them at home, and in the presence of his friends, regardless of the tastes and the comfort of the people who were obliged to listen to him. Even here he is childishly thoughtless, however, not wickedly selfish. He simply had to have an audience. He had lived in the spotlight so long that he must now do his very thinking aloud, and if there had been no human beings to listen to him, he would have preached to the birds, as St. Francis did. Before the death of Mrs. Clemens, he had come to realize this failing, and, as was his habit, he heaped exaggerated abuse upon his head. "I WISH—I WISH—but it is too late. I drove you to sorrow and heart-break just to hear myself talk. If ever I do it again when you get well I hope the punishment will fall upon me the guilty, not upon you the innocent."

Like many men of marked individuality, he did not always allow as carefully as he might have done for the rights of others, or perhaps it would be fairer to say that he did not sufficiently realize how much the habits and desires of others might differ from his own. "I have known him to sit for hours in a smoking car on a cold day," writes J. B. Pond, "smoking his pipe and reading his German book with the window wide open." Once Pond remonstrated in behalf of the other passengers. Mark blustered a bit, tried to justify himself, but he closed the window. "Whenever he had been a few days with us," W. D. Howells tells us, "the whole house had to be aired, for he smoked all over it from breakfast to bedtime. He always went to bed with a cigar in his mouth, and, sometimes, mindful of my fire insurance, I went up and took it away, still burning, after he had fallen asleep."[6]

However, Mark Twain could be exquisitely, even quixotically courteous in other things, as he was when, while he was living in Riverdale, Norman Hapgood invited him to come into New York to see Duse. On the night set there was a terrific storm. At the end of the first act, Mark Twain appeared at the theater. "It was impossible to reach you, by telephone," he said, "or in time by telegram, so I have come to explain that Mrs. Clemens is so unwell this evening that I ought not to be away." And thereupon he went back to Riverdale, through the storm.

I have several times already compared Mark Twain and Bernard Shaw; let me make one more comparison here. I yield to few in my admiration for the great Irish playwright; he is, to my way of thinking, one of the major prophets of our time. But if he is a great prophet, is he not also a great boor, and does he not often show the worst possible taste in the discourtesy displayed both in his private and his public utterances? Mark Twain was at least as temperamental as Shaw, at least as fond of making a grandstand play. He was a pessimist, as Shaw is an optimist, and in the abstract, he had a very low opinion of the human race. His witticisms and his foolishments filled the newspapers for a generation, but when did he ever hurt anybody's feeling or tread on anybody's toes? There are times when the frontier may give lessons in good manners to Mayfair.

The Damned Human Race

I

THEORETICALLY, Mark Twain is the Devil's Advocate in the case of the Universe versus Humanity; no man ever poured fiercer scorn upon his own kind. He is willing to admit that he himself rests under this self-pronounced condemnation, for "what a man sees in the human race is merely himself in the deep and honest privacy of his own heart. Byron despised the race because he despised himself. I feel as Byron did, and for the same reason." His heart would need to be pretty black on that basis. "Man is a museum of diseases, a home of impurities; he comes to-day and is gone to-morrow; he begins as dirt and departs as stench." Of all animals, he is least adapted to life on this planet, and if he was made for any purpose at all, it must have been for the support and entertainment of the microbes. Probably he was not made intentionally; he worked himself up from the primeval slime, through some unhappy accident, much to the surprise and grief of the Creator. In any event, the evolutionary process failed when he came on the scene, for his is the only bad heart in the whole animal kingdom; he alone is capable of malice, drunkenness, vindictiveness, and when he is not cruel by nature, he is a mere stupid sheep. What can be said of such a race, save that it would be better dead? "Often it does seem such a pity that Noah and his party did not miss the boat." And he wondered whether it might not be possible to exterminate the race by means of an invention which should withdraw all the oxygen from the air for a period of two minutes.

So much for humanity in the abstract; when he comes to deal with individuals, there is another story to tell. The race might be contemptible, but even a contemptible creature must be looked after and cared for when he is in need. "He would listen, no matter what you wanted to say," Katy Leary tells us, "just like he would listen to a little child's story, and help you. He was never too tired or busy to hear what you had to say." He was generous with money; he gave more than money; he gave time and understanding. An afflicted woman writes to him, asking for his autograph and a picture. He mislays the request, and when he finds it again, it is not enough that he shall send what she asks for; he must write a letter explaining carefully and in detail, why he has delayed so long. A boy writes, boy-fashion, to invite him to dinner; he replies courteously, explaining that since he is in mourning just now, he is not dining out. In New Zealand, an old man is taken ill during his lecture. He stops talking and goes back stage to offer assistance, nor will he resume until the man is better. A storm comes up while an artist is visiting him, painting his portrait; when the man is about to leave, he insists on loaning his overshoes. He will not miss them, he says, for he is old enough now to be able to refuse any invitation on the ground of bad weather. When young authors come to him, he gives them his time and his thought, encourages them as much as he conscientiously can, and if he is especially struck by what they have written, he is not averse to making a personal effort toward bringing it before the public.

The truth is that he is drawn powerfully in two directions at once: he admires noble deeds and aspirations and he thoroughly detests mean ones. If he had been less sensitive to fineness of spirit, if the standard he set up for the human species had not been quite so high, perhaps he would not have minded it so much when people behaved disgracefully. This dual aspect comes out perfectly in his comment on the murdered Empress of Austria: "She was so blameless, the Empress; and so beautiful, in mind and heart, in person and spirit; and whether with a crown upon her head or without it and nameless, a grace to the human race, and almost a justification of its creation; *would* be, indeed, but that the animal that struck her down re-establishes the doubt." There you have it. It was "the damned human race," yet after all it had produced Anson Burlingame and Henry H. Rogers and John Hay and Dr. John Brown—and Livy Clemens—and Joan of Arc.

It was impossible to avoid admiring such people, and he was aware that there were many others like them whom he personally had not had the good fortune to know. He could be thrilled by a deed of unselfish heroism, and when it was reported to him, he would walk the floor, his eyes filled with tears: "What noble generosity! By gosh! that's a fine man for you!" So it comes about that for all the blasting pessimism of his generalizations, practically speaking his books exemplify a high standard of moral idealism. He admires King Arthur risking his life in the smallpox hut; he admires Huck Finn when he refuses to surrender Nigger Jim; and he expected his readers to admire them also. What Albert Schweitzer calls "reverence for life" possesses him. His philosophy being what it was, he knew that theoretically he had no right either to praise man or to blame him, for theoretically man is a machine, and in no sense responsible for his deeds.[1] Yet he goes on doing it just the same, he does it even in *The Mysterious Stranger,* where we have Marget and Wilhelm Meidling and the good priest, side by side with Satan's fiercest denunciation of the human nature which, in the last analysis, they share. Like many another man, he is bigger than his philosophy, and Bradford sums it all up when he remarks, "No man ever more abused the human heart, or railed at the hollowness of human affection, and no man ever had more friends or loved more."

II

HE wanted friends, and needed them. He hated solitude; he could not bear to be left alone. Had he lived in Eden, he was sure he would have greeted the Serpent as "a welcome change —anything for society." Even in grief, the consciousness of human sympathy was precious. "They cannot heal the hurt, but they take away some of the pain." It was, in some respects, unfortunate that so sensitive a man should have needed humanity

quite so much, for while, as Huckleberry Finn observes, "the
more you join in with people in their joys and their sorrows,
the more nearer and dearer they come to be to you," it is also
true that the more you join in with them, the better chance they
have to hurt you. Clemens was not always fortunate in his
friends—what man is who assumes that everybody he has to
deal with is just as honest as he is himself? With Bret Harte, to
whom originally he had been under some obligations, there
was, in the end, something like a break. But Harte was an impossible person, and Mark Twain's life is, on the whole, singularly free from the quarrels and disagreements one expects, almost as a matter of course, with artists and literary men. His
quick sympathy is well suggested by Helen Keller: "He knew
with keen and sure intuition many things about me; how it
felt to be blind and not to be able to keep up with the swift
ones—things that others learned slowly or not at all. He never
embarrassed me by saying how terrible it is not to see, or how
dull life must be, lived always in the dark."

It will be worth while to look at his social life, to study its
conditions without too many preconceived ideas. In his teens,
he seems to have been shy, but he became a social lion as early
as the Carson City days, and after marriage and fame there
were naturally many temptations along this line. One observer
testifies: "The Clemens house was the only one I have ever
known where there was never any *pre*occupation in the evenings, and where visitors were always welcome." As late as the
turn of the century, we hear of one week when guests were entertained at seventeen out of the twenty-one meals and on three
out of the seven evenings.

To be sure, he could be bored, or, rather, he could be enraged,
for boredom was too mild a feeling to touch that ardent soul.
"All the old cats in Christendom seem to have chosen this particular day to visit here. . . . Miss S. (whom I delight to hate)
called first, and she was no sooner gone than Mrs. B. (whom to
hate is an unspeakable luxury) came. When I get sight of either
of these women I am 'done' for that day. When they both come

in one evening I degenerate into pure lunacy." Yet on the whole congeniality far outweighed annoyance. Katy Leary describes his sessions with Howells: "Well, you couldn't hear a thing from the Billiard Room but peals of laughter from them two men when he was visiting there. Oh, how they'd laugh!" Chauncey M. Depew says he was very uneven as a conversationalist. "Sometimes he would be the life of the occasion and make it one to be long remembered but generally he contributed nothing. At this dinner, whenever he showed the slightest sign of making a remark, there was dead silence, but the remark did not come." It is no wonder—in the dead silence; Mark Twain always had considerable difficulty in doing what he knew he was expected to do. On the whole, his personality seems to have been quite impressive enough without his reputation. Bernard Shaw tells us that when he visited Adelphi Terrace, the parlor maid did not know him from Adam, yet she admitted him without question and unannounced.

To many of the amusements toward which men turn to reinforce their social life, Mark Twain was altogether indifferent. Physically he was much too fond of his ease to be drawn to sports. Even in childhood, only swimming—plus skating in the winter time—seems to have attracted him very much. He did some fencing in his Virginia City days. In Hartford, he used to go to baseball games. He once went to see Corbett box, and was impressed by the fine form he displayed. Neither golf nor yachting interested him. He was quite indifferent to horseflesh, and though he experimented briefly with the bicycle, this is simply an example of his unfailing curiosity concerning newfangled machinery. He always preferred walking to riding, liked to take his guests to ramble over the hills and fields around Stormfield, and told Dan Beard that he intended to do his traveling on his own "hind legs."

In his boyhood, his uncle and his cousins sometimes took young Sam out hunting, but he never hit anything, nor did he show any great eagerness to learn. It never occurred to him that pleasure could be derived from inflicting suffering and death on dumb creatures. He once went to a cockfight, but he had to leave before it was over. The bullfight was, to him, a spectacle of horror. Huck's beautiful sensitiveness is used here, as so often, to pass judgment on those who imagine themselves to be civilized: "I see a bird setting on a limb of a high tree, singing with its head tilted back and its mouth open, and before I thought I fired, and his song stopped and he fell straight down from the limb, all limp like a rag, and I run and picked him up and he was dead, and his body was warm in my hand, and his head rolled about this way and that, like his neck was broke, and there was a little white skin over his eyes, and one little drop of blood on the side of his head; and, laws! I couldn't see nothing more for the tears; and I hain't never murdered no creature since that warn't doing me no harm, and I ain't going to." Lest there be any question as to this being purely a dramatic utterance, may I add Howells' testimony: "He abhorred the dull and savage joy of the sportsman in a lucky shot, an unerring aim, and once when I met him in the country he had just been sickened by the success of a gunner in bringing down a blackbird, and he described the poor, stricken, glossy thing, how it lay throbbing its life out on the grass, with such pity as he might have given a wounded child."

Indoor amusements interested him more, though, except for billiards, which, toward the end, became a kind of religion, they did not take a very deep hold on him either. He danced in his youth and sometimes in later life also. In his mining-camp days, he played euchre and seven-up, and there are a few references to poker, but he was no gambler, and he preferred solitaire or hearts. I find some mention of chess but none of checkers. He never needed stakes to make the game interesting. "Father," writes Madame Gabrilowitsch, "was like a little child in his capacity for getting angry over cards. Continuous bad luck would start those little twitching muscles under his eyes that signified a growing storm, and then suddenly followed an avalanche of cards on the table and Father would sing out: 'By the humping jumping —— who can play with a hand like that? Look at those cards! Just look at them! Products of the devil and his ancestors." But better than any card game, he enjoyed charades, for they brought his dramatic gift into play, and he liked nothing better than to devise curious methods to help his children learn their lessons, as may be seen best of all in his history games.

It seems hardly necessary to say that he did not always follow the accepted rules of social behavior. In the early days, he disregarded them sometimes because he did not know them, later often because he did not choose to consider them important. Once, at a dinner given in his honor, he pushed back his chair midway through the meal, declared that he had had enough, called for a cigar, and walked up and down the room talking while the rest of the guests finished their meal. Laurence Hutton tells, too, how he once walked in on a dinner to Sir Henry Irving. He had not been invited, because it was not known that he was to be in the city. "He had arrived from Hartford late in the afternoon, had discovered from the gossip at the Club that the Huttons were having 'a rather unusual dinner-party,' was told who were to be present, and decided that it was too good a thing to lose. So he dressed hurriedly, walked in without ceremony just as the feast began, drew up a chair by the side of his hostess, helped himself to her oysters, and for the rest of the evening was the life of the party."

Nor will it surprise us in a man so much given to violent expression of his dislikes, if we find him sometimes proceeding to the opposite extreme, going over into sheer extravagance and sentimentality. Let us leave out the more personal, the more poignant matters here; let us take a literary problem—his portrait of Joan of Arc. "Hearing the M.S. read aloud," writes Susy, "is an uplifting and revealing hour to us all. Many of Joan's words and sayings are historically correct and Papa cries when he reads them. In fact he almost always fills up when reading any speech of hers." Joan is a great heroine, a great genius, yet he cannot resist the temptation to sentimentalize her—"the noble child, the most innocent, the most lovely, the most adorable the ages have produced." People gaze upon her, half-wonderingly and half-worshipfully: "How sweet—how lovely—how divine!" If the verdict of time finally sustains the judgment of those who feel that Mark Twain failed in the book he himself regarded as his masterpiece, such passages as these will play a large part in the decision rendered.

III

THOUGH the shortcomings of women have always been one of the principal themes of the professional humorist, Mark Twain is very rarely cynical in this regard. There is one speech on "Woman," delivered at a banquet of the Washington Correspondents' Club, which verges on ribaldry; and when he went to Washington to speak in behalf of copyright, he stated as one of the reasons why he needed money the fact that he had reared his daughters as young ladies and that therefore they didn't know anything and couldn't do anything. In *Eve's Diary,* he makes fun of woman's social proclivities and her passion for hanging ornaments on her person, and Adam is right down Mr. Brooks's street when he speaks of the hampering effect of domestic relations, and complains of Eve's disposition to interfere with the things he likes to do.[2]

These passages seem very inconsequential, however, when compared to those in which Mark Twain expresses his respect and regard for women.[3] When he encountered a man who lacked such respect, he felt that he had learned nothing about women but a good deal about men. So he hated Strindberg for the unpleasant women encountered in his plays, "a dead give-away on the author's part, for a writer who sees no good in women confesses that he was found out by the sex he wars on and that the female of the species pronounced him n.g. before he had time to out-Ibsen the Norwegian."[4] He was especially impressed by the endurance of women, in the painful business of childbirth. "I do admire Katharine's courage. I hope I shall never have a baby, for I know I should dread it so that every one would be ashamed of me." He declares bluntly that the average woman is superior to the average man: his notion of the form that superiority was likely to take is shown very clearly in *The $30,000 Bequest*. Both husband and wife make fools of themselves as they dispose of their imaginary fortunes, but the woman's dreams are on a far higher level than the man's.

In sexual matters, so far as he considers them at all, he is distinctly on the woman's side. He is proud of the purity of American women; he is also proud of the fact that "even the most degraded woman can walk our streets unmolested, her sex and her weakness being her sufficient protection." When Professor Dowden permits himself to blacken the good name of Harriet Shelley in an attempt to make the best case that can be made for her husband, he writes his reply in a white flame of anger: "The charge insinuated by these odious slanders is one of the most difficult of all offenses to prove; it is also one which no man has a right to mention even in a whisper about any woman, living or dead, unless he knows it to be true, and not even then unless he can also *prove* it to be true." Mark Twain himself once had a share in forcing matrimony upon an unwilling bridegroom, and the dubious experiment seems to have turned out fairly well. And there is an amazing and little-known magazine article in which he proposes to disregard "consent" as minimizing the guilt of seduction. "Consent" is not adduced as a palliating circumstance in connection with murder or arson; why should it appear here? "I should say simply that commerce *with a spinster,* of whatever age or condition, should be punished by two years of solitary confinement or five years at hard labor; and let the man take his choice." Himself he would prefer an even heavier penalty; the monster should be flayed alive, but that, he knows, is more than could reasonably be hoped for.[5] And do you not hear an echo of the bitter wisdom of the Shakespeare of *Measure for Measure:* "Does your worship mean to geld and spay all the youth of the city?"

Many men profess great respect for women in sexual matters

who still, when it comes to a showdown, manifest a very clear
determination to keep the control of the world in the hands of
men. It was not so with Mark Twain. The question of careers
for women intrudes as early as *The Gilded Age,* though here
no definite conclusions can be drawn. When it comes to woman
suffrage, however, he declares quite unequivocally, in an address of 1901: "I should like to see the time come when women
shall help to make the laws. I should like to see that whip-lash,
the ballot, in the hands of women. As for this city's government, I don't want to say much, except that it is a shame—a
shame; but if I should live twenty-five years longer—and there
is no reason why I shouldn't—I think I'll see women handle the
ballot. If women had the ballot today, the state of things in this
town would not exist."

It is a pity that Mark Twain's faith was, in this instance, not
justified. The world is little, if any, better today, than it would
be if no woman had ever cast a ballot in it.

IV

MARK TWAIN loved children always: it is significant that when
he wishes to describe a group of beautiful women he should
say, "They fasten one's eyes like a magnet—or a baby—or a
wood-fire in the twilighted room." "The darling mispronun-
ciations of childhood!" cries the Connecticut Yankee, "—dear
me, there's no music that can touch it . . ." and there can be
no doubt that here, as in the preceding description of the serious illness of his child, he is speaking for Mark Twain. His
love of children informs also his ecstatic appreciation of Titian's
"Moses," in *A Tramp Abroad.* Indeed, I think one reference to
"trundlebed trash" in an 1853 letter to his mother is the only
unkind word Mark Twain ever gives to childhood.

This kindliness appears most clearly in his relations with his
own children. In later years, after the death of Susy, he up-
braided himself for having neglected her, but that was his way;
after he had done all, he must still insist he was the unprofitable
servant. While the children were small, he frolicked with them

and played with them, and took part in amateur theatricals, and rejoiced when they abused him and tyrannized over him, and was never bored when they insisted that he tell them very long stories. Discipline was entirely in the hands of Mrs. Clemens, who seems to have combined absolute firmness with complete gentleness and justice. When Grace King visited the Hartford home, she was surprised and charmed at the freedom permitted, "Susy and Clara taking the lead in their bright, girlish way, expressing themselves boldly, without fear of criticism or correction, making keen remarks on the people they knew or had met." Mark Twain himself was, of course, far too temperamental ever to be a good disciplinarian; he showed common sense by simply letting the matter alone. On the one hand, he was capable of playing practical jokes on his children, as when he got Clara to believe that the calf Jumbo was going to grow up into a pony; on the other hand, he permitted her to keep a pair of squirrels in her room, even though they gnawed the woodwork until it seemed that the walls must fall in. When illness came to the children, he was nearly beside himself. Mrs. Fields tells a story which might almost serve for a page out of the biography of Mrs. McWilliams,[6] and it would be difficult to carry solicitude much further than Mark himself carries it in an 1877 letter to J. R. Clemens: "We should all greatly like to make the Richmond excursion Sunday, but Clara has had a fall at the gymnasium and we are afraid to have her go, and so the rest of us will have to stay at home and keep her company."[7]

Susy was undoubtedly his favorite, as how could she help being, when she had inherited so much of his gift and his temperament? Clara inherited his temperament also—the first two syllables of it, at least—and he loved her for it—"a very dear little ashcat, but has claws." After she had grown up, there was a good deal of friendly sparring between them; Mr. Paine found it "always a delight to see them together when one could be just out of range of the cross-fire." Once his sense of humor deserted him with Clara, and he literally locked her up in her room in order to keep her away from a suitor he happened to dislike. Perhaps he knew her best of all at the end. "You must know Clara better;" he writes Mrs. Rogers, "she is one of the very finest and completest and most satisfactory characters I have ever met." Certainly the letter he wrote her after the death of Jean is as beautiful as any father ever wrote or daughter received. Jean, too, he knew best at the end, and of his love for her he has made a record that all the world may read—and has read.

In his writings, Mark Twain succeeds much better with boys than he does with girls—the little heroine of "The Death Disk" is a quite impossible creature—but in life he seems distinctly to have preferred girls. This was true especially in his old age, after his own girls had grown up or died; through his child-friends, he tried to recapture the past. In *Mark Twain and the Happy Island,* Miss Elizabeth Wallace has written engagingly of his frolics in Bermuda, and he did not forget the friends he made there. He had his "Aquarium," made up of "Angel Fish," that is, girls in their early teens, and he found much pleasure in the Juggernaut Club, which consisted of a number of little girls, no more than one from any single country, he himself, the only male member, being designated the Chief Servant. Benjamin De Casseres tells how, one afternoon in 1908, he chanced to see Mark Twain arrive at an Empire Theater matinee, accompanied by a whole raft of children, to see Maude Adams in *Peter Pan.* "Girls are charming creatures," he declares. "I shall have to be twice seventy years old before I change my mind as to that."

V

OF Mark Twain's servants, the shrewd Katy Leary is by far the best known. He watched over her and guarded her carefully, though she may not always have appreciated it when he sent her suitors home and locked up the house at ten o'clock. That there were hardly any limits to her devotion to him, her whole book testifies eloquently, but she knew his peculiarities also, humored him when necessary, played up to him, and well understood how to evade directions she did not care to carry out. He seems never to have been unreasonable with her except when he would mislay one of his own manuscripts and then accuse her of having burned it—after which there would be grand high passages of words between them—but he had certain services which she must always perform in his behalf, and if she failed, there was the devil to pay. "He always had three sets of cuff buttons and shirt buttons fixed, so there'd always be a shirt ready for him. My goodness! I used to have to fix three shirts at the same time, because if he found one shirt that didn't have the proper cuff buttons in, he'd tear it up." Katy wouldn't have that, for she thought him far too extravagant already, and when he told her a shirt was worn out and she must throw it away, she would mend it instead and put it back in his drawer, and Mark would go on wearing it without ever knowing the difference. Yes, a clever servant is like Chaucer's Manciple: the brightest man is putty in her hands.

In the East, Mark Twain loathed the jinricksha because he could not feel it right that one man should draw another about. He employed a colored butler, because he did not like to give orders to a white man, but George was not much troubled by orders, much less indeed than nine persons out of ten would have said a proper regard for discipline and decorum required. And when the coachman, Patrick McAleer died, Clemens acted as a pallbearer in company with his own gardener, and, in a public address, lauded Patrick as the ideal gentleman. It was not an unkind way to treat a member of the damned human race.

VI

PROBABLY no man ever loved animals better than Mark Twain, and—as everybody knows—his favorite animal was the cat. Indeed, he ranks with Doctor Johnson, Cardinal Richelieu, and others, among the greatest cat lovers of all time. He began to love cats as a boy—though, if the painkiller incident in *Tom Sawyer* is from his own experience, there must have been times when his sense of humor got the better of his affections, and he liked to recall, in later years, how, one Sunday morning, he had seen a cat walk into some flypaper placed close to the pulpit, "saw her struggle and fall down, more and more unreconciled, more and more mutely profane." His own opinion is summed up categorically: "I simply can't resist a cat, particularly a purring one. They are the cleanest, cunningest, and most intelligent things I know, outside the girl you love, of course." Or, as Susy puts it, in her own charming way: "The difference between papa and mama is, that mama loves morals and papa loves cats."

It might be expected that such a man as Mark Twain would invent ingenious names for his cats, and he does not disappoint us. Four kittens at Quarry Farm were called Sour Mash, Apollinaris, Zoroaster, and Blatherskite. He chose the names, he said, to give the children practice in pronunciation, and when all four animals died young, he was sure their names had killed them. When he came to spend a summer at Dublin, New Hampshire, he simply could not consider getting along without a cat, but he could not disregard the problem of what would happen to the animal after he went home again. He solved it triumphantly by renting a cat instead of adopting one, renting two in fact—Sackcloth and Ashes, he called them—and paying enough to insure their care after the autumn should have come. In a man as absent-minded, as careless concerning detail as Mark Twain was habitually, one could hardly ask for more. "Once," writes Mr. Paine, "as he was about to enter the screen-door that led into the hall, two of the kittens ran up in front of him and stood waiting. With grave politeness he opened the door, made a low bow, and stepped back and said: 'Walk in, gentlemen. I always give precedence to royalty.' And the kittens marched in, tails in air."

Danbury and Tammany were great favorites in Stormfield days. "Mark Twain might be preoccupied and indifferent to the comings and goings of other members of the household; but no matter what he was doing, let Danbury appear in the offing and he was observed and greeted with due deference, and complimented and made comfortable. Clemens would arise from the table and carry certain choice food out on the terrace to Tammany, and be satisfied with almost no acknowledgment by way of appreciation." And how fine and tender is his own story of the kitten on the billiard table. "If I can find a photograph of my 'Tammany' and her kittens, I will enclose it in this. One of them likes to be crammed into a corner-pocket of the billiard-table—which he fits as snugly as does a finger in a glove and then he watches the game (and obstructs it) by the hour, and spoils many a shot by putting out his paw and changing the direction of a passing ball. Whenever a ball is in his arms, or so close to him that it cannot be played upon without risk of hurting him, the player is privileged to remove it to any-one of the 3 spots that chances to be vacant."

Sometimes the family cunningly played on this love of cats, as when they rented an apartment in an undesirable neighborhood in Berlin without consulting him. "The women took that apartment in Slumland over my head, and lured me to approve of their choice by having two purring cats on the hearth when I first saw the place." Madame Gabrilowitsch tells us that if, as a child, she was obliged, for any reason, to disturb him at his work, and was in any doubt concerning her reception, she always took a kitten with her in her arms.

Dogs were quite another story. His great sensitiveness to sound made their barking very trying to him, and he sometimes declared he wished he could exterminate them all. Like many persons who have learned to appreciate the independent spirit of the cat, he disliked the dog's servility,[8] and he had the same opinion as O. Henry about people who take dogs out at the end of a string. Yet there is no tenderer dog story in literature than "A Dog's Tale"—written as an argument against vivisection—and one of the most touching passages in "The Death of Jean" relates how he and his daughter's dog were drawn together in their common grief.[9]

Mark Twain, indeed, did not know how to be unkind to any

animal. When Edmund Yates visited him, he found in the
greenhouse a cage containing a pair of California quails: Mark
had bought them from a boy in order to save them, and when
spring came, he planned to set them free. In 1904, there is a
characteristic entry in his journal. He is staying at Tyringham,
in very unpleasant weather. "We built a fire in my room. Then
clawed the logs out and threw water, remembering there was a
brood of swallows in the chimney. The tragedy was averted."
When he was abroad with Twichell, he would, on no account,
permit the drivers to whip their horses. "Never mind that! We
are going fast enough. We are in no hurry." Not even snakes
and bats were excluded from his sympathies, though he detested flies and spiders.

Like most lovers of animals, Mark Twain refuses to believe
that they cannot think, or that they do not converse with one
another. He thinks of them as individuals, describes their individual characteristics in such a way that they seem almost human.[10] I find no indication that he ever read, in any of its forms,
the great folk epic of "Reynard the Fox," or even the two beautiful poems it inspired in English literature—"The Nonne
Preestes Tale" of Chaucer and Spenser's "Mother Hubberd's
Tale"—but he would certainly have relished these masterpieces
in which human and animal characteristics are so ingeniously
mingled and animals are used for satirical commentary on human nature and human institutions. And what a pity he did not
live long enough to enjoy George Herriman's "Krazy Kat"—
"the most tender and most foolish of creatures, a gentle monster
of our new mythology," as Gilbert Seldes has called him—and
the infinitely ingenious "Mickey Mouse" of Walt Disney.

With Mark Twain, the emphasis of such satire would always
have been rightly pointed, for—let there be no mistake about it
—he was completely, and quite seriously, convinced that man
is the least admirable figure in the animal kingdom. "Man isn't
even handsome, as compared with the birds; and as for style,
look at the Bengal tiger—the ideal of grace, physical perfection,
and majesty. Think of the lion and the tiger and the leopard,

and then think of man—that poor thing!—the animal of the
wig, the ear-trumpet, the glass eye, the porcelain teeth, the
wooden leg, the trepanned skull, the silver wind-pipe, a creature that is mended and patched all over from top to bottom."
Test his character and he shows no more attractively: what animal would be guilty of the refined, useless cruelties that human
beings inflict upon one another. This inferiority is most seriously argued in *The Mysterious Stranger;* it is most epigram-
matically summed up in the words of Pudd'nhead Wilson: "If
you pick up a starving dog and make him prosperous, he will
not bite you. This is the principal difference between a dog and
a man."

There is something very touching about Mark Twain's attitude toward animals at the end of his life: as his pessimism
grew upon him, as he became more and more disgusted with
the damned human race, he turned to them for comfort. Here
he suggests Cowper, who needed refuge, to be sure, not so
much from other men as from himself, Cowper who loved his
hares and his cats so tenderly, and who could write: "The season has been most unfavorable to animal life; and I, who am
merely animal, have suffered much by it." Also, as has already
been suggested, he recalls Swift, who came, at last, in his utopia,
to the ideal of a land ruled by the horses, with vicious, degraded
human creatures subordinated to their proper place. When, in
The Prince and the Pauper, young royalty is cast out by men,
he finds comfort in a calf who is thrown in his way, and Clarence suggests to the Yankee—here the closest parallel with
Swift—that, since mankind apparently will not consent to be
deprived of the gewgaws of royalty, a race of cats to rule us
would be the best.

CHAPTER IV

The Root of Evil

I

THERE is high authority for the statement that the love
of money is the root of all evil, but this world is a much
less simple place than most of us would like to have it,
and in actual experience we all find a good deal of evil that is
inspired by the lack of money. Mark Twain was quite familiar
with this Janus-faced aspect of the money problem, as these entries in his notebook show:

Saturday, January 3, 1903. The offspring of riches: Pride,
vanity, ostentation, arrogance, tyranny.

Sunday, January 4, 1903. The offspring of poverty: Greed,
sordidness, envy, hate, malice, cruelty, meanness, lying, shirk-
ing, cheating, stealing, murder.

There was no chauvinism in his own attitude toward money.
He saw a particularly ugly aspect of money lust in the Western
mining camps of his early days, and as he grew older, he was
saddened to observe even uglier manifestations of it in the increasing commercialism of modern society. There never was a
more effective parable of the corrupting effects of greed on human character than in *The Man That Corrupted Hadleyburg.*

But he came out of a household which knew poverty. He had
a most worthy but impractical father, and an equally worthy
and impractical brother. He did not want to be like them. He
made up his mind to push out into the great world of active
humanity, as they had never done, to get a share of the good
things of life not only for himself but for them. As pilot, he
came into a large salary, which he spent freely and generously.
From piloting, he went on to prospecting, then, through the
antechamber of his newspaper days, to the *Innocents* tour, to
the lecture platform, to his prosperity as a man of letters, to his

many adventures in business and in speculation. For money, dangerous though it may be, is "a good and strong friend," and when business fails, he is haunted by the fear of poverty. To the last, he dreams recurrent dreams of being obliged to go back to the river or to the lecture platform, to earn a living.

II

HE considered the economic aspects of literature carefully. In his early days, he agreed to write some letters for the Keokuk *Post*. Five dollars each was the price agreed upon. After writing the first, he asked seven dollars and a half for the second, which was granted. When he came to the third, he pushed the honorarium up to ten, and the publishers refused.[1] Mark was born with the writing urge in his bones, but he had no intention of devoting himself to authorship unless there was money in it. When the American Publishing Company approached him with the suggestion that he make a book out of the travel letters he had written home from his excursion to the Mediterranean and the Holy Land, he made this perfectly clear. "But I had my mind made up to *one* thing—" he explains to his mother, "I wasn't going to touch a book unless there was *money* in it, and a good deal of it. I told them so."

This is no exceptional note. He would like to sell *Tom Sawyer* to the *Atlantic,* but he does not think the magazine could afford to pay what he can get elsewhere, and he is indisposed to sacrifice cash for glory. "You see I take a vile, mercenary view of things—but then my household expenses are something almost ghastly." Elsewhere, he asks of a publishing venture: "Why should we assist our fellowman for mere love of God?" And when it comes to *Pudd'nhead Wilson,* you would think he was selling cordwood or potatoes. "Now, then what is she worth? The amount of matter is but 3,000 words short of the American Claimant, for which the syndicate paid $12,500. There was nothing new in that story, but the finger-prints in this one is virgin-ground—absolutely *fresh,* and mighty curious and interesting to everybody." Only with *Joan of Arc* is this consideration neglected. "Possibly the book may not sell, but that is nothing—it was written for love."

When he died, his estate, despite his not-so-distant bank-ruptcy, was valued at about $600,000, including the value of his copyrights. It was not a bad showing for the boy from Hanni-bal. He had bargained well with his publishers, on the whole, disastrous as some of his other financial transactions had been. The terms of his final contract with Harpers, arranged for him by H. H. Rogers, were very generous. The publishers were to pay royalties on a minimum of 50,000 volumes per year, whether they sold that many or not, and every time they left an adver-tisement out of their magazine, it cost them $200. Some crit-ics of Mark Twain are inclined to attribute his interest in the commercial aspects of literature to his frontier background; he grew up—they tell us—in a world where the material standard was the only criterion of success. But Scott and Dickens were equally interested in this aspect—though neither was born on the frontier—and so is Bernard Shaw, his socialistic convictions concerning the iniquities of capitalism notwithstanding. The pure, disinterested idealism of a Van Wyck Brooks is, un-happily, not the necessary concomitant development of a com-plex social environment.

III

By nature Mark Twain was extravagant; he always wanted plenty of money, to spend and to give away. In his pilot days, "a ten dollar dinner at a French restaurant—breathe it not unto Ma!" was so great an event that he had to write home about it, but he soon came to the place where his indulgences, though different in character, cost a great deal more money than that. As early as 1868, when he goes to California to try to persuade the *Alta* to release his travel letters for book publication, one stateroom is not enough for him, he must have two. When he is married, his bride tells him not to worry about finances, they can live on a very moderate sum, and he comments signifi-cantly, "I know very well that she can . . . but I am not so sure about myself." Careful computation of costs was not for him. He ordered clothes and household accessories by the dozens, by the hundreds; when he decided to wear white clothes, he immediately ordered fourteen suits, so that he would always have seven for each week—seven at the cleaners' and seven at home. Take the mere detail of barbering. While he was in Hartford, the barber used to come to the house every morning to shave him, for which service he paid a dollar and a half per shave. His household expenses were enormous always; he entertained on a lavish scale; in the year 1881 alone, $30,000 were swallowed up in improvements on the Hartford property, including $12,000—a highwayman's price—for an adjoining strip of land where building was threatened. Even in his last years, when he and Jean were living alone at Stormfield, his household expenses ran up to fifty dollars a day.

I am not forgetting that there were times when Mark Twain and his family went to Europe to live because they could not afford to remain in America. But even on such occasions they did not live quite like paupers. In 1898, they settled in Vienna, paying $600 a month for "4 bedrooms, a dining-room, a drawing-room, 3 bath-rooms and 3 Vorzimmers, (and food)" at the best hotel in the city. A few years later, he paid $2,000 a year for the Villa Quarto in Florence. No wonder Mrs. Clemens found it necessary to remind him, during one financial crisis, when, with his excited imagination, he saw them settled in the poorhouse, that even if it came to the worst, they would still have an income of $6,000 a year, and what he could earn with his pen besides! Did Mark Twain, in all his frenzied taking thought for the morrow, ever have the slightest understanding of what the financial problem was like for the overwhelming proportion of his countrymen? Of this, too, his wife sought to remind him. "What should we do, and how should we feel if we had no bright prospects before us, and yet how many people are situated in that way?"

Mrs. Clemens' attitude becomes a matter of vital interest in this connection, for those who see her as the antiartistic force in her husband's life are firmly persuaded that he would never have devoted himself as he did to the pursuit of the almighty dollar if he had not been married to her. This idea seems to be based on the fact that Mrs. Clemens was the daughter of a very wealthy man. Jervis Langdon's household expenses, at Elmira, New York, ran up to the dizzy heights of $40,000 a year, and it is assumed that the sum stood, somehow, as a challenge to Mark Twain. I cannot quite follow this reasoning. Mark Twain's position was not impressive at the time he won Olivia Langdon, and he had no intention, as the saying is, of trying to support her in the style to which she had been accustomed. He even dramatizes his poverty—a bit unnecessarily, it would seem, in the light of some of his other expenditures: "I gave her only a plain gold engagement ring, when fashion imperatively demands a two-hundred dollar diamond one, and told her it was typical of her future lot—namely, that she would have to flourish on substantials rather than luxuries." When they were prosperous, she wore beautiful clothes, but that she was not extravagant we learn incidentally from a remark of her daughter's, that Mark seldom noticed a new gown until after she had been wearing it for six months. It is not fair to blame her for the worldly splendor of their hospitality; it was her husband, not herself, who was the more social being of the two, and had her own inclinations ruled, they must have led a much simpler life than they did.[2]

Mrs. Clemens comes in for special consideration here in connection with Mark Twain's business failure—a failure, it should be remembered, which carried away her fortune as well as his own. It was difficult for her to accept the idea that her husband had actually gone through bankruptcy. "I have a perfect *horror* and heartsickness over it," she writes her sister. "I cannot get away from the feeling that business failure means disgrace." So she is presented as an extremely conventional person, a child of the Gilded Age who finds it impossible to believe that values can exist without money. This interpretation is not impossible, though I think allowance must be made also for Mrs. Clemens' stern sense of honor, and possibly if a few more business men had felt as she did about such matters, our present economic mess might never have become so bad as it is. In any case, she seems to have been very careful not to add to her husband's burden. We need not give her the full credit for his determination to pay one hundred cents on the dollar instead of the fifty cents with which he could have escaped. Mark Twain did not need a wife to teach him to be an honest man. But it is something that she should have stood by him as she did. He could not help knowing that she was desperately grieved over the whole affair—"I seem to see you grieving and ashamed, and dreading to look people in the face"—but he rejoiced in her courage and her loyalty.

IV

But the thing that really wrecked Mark Twain financially was never his extravagance; it was his investments. All through his mature life, he had the gambling fever in an aggravated form. He did not gamble with cards, but he was never able to resist a speculation. Pudd'nhead Wilson's advice on the matter is sage enough: "There are two times in a man's life when he should not speculate: when he can afford it, and when he can't." But Mark Twain himself seems to have been quite unimpressed. In the single year 1881, he invested no less than $46,000, mainly in abortive projects. It was exciting entertainment while it lasted, though clearly the most expensive he could buy. "I was always taking little chances . . . —a thing which I did not greatly mind because I was always careful to risk only such amounts as I could easily afford to lose." Among the world-revolutionizing inventions which he sponsored were a steam generator, a steam pulley, a new method of marine telegraphy, a new engraving process, a patent cash register, and a spiral hat pin. When he died, the appraisers of his estate found only $8,000 of his investments in bonds. Among his assets were 375 shares of capital stock in the Plasmon Milk Products Company. The appraisers estimated the total value of these shares at $100.00.

In other words, as he himself puts it, "all through my life I have been the easy prey of the cheap adventurer." Only once does he seem to have been cautious, and that was when a young man named Alexander Graham Bell came to him with a crazy newfangled Arabian Nights' kind of invention called the telephone. He could have had any number of shares, virtually at his own price, but he turned the offer down. He was too old and too wise a bird to be caught with a thing like that.

We have had occasion elsewhere to observe the absence of any carefully formulated direction in his literary career. He had not analyzed his gifts with sufficient care, had never thought his problem through. A literary man? He knew what a literary man was. Undoubtedly to those utterly lacking in such ability, it must seem something of a miracle that a man should be able to put a book together, to make something exist where nothing had been before. But once you had done it—shucks! it was nothing. He knew a trick worth two of that. Over there on the other side of the fence were those astonishing business men. Business was not what it had used to be. It was expanding, developing, running out in infinite ramifications. If you were in business, you could feel power under your hands—you were the force that made things go—you even made these damned kings crawl in the dirt beneath your feet. "Unconsciously," he says, "we all have a standard by which we measure other men, and if we examine closely we find that this standard is a very simple one, and is this: we admire them, we envy them, for great qualities which we ourselves lack." When he finds in himself even a little aptitude along this line, he swells up like a pouter pigeon; no purely literary achievement could for a moment be compared with it. He plans to take the manuscript of *The Gilded Age* to England, so as to print simultaneously on both sides of the Atlantic, and foil the pirates: "Some people think I have no head for business, but this is a lie."

He had, to be sure, one great triumph as a business man, when he "stole" the Grant Memoirs from the Century Company, by offering far more liberal terms and backing up his faith with a check for $25,000 advance royalties. Here, again, the speculative element appealed to him strongly; he saw a long chance and he took it, and this time he was fully justified. The sales of the book quite reached his most sanguine expectations and ultimately about $425,000 was paid out in royalties. This was during the period when, in his own words, he was frightened at the proportions of his prosperity. "It seems to me that whatever I touch turns to gold." But even then he was out of his orbit; he was planing against the grain of the wood; he was carrying burdens that were much too heavy for him. "Life has come to be a very serious matter with me. I have a badgered, harassed feeling, a good part of my time." In his heart he knew—or he soon learned—that he had no place in business—and the conviction gained upon him as time went on. "I am terribly tired of business. I am by nature and disposition unfit for it, & I want to get out of it." When the crash came, there was a part of him—way down inside—that was actually glad. "Now and then a good and dear Joe Twichell or Susy Warner condoles with me and says 'Cheer up—don't be down-hearted,' and some other friend says, 'I am glad and surprised to see how cheerful you are and how bravely you stand it'—and none of them suspect what a burden has been lifted from me and how blithe I am inside."

V

IT will be seen, then, that there was a visionary quality in Mark Twain's adventures with money, and only when this element appeared to stimulate his imagination was he greatly interested. Howells is, therefore, perfectly justified, when he says: "He was never a man who cared anything about money except as a dream, and he wanted more and more of it to fill out the spaces of this dream." And this is what I mean when I say that Mark Twain sometimes appears as Colonel Sellers. In *Roughing It,* he tells of the pipe dreams that came to him when, in his mining days, he once thought that he and Calvin Higbie had struck it rich, and though there is probably some exaggeration here for literary purposes, Higbie's own version of the story gives us quite as much corroboration as we need: "He was determined . . . to have a marble mansion several stories high with ample grounds, fine horses and carriages, and a pack of hounds. He was very emphatic about the hounds, and a steam yacht he could steer himself. We talked all night long in this strain."

Mr. Paine himself points out the Sellers element in Mark Twain's attitude toward the Paige typesetting machine: "He immediately began to calculate the number of millions he would be worth presently when the machine was completed and announced to the waiting world. He covered pages with figures that never ran short of millions, and frequently approached the billion mark. Colonel Sellers in his happiest moments never dreamed more lavishly. He obtained a list of all the newspapers in the United States and in Europe, and he counted up the machines that would be required by each." The same Sellers-like quality entered into his book schemes, especially the bad ones. Once, with Howells, he projected a fearful thing to be known as "Memorable Murders," and, writes his partner in crime, "by the time we reached Boston we were rolling in wealth so deep that we could hardly walk home." And once he got the idea that there would be millions in a play to be written about Kathi Schratt, mistress of the Emperor. He would write it with a collaborator, and it would be translated into all the languages of Europe.

But the Sellers quality comes out best of all in his interest in the carpet-pattern machine of the young Austrian inventor, Sczezepanik. Here, if anywhere, he proves himself utterly incorrigible, for the burned child dreads the fire, and he had just recovered from the Paige disasters. Yet he is off again, asking an option on world rights and covering pages with figures summing up the enormous profits that are to accrue. Fortunately, H. H. Rogers came around to prick the balloon of his enthusiasm, or he might have gone through the Paige fiasco all over again.

It can hardly be necessary to point out that at no time did the visionary part in Mark Twain's schemes interfere with a most scrupulous honesty. He was "businesslike" in this particular at any rate, and what he had promised he performed to the letter —or is "businesslike," perhaps, not quite the word to use? The story of his heroic conduct in bankruptcy is familiar enough, yet it can never be told too often, for it was an illustrious and a salutary example of the kind of thing that holds society to- gether, of the honesty, the character, and the courage for lack of which our economic system today is crumbling before our very eyes. His punctiliousness appears in lesser matters also. When Frank Harris praised Bret Harte, Mark denounced him and told a story about how he had cheated his publishers. "I told the publishers," he said, "that they ought to have put him in prison. A man should be honest, above everything." Harris complained about writers being underpaid, but Mark Twain was unmoved. They did not need to write unless they cared to, he insisted; "they could make shoes or do manual labor of some kind." But the best story in this connection relates to the occasion when a New York paper offered to pay $100 to any charity he might name in return for a fifteen-minute interview on a subject he did not wish to discuss. "The refusal worried him during the rest of the afternoon," says S. J. Woolf, who was in his house at the time, "and before I left he gave me a note to mail to a certain hospital, enclosing a check as con- tribution to its 'conscience fund.'"

CHAPTER V

Literature and Love

"It takes a character of vast proportions to be equal to a wife and
literature both."

PETRARCH.

UNTIL 1920, Olivia Langdon Clemens was an idyl, a
benediction in the record of her husband's life, heroine
of one of the loveliest true romances in American literature, a deservedly conspicuous example of the *Ewig-Weibliche*
that leads us upward for our good. But in that year Mr. Van
Wyck Brooks published a disturbing book, already several
times referred to in these pages, *The Ordeal of Mark Twain,* in
which he presented "that simple Delilah," as he called her, in
an astonishingly new rôle, ranging her along with the wicked
forces of Puritanism and capitalism that enslaved the soul of
Mark Twain, broke his courage, plunged him at last into utter
pessimism and despair, and robbed American literature of its
rightful king-figure.

One may agree with Mr. Brooks or one may disagree with
him. One may even disagree with him acrimoniously. The only
thing that one cannot do with Mr. Brooks is to ignore him. Nobody can write about Mrs. Clemens in 1935 as he might have
written in 1919. She is no longer an idyl; she is a problem.

I

SAMUEL L. CLEMENS was one of those favored men who taste
all the sweets of love with none of its bitter cruelties. There was
in his life no Dark Flower, as Galsworthy calls it, no night-
blooming cereus, permeating his experience with a strange, exotic odor, inflaming the imagination, maddening the senses, so
that at last a man cannot tell which predominates—the pleasure

or the pain. "Would I had never seen her!" cries Antony. And
the wise Enobarbus replies, "O, sir, you had then left unseen a
wonderful piece of work; which not to have been blest withal
would have discredited your travel." That cry finds no echo in
the life of Mark Twain, nor did he ever have cause to share the
grief of the Wife of Bath, as expressed in the words which, as
Professor Lowes has remarked recently, sum up "half the passion and pain of the world":

> Allas! allas! that evere love was synne!

It never was for him. He grew a White Rose in his own garden,
and his feet were never tempted beyond the happy pale.

Some of his biographers, to be sure, have taken pains to ex-
aggerate his indifference to feminine allurements. Sam had the
usual assortment of child sweethearts, one of whom, Laura
Hawkins, afterward Mrs. Frazer, gained considerable notoriety
in later years as the original of Becky Thatcher. In 1859 he
writes from St. Louis: "All the family are well except myself—
I am in a bad way again—disease, *Love,* in its most malignant
form." The next year, when his mother visited him on the river,
he writes that she "was delighted with her trip, but she was disgusted with the girls for allowing me to embrace and kiss them
—and she was horrified at the Schottische as performed by Miss
Castle and myself." In Virginia City, he was fascinated, briefly,
by the actress Adah Isaacs Menken. He admired beauty, in
women as in all lovely things, and he admired it in age as he
had admired it in youth. But there was nothing sensual about
this admiration. Howells is right when he tells us that Mark
Twain "loved the minds of women, their wit, their agile clever-
ness, their sensitive perception, their humorous appreciation, the
saucy things they would say, and their pretty temerarious de-
fiances." How charming, in this connection, is the letter he
wrote his fiancée in the early days of their engagement: "Livy,
you are as kind and good and sweet and unselfish and just, and
truthful, and sensible and intellectual as the homeliest woman
I ever saw (for you know that these qualities belong peculiarly

to homely women). I have so longed for these qualities in my
wife, and have so grieved because she would have to be necessarily a marvel of ugliness—I who do so worship beauty. But
with a good fortune which is a very miracle, I have secured all
these things in my little wife to be—and beauty—beauty beyond
any beauty that I ever saw in a face before."

II

THE story is well known of how he fell in love with her, fell in
love with her before ever he saw her, when her brother, Charles
Langdon, a fellow Innocent, showed him her picture in the Bay
of Smyrna. Many young men have fallen in love with a picture;
fewer have found the original so alluring as they had hoped;
fewest of all have been able to write late in life, as he wrote with
entire truthfulness: "It is forty years ago. From that day to this
she has never been out of my mind."

He was full of tenderness and reverence for her, those first
precious days of their engagement. "These several times today
this face has amazed me with its sweetness and I have felt so
thankful that God has given into my charge the dear office of
chasing the shadows away and coaxing the sunshine to play
about it always." She seems altogether too good for him, too
pure, indeed, for this world that they inhabit. "Oh, Livy darling, I could just worship that picture, it is so beautiful. . . .
But its beauty startles me—it somehow makes me afraid. It
makes me feel a sort of awe—and affects me like a superstition.
For it is more than human, Livy—it is an angel-beauty—something not of earth—something above the earth and its gross-
ness."

This was, you say, a sentimental engagement mood. But the
interesting thing about Mark Twain is that he never felt differently to the end of his life. He had found the pearl of great
price, and all the honors and triumphs that life was to bring
him were dust in comparison. The beautiful letter he wrote his
wife on her thirtieth birthday, the article he sent to the *Chris-*

tian Union without permitting her to see it, "to save it from getting edited into the stove," his public tribute to her in the sixty-seventh birthday speech—they all speak with the same voice. He had loved quickly, eagerly, at first sight, but it was no mere "love of the eyes" that had satisfied him. "Love," he wrote in one of his notebooks, "seems the swiftest but is the slowest of all growth. No man and woman really know what perfect love is until they have been married a quarter of a century." And the Yankee's love for Sandy is clearly a piece of autobiography: "People talk about beautiful friendships between two persons of the same sex. What is the best of that sort, as compared with the friendship of man and wife, where the best impulses and highest ideals of both are the same? There is no place for comparison between the two friendships; the one is earthly, the other divine."

She brought him great happiness, and, in the end, she brought him great pain, for, as we all know, the only way to avoid pain is never to care for anyone. "Last night at 9.20 I entered Mrs. Clemens's room to say the usual goodnight—and she was dead—tho' no one knew it. . . . I bent over and looked in her face, and I think I spoke—I was surprised and troubled that she did not notice me. Then we understood, and our hearts broke. How poor we are to-day!" So, with quiet dignity, he announces her death to Howells. And he adds simply, "I am tired and old; I wish I were with Livy."

He never recovered. When he went to Washington with Mr. Paine to speak in behalf of the copyright bill, "He was light-spirited and gay; but recalling Mrs. Clemens saddened him, perhaps, for he was silent as we drove to the hotel, and after he was in bed he said, with a weary despair which even the words do not convey: 'If I had been there a minute earlier, it is possible—it is possible that she might have died in my arms. Sometimes I think that perhaps there was an instant—a single instant—when she realized that she was dying and that I was not there.'" And sadder still is the letter he wrote, two years before his death, to a friend about to be married:

"DEAR FATHER FITZ-SIMON,—Marriage—yes, it *is* the supreme felicity of life, I concede it. And it is also the supreme tragedy of
life. The deeper the love the surer the tragedy. And the more
disconsolating when it comes.

"And so I congratulate you. Not perfunctorily, not luke-
warmly, but with a fervency and fire that no word in the dic-
tionary is strong enough to convey. And in the same breath and
with the same depth and sincerity, I grieve for you. Not for
both of you and not for the one that shall go first, but for the
one that is fated to be left behind. For that one there is no recompense—For that one no recompense is possible.

"There are times—thousands of times—when I can expose
the half of my mind, and conceal the other half, but in the matter of the tragedy of marriage I feel too deeply for that, and I
have to bleed it all out or shut it all in. And so you must consider
what I have been through, and am passing through and be
charitable with me.

"Make the most of the sunshine! and I hope it will last long
—ever so long.

"I do not really want to be present; yet for friendship's sake
and because I honor you so, I would be there if I could.

"Most sincerely your friend,

"S. L. CLEMENS."

III

SUCH, then, was their marriage, from his point of view. What,
now, of her opinion? She was not a professional writer, and
only a few of her letters have been printed; her testimony is,
therefore, not abundant. But, fortunately, what there is is unmistakably clear. Unlike her husband, she was demonstrative in
her love, poured out kisses, caresses, and endearments with a
prodigality which at first astonished and bewildered him.
When J. R. Clemens announced his engagement, she wrote to
him: "I feel entirely with Browning when he says 'Love is

best.' Surely it is far and away the best, there is nothing that in the very least approaches it."¹ One day, Clara asked her whether if father died, she would die too. "Unfortunately, no" was her reply. But I don't know that anything here is more impressive than the remark Grace King reports her as having made, one day, when Mark Twain confessed that though intellectually he did not believe in hell, emotionally he was still often afraid that he was going there. "Why, Youth," she exclaimed, "who, then, can be saved?"

The judgments of third parties are never worth very much where marriage is concerned, but there can be no harm in glancing toward them in passing. Her husband was of the opinion that Mrs. Clemens possessed the most perfect character he had ever come in contact with, and there are others who practically reaffirm this judgment. "She was in a way," wrote Howells, "the loveliest person I have ever seen, the gentlest, the kindest, without a touch of weakness; she united wonderful tact with wonderful truth. . . ." After her death, when Mark wrote him how she had kept his letter about Susy in her New Testament, he replied: "You know how it must humiliate a man in his unworthiness to have anything of his so consecrated. She hallowed what she touched, far beyond priests." J. B. Pond came to know her when he accompanied the Clemenses, on the world lecture tour, as far as Victoria, B.C. "The more I see of this lady," he declares, "the greater and more wonderful she appears to be. There are few women who could manage and absolutely rule such a nature as 'Mark's.' She knows the gentle and smooth way over every obstruction he meets, and makes everything lovely."

It is clear that Mrs. Clemens' goodness was not motivated by weakness; she was never one of those distressing persons who are perfectly good because they haven't sufficient spunk to be anything else. Her daughter tells us that she "could blaze out at times if occasion warranted," though she immediately adds that "such instances" were rare, and Mark Twain himself once refers to her as "that turbulent spirit." Absurdly overconscientious, he accused himself, especially in his later years, of having been a bad husband, and in the last talk he had with her, he begged her to forgive him for all the tears he had brought into her life. Every man needs to beg forgiveness of the woman who is generous enough to live with him and put up with him, but Mark Twain was one of the best of husbands. Yet for all his kindliness, he must have been, in many ways, a difficult man to get on with, as, in his own very different way, was Lincoln. "Being very shy and noncommunicative myself as a child," writes Madame Gabrilowitsch, "I used to marvel at my father's ability to sit at the table and pour out uninterruptedly a flow of words expressing his feelings on matters intimately connected with himself, in the presence often of comparative strangers, who were wide-eyed with interest and surprise. Yet this was but one side of the medal, for he could be forbiddingly reserved and locked away from the most vivacious attempts of visitors to enter his personality ever so tiny a distance. He was a constant surprise in his various moods, which dropped unheralded upon him, creating day or night for those about him by his twinkling eyes or his clouded brows. How he would be affected by this or that no one could ever foresee." His absent-mindedness and his capacity for self-absorption sometimes created difficulties. He always held himself responsible for the death of his son Langdon, having exposed the child during a sleigh ride on a cold winter day. "I was not qualified for any such responsibility as that. Some one should have gone who had at least the rudiments of a mind." And once when Clara was a baby, he took her out for a ride in her carriage, and then, forgetting his responsibility, he released the handle suddenly, and the carriage started off downhill, spilling the child by the roadside. These are not helpful things for a husband and father to do, nor can Mrs. Clemens have particularly enjoyed the Sunday morning when, annoyed at finding a button missing from his shirt, he threw shirts, collars, and ties out the bathroom window, decorating the shrubbery with them for the benefit of persons passing on their way to church. Fortunately she had a sense of humor, and on this occasion she made no protest whatever, save that, lying quietly and peacefully in her bed, she repeated all his swear words, in order as he had uttered them. "Livy," he said, "it would pain me to think that when I swear it sounds like that. You got the words right, Livy, but you don't know the tune." What can you do with a man like that except to forgive him?

That he was ever consciously inconsiderate of her, I do not believe. Unconsciously, he probably was, in many ways, for, as Katy Leary observes, that is "the way with men—even the best of them." In later years, when he was beginning to luxuriate in the pessimism that did not take full possession of him until after she had died, he would distress her sometimes by holding forth at length on the subject of the dismal failure that is life, for he loved the sound of his voice always, and he had a burning interest in developing his ideas. Mrs. Clemens seems to have stood it very well, though there is a good deal to be read between the lines of her quiet remark upon taking to her sickbed on one occasion, that at least she would not now have to hear quite so much about "the damned human race." It is not often that a member of a great man's family can be trusted to speak the final word on so delicate a matter as this, but Madame Gabrilowitsch is exceptional, both in her honesty and her penetration. "It was remarkable," she writes, "that two people like my father and mother, possessing highly sensitive and emotional natures, managed so to live that in my memory *few discords stand out* and those of but a superficial nature." And again she says of her father, "He *almost never* permitted his wrath to rise toward my mother."[2]

IV

It is time now to turn directly to the crucial question of Mrs. Clemens' editorship of her husband's work. Of the fact there can be no question. She is "a hard critic to content," and his stuff "generally gets considerable damning with faint praise out of her." It was his habit to read aloud to her each evening whatever he had written during the day, or to leave his manuscripts beside her bed for her approval, and she often called for a good deal in the way of expurgation and revision. When she is ill and unable to read manuscripts herself, she suggests that he send them to Stedman or to Howells. Once Clara serves as her deputy. Occasionally she extends her supervision over letters, illustrations, and interviews. When the Mississippi book is going through the press, she insists on suppressing a cut showing her husband in hell fire, even though part of the edition has already been printed.[3] Hamlin Garland gets an interview, but he must promise not to print it without Mrs. Clemens' approval, and Mrs. Clemens' approval is permanently withheld. Perhaps Mark Twain's dependence on her appears most clearly in his hesitancy over a proposal to write an article concerning Queen Victoria's Jubilee because she was not there to look over it. "Ever since we have been married," he told F. M. White, "I have been dependent on my wife to go over and revise my manuscript. I have written scarcely anything in twenty-five years that she hasn't edited. Not but that I can do the spelling and grammar alone—if I have a spelling-book and a grammar with me —but I don't always know just where to draw the line in matters of taste. Mrs. Clemens has kept a lot of things from getting into print that might have given me a reputation I wouldn't care to have, that I wouldn't have known any better than to have published."

Mrs. Clemens' influence being indisputable, how, then, did she use it? Obviously, against burlesque, against extravagance, against blasphemy and irreverence of all kinds, whether it shocked her personally or whether she merely thought it might prove shocking to others. In the first place, it should be clearly understood that she believed in her husband's work. It was, in her eyes, no mere method of making a livelihood, nor was it a pretty toy with which he amused himself when he had nothing better to do. She believed in him, she believed he had great gifts, but she believed also that he was definitely in need of guidance to bring out the best that was in him. "You see, the thing that gravels her is that I am so persistently glorified as a mere buffoon, as if that entirely covered my case—which she denies with venom." When he was on tour with Pond, she suggested that too many humorous selections in his programs tired an audience with laughter. Accordingly, he worked in a few serious pieces, and Pond thought the result distinctly an improvement. When he wrote a wild piece of burlesque like "The Undertaker's Love Story," and came down happily to read it to the family, under the delusion that it was good, it was she who saved him from printing it.

But it was not always on the score of ineptitude that she made her rejections. His paper on the idea of God, which seems sensible and reverent enough today, she would not permit him to print under any circumstances, and she could not even hear his "Gospel," now known as *What Is Man?* mentioned without a shudder. Often, however, she was preoccupied with mere questions of lady-like detail. Mr. Paine's biography gives a list of some of her comments on the manuscript of *Following the Equator,* together with Mark Twain's annotations on them:

"Page 597. I hate to say it, but it seems to me that you go too minutely into particulars in describing the feats of the aboriginals. I felt it in the boomerang-throwing."

"Boomerang has been furnished with a special train—that is, I've turned it into 'Appendix.' Will that answer?"

"Page 1002. I don't like the 'shady-principled cat that has a family in every port.' "

"Then I'll modify him just a little."

"Page 1020. 9th line from the top. I think some other word would be better than 'stench.' You have used that pretty often."

"But can't I get it in anywhere? You've knocked it out every time. Out it goes again. And yet 'stench' is a noble, good word."

"Page 1038. I hate to have your father pictured as lashing a slave boy."

"It's out, and my father is whitewashed."

"Page 1050. 2d line from the bottom. Change breech-clout. It's a word that you love and I abominate. I would take that and 'offal' out of the language."

"You are steadily weakening the English tongue, Livy."

"Page 1095. Perhaps you don't care, but whoever told you that the Prince's green stones were rubies told an untruth. They were superb emeralds. Those strings of pearls and emeralds were famous all over Bombay."

"All right, I'll make them emeralds, but it loses force. Green rubies is a fresh thing. And besides it was one of the Prince's own staff liars that told me."

V

BUT it was not only Mark Twain that Livy edited; she edited Samuel L. Clemens also. Here she possessed a distinct advantage, for if she would assume supremacy in the professional phase of his life, where she was certainly no expert, how much more completely would she be bound to dominate him in his social relations, a field where she was so much better versed than he. At home, partly as a result of her invalidism, she had been treated like a princess. Her lover, coming out of a more austere environment, seems to have wondered at it, much as he loved her and considered her to deserve such homage. "Her father and mother and brother embrace and pet her constantly, precisely as if she were a sweetheart, instead of a blood relation." Once they were married,[4] she assumed full control of their domestic establishment, and so long as her always delicate health permitted her to be up and about, she managed things completely to her own satisfaction, and without any suggestions or criticisms from her husband. Let us run briefly down the record of the years:

1875: "I mean to try to go down the Mississippi river in May or June. . . . But there's nothing certain about it—except that at the last moment Livy will put her foot on it."[5]

1882: "I cannot come, because I am not Boss here, and nothing but dynamite can move Mrs. Clemens away from home in the winter season."

1891: "I'm going to do whatever the others desire, with leave to change their mind without prejudice, whenever they want to."

1895: "According to Mrs. Clemens's present plans—subject to modification, of course—we sail in May."

1901: "If Livy will let me I will have my say."

1903: "Livy is coming along . . . and, in the matter of superintending everything and everybody has resumed business at the old stand."[6]

It never occurred to him that he could have any life apart from her. "This is a secret," he writes Howells, "to be known to nobody but you." And he immediately adds: "(of course I comprehend that Mrs. Howells is part of you)."

He tells us, both generally and in detail, just how she handled her problems. "I was always heedless. I was born heedless, and therefore I was constantly, and quite unconsciously, committing breaches of the minor proprieties, which brought upon me humiliations which ought to have humiliated me, but didn't, because I didn't know anything had happened. But Livy knew; and so the humiliations fell to her share, poor child, who had not earned them and did not deserve them. She always said I was the most difficult child she had. She was very sensitive about me. It distressed her to see me do heedless things which could bring me under criticism, and so she was always watchful and alert to protect me from the kind of transgressions which I have been speaking of." They visit the Howellses, and when they get home again, she enumerates for him carefully all the errors he has made. "I 'caught it' for letting Mrs. Howells bother and bother about her coffee when it was 'a good deal better than we get at home.' I 'caught it' for interrupting Mrs. C. at the last moment and losing her the opportunity to urge you not to forget to send her that MS when the printers are done with it. I 'caught it' once more for personating that drunken Col. James. I 'caught it' for mentioning that Mr. Long-fellow's picture was slightly damaged; and when . . . I con-fessed, shame-facedly, that I had privately suggested to you that we hadn't any *frames,* and that if you wouldn't mind hinting to Mr. Houghton, &c., &c., &c., the Madam was simply speech-less. . . ."

When he is in New York without her, she writes from Paris, urging him not to go out too much and not to be rude to Mr. Rogers. "You must not think I am ever rude with Mr. Rogers," he writes back without a trace of resentment, "I am not. He is not common clay, but fine—fine and delicate—and that sort do not call out the coarsenesses that are in my sort." As soon as they were old enough, the children seem to have assisted Mrs. Clemens. Susy once told Henry Fisher that "Pa . . . was an awful man before Mamma took him in hand and married him." They had a name for the address she would give him after a dinner party—"dusting off papa," they called it—and they helped her with a series of signals devised at Mark Twain's own suggestion, so that they might advise him in a moment what particular crime he happened just then to be committing.

She did not always approve his reading. Says Mr. Paine: "That he should be fond of history and the sciences was natural enough, but when the *Life of P. T. Barnum, Written by Him-self,* appeared, and he sat up nights to absorb it, and woke early and lighted the lamp to follow the career of the great showman, she was at a loss to comprehend this particular lit-erary passion, and indeed was rather jealous of it."

VI

WHAT, now, was the influence of all this upon Mark Twain, as a man and as a writer. The answer is by no means simple. At the outset we must keep in mind that we are dealing with a humorist. Such statements as the foregoing, for example, un-equivocal though they seem, must surely be subject to discount; the problem is to decide just what percentage to take. It is al-ways extremely difficult to tell when Mark Twain is reporting and when he is elaborating, when he is actually conveying information to his auditor, and when he is "stringing him along." Nothing made him more happy, when he was with those he felt sure would understand his fooling, than to represent the gentle, ladylike Mrs. Clemens as a fearsome Amazonian virago. "George was the first person she stumbled on in the hall, so she took it out of George. I was glad of that, because it saved the babies." And again: "My wife was afraid to write you—so I said with simplicity, 'I will give you the language—and ideas.' Through the infinite grace of God there has not been such another insurrection in the family before as followed this."

Again, it must be remembered that Mrs. Clemens was a very skilful manager. She understood her husband; she had the great gift of making him feel that all the suggestions she made were altogether for his good. Nothing could be further from the truth than to imagine that she made Mark Twain live in an atmosphere of nagging; on the contrary, she was always poised, always self-controlled, and consequently when she did have occasion to offer a criticism, she made every word count. She was one of those persons who never need to be rebuked themselves because they are never off guard. This does not mean that she was calculating. It means simply that she lived in perfect self-possession. Her love was the thing that had blessed her husband's life above everything else that had been given to him; her displeasure was, therefore, the thing he wished primarily to avoid. "In her mouth," he writes, "that word 'disapprove' was as blighting and withering and devastating as another person's damn." She gives him a letter to mail to Mrs. Howells. She ought to have known better, for of course he mislays it. But he remembers the contents, so he writes to Mrs. Howells himself. She must not tell Livy what happened, but "just answer her the same as if you had got it." Yet she seems always to have known just how far she could go, always to have realized, for example, that he could not be happy unless she left him free to *express* his ideas, regardless of whether or not she agreed with him. "He'd say hard, severe things about religion," says Katy Leary, "and Mrs. Clemens, although she hated to have him talk that way, said she'd made up her mind when they first married, that her husband was going to be *free* to *say* anything and everything that he wanted to—no matter what it was; that he wasn't ever going to dread her criticizing him—there was never going to be any 'curtain lectures' or nothing like that; that his home was going to be a place where he could say and do what he wanted. It struck me as kind of wonderful for her to think all that out when she was just a young wife. It showed how much she loved him and what a lot of common sense she had and how she never believed in interfering with other people's rights —even if they was her husband's."

Again, if Mrs. Clemens played the censor to her husband, it is impossible to avoid feeling that in many instances it must have been inevitable. We have already seen how weak his capacity for intelligent self-criticism is, how utterly lacking his sense of social graces. From this point of view, Susy is perfectly correct: he was "an awful man" when Mrs. Clemens married him, and this was true not merely from the limited, upper bourgeois standpoint of Elmira, New York, but from the point of view of any cultivated group anywhere in the Western world. Often when Mrs. Clemens seems to dominate, she is simply doing what needs to be done, what, to be sure, the husband, not the wife, ought to do—only Mark Twain would never have done it. He speaks of "her plans" in a letter to Mrs. Howells, "hers, mind you, for I never have anything quite so definite as a plan." It was true: there are a thousand passages in his life to prove that it was true. Juliet proposed marriage to Romeo, not because Shakespeare wished to convey the idea that she was a bold young hussy, but because she knows that, wrapped up as he is in the mystery and beauty of the night, her lover is quite incapable of taking charge of the situation: unless she does it for him, he will wander off into the darkness again with nothing arranged, and all their love for each other will be in vain. I attempt no denial that Mrs. Clemens sometimes overestimated the importance of the conventionalities. But no blame attaches to her for seeking to discipline and to regularize Mark Twain. If such regulation is subversive of some genius and destroys it, then that particular kind of genius ought to live unwed.

Occasionally one catches a suggestion of annoyance or evasion on his part. "I never knew a woman," he writes Howells, not too seriously, "so hard to please about things she doesn't know anything about." Once he developed a wild fantasy of which she did not approve. Himself he thought it entirely too good to lose; so he laboriously translated it into German, with the idea of printing it without her knowledge, but his conscience got the better of him, and the work did not appear. On one occasion at least, he exercised a quite uncommon tact of his own: "When I started to write this note my wife came up and stood looking over my shoulder. Women always want to know what is going on. Said she: 'Should not that read in the third person?' I conceded that it should, put aside what I was writing, and commenced over again. That seemed to satisfy her, and so she sat down and let me proceed. I then—finished my first note—and so sent what I intended." I doubt that he did such things very often, though he must have written a good deal, first and last, that he knew she would not approve. Once, at the home of Mr. and Mrs. James T. Fields, he spoke of the autobiography he intended to write. "His wife," writes Mrs. Fields, "laughingly said she should look it over and leave out objectionable passages. 'No,' he said, very earnestly, almost sternly, '*you* are not to edit it—it is to appear as it is written, with the whole tale told as truly as I can tell it.'" And as for *What Is Man?* her influence kept him from printing it, but the force of her disapproval did not modify his opinion of it, and he seems to have talked it freely.

Generally, however, he encouraged her. "Do you know, Sue," he once remarked to her sister, "whenever I have failed to follow the advice of Livy to change this or that sentence or eliminate a page, I have always come to regret it, because in the end my better taste in thoughts and their expression rises up and

says: 'You should have done as she said; she was right.' " Was
it really his "better taste," I wonder, or was it that "trained
Presbyterian conscience" of his, that terribly uxorious fear of
displeasing his wife? Even in matters of style, he considered her
nearly infallible. "I am notorious," he writes her, "but you are
great—that is the difference between us. . . . You had a sentence in your letter that all the culture and all the genius and
all the practice in the world could not improve. It was admirable." He was in no sense ashamed of her careful surveil-
lance of him: he flaunts it, he boasts about it, he describes it in
detail even to persons who, in the normal course of events need
never have heard of it. On his own account, he seems to have
been anxious that she should not overlook anything. When he
read *Huckleberry Finn* to her, she passed over a bit of profanity, where Huck is made to say, "they comb me all to hell."
It worried him, and we find him, a little later, writing Howells
to ask what he thinks of the propriety of it.

At Quarry Farm, Mrs. Clemens would sit on the porch, pencil in hand, reading aloud from her husband's manuscripts, and
whenever she came to "a particularly satisfactory passage," she
would strike it out. Mark Twain's humor—which spared nothing and nobody else—could not quite consent to spare his editor either. Aided and abetted by the children, he often "inter-
larded remarks of a studied and felicitously atrocious character
purposely to . . . see the pencil do its fatal work. I often joined
my supplications to the children's for mercy, and strung the
argument out and pretended to be in earnest. They were deceived, and so was their mother. It was three against one, and
most unfair. But it was very delightful, and I could not resist
the temptation. Now and then we gained the victory and there
was much rejoicing. Then I privately struck the passage out
myself." If Mark Twain was a suppressed genius, he died without ever finding it out.

This special tractableness on the part of Mark Twain was
partly the result of his modesty; it was also partly due to the
fact that he was so constituted that he simply must rely on

somebody. When Mrs. Clemens could not serve him, he turned to others. On the *Innocents* excursion, before ever he saw Livy, he relied on Mrs. Fairbanks. "I am glad, & grateful, to be placed upon your list of friends," he wrote her afterwards, "for I honor & esteem you more than I can tell. I am *bound* to wander out of the straight path & do outrageous things occasionally, & believe I have a genuinely bad heart anyhow—but in the course of time I will get some of the badness out of it or break it."[7] And he was afraid *Roughing It* was an utter failure until Joe Goodman had assured him of the contrary.

Even when we come to the more disputed questions, it is not impossible to defend Mrs. Clemens. She sensed the merit of *The Mysterious Stranger,* but she feared its effect. "It is perfectly horrible—" she said, "and perfectly beautiful!" Concerning *What Is Man?* there can be no question at all. She was abundantly justified in the effect the thing had upon Mark Twain himself, as described in his own words: "Since I wrote my Bible (last year)—which Mrs. Clemens loathes, and shudders over, and will not listen to the last half nor allow me to print any part of it, Man is not to me the respect-worthy person he was before; and so I have lost my pride in him, and can't write gaily nor praisefully about him any more." It is mere cant to pretend that Mrs. Clemens' primary business in life was to foster the development of American literature. It was her business to look after her husband, and she was sufficiently familiar with his temperament to realize that the effort of formulating any such philosophy of life as he set forth in *What Is Man?* was not going to contribute notably to his well-being.

VII

SUCH is the case for Mrs. Clemens, and I regard it as rather a strong one. This is not the whole story, however, nor can our inquiry end just here. Mark Twain's special need of guidance, as a writer and as a man, manifests his weakness, not his strength, and a slave may grow so accustomed to his fetters that he never feels their weight, would indeed be very uncomfortable if they were to be lifted from him. In matters of detail, Mrs. Clemens' taste was probably good; as Mr. DeVoto observes, the publishers must have deleted many of the passages to which she objected if she had not saved them the trouble. I confess I should not in the least have minded, had Huck been permitted to say "they comb me all to hell," instead of "to thunder," as it now stands in the text,[8] but such things are of quite too insignificant import to disturb me very much one way or the other, and a genius which could be suppressed, destroyed, deflected out of its natural channel by any such criticism of details must surely be a genius of very tender growth.

But, granting all this, there is still one thing that must be said against Mrs. Clemens as an editor of her husband's work. She did not understand his art. She liked good literature, but she liked literature of a much prettier, much more conventional order than that which the gods had designed her husband to write. She had her doubts about *Tom Sawyer,* and she utterly failed to recognize the power of *Huckleberry Finn.* She liked such things as *Joan of Arc* and *The Prince and the Pauper.* *Huck* and *The Prince* were in the making together: she was enthusiastic about the one and almost completely indifferent to the other. "I have two stories," Mark Twain wrote his mother, "and by the verbal agreement they are both going into the same book; but Livy says they're not, and by George I. she ought to know. She says they're going into separate books, and that one of them is going to be elegantly gotten up, even if the elegance of it eats up the publisher's profits and mine too."[9]

This means no special discredit to Mrs. Clemens: indeed, it was almost inevitable in a woman of her class, her period, and her bent of mind. But it leaves us no alternative save to say, as I have said already, that she did not understand the full significance of her husband's work, or, in other words, that her influence was negative rather than positive. Of course, very few of the great writers of the world have had wives who perfectly understood their art or completely sympathized with it, but then very few great artists have submitted what they wrote to their wives for approval. Mark Twain did. I am not inclined to feel that, so far as his actual choice of themes was concerned, or the general bent and balance of his work, her influence was really determinative. After all, he did attack the missionaries, he did write *Huckleberry Finn,* he did formulate his philosophy of determinism. There was too much virility in him for him to permit himself to be pushed very far from his native bent; his qualities and his limitations were alike such that he could never have been the conventional man of letters under any circumstances. What he would have been like had he married another woman, we shall never know. But it would have been very unreasonable to expect any woman—at least any eastern American woman—of his time to do more for him than Olivia Langdon did. Very few could have done so much.

III

THE SAGE OF REDDING

CHAPTER I

Charts of Salvation

I

IN his later years, Mark Twain loved to think of himself as a
philosopher; there was nothing he enjoyed more than to ex-
pound what he thought of as the original and highly ingenious world-view that he had worked out for himself. A very different world-view had been presented to him, however, in his
early days, and this was the view of the Christian religion, as
interpreted in the form of the popular mid-western Calvinism
of the early nineteenth century. To be sure, the Calvinism of
Hannibal, Missouri, has often been grossly exaggerated by
writers who understand neither Hannibal nor Calvinism very
well. As we have observed already, eighteenth-century rational-
ism was by no means wholly without influence in the community, Mark Twain's mother was not intolerably narrow in her
convictions on these matters, his uncle, John Quarles, was far
from being a Calvinist,[1] and his father stood outside organized
religion altogether. But we must not allow these newly and
justly emphasized facts to destroy our balance. After all is said
and done, Mark Twain *was* brought up on the old theology.

Late in life, Mark Twain once said that we have no morality
except artificial morality. Mr. Brooks has justly remarked that
this statement is not in any sense true of the civilized man who
is morally and spiritually mature, but his conclusion does not
necessarily follow: that the situation appeared as it did to Mark
Twain because he had stultified himself, refusing to develop in
his own orbit, accepting instead the unjust and indecent code
of the world about him. A boy who had been reared a Calvinist could hardly have thought of morality except as Mark
Twain did. All his youth he must have been trained to suppress
his natural instincts, to fight them down, to regard them as so

many snares of Satan. Those are moving passages in the *Auto-biography* and in *Life on the Mississippi* where Mark Twain tells how, after some innocent peccadillo, some boyish prank, he would hear the voice of the thunderstorm as the messenger of God's wrath against him, fully convinced that one small boy had been singled out in heaven as the special object of divine vengeance, and how, under the spell of terror, he would reck-lessly promise to do all the things a perfectly arbitrary deity wanted him to do, even though in his heart he knew that there was very little sense to most of them.

Growing up, he grew away from Calvinism, though he did not at once throw off the yoke. Even in the most critical passages of *The Innocents Abroad,* he writes as a believer, and the letter he wrote his brother's wife after Henry Clemens had been killed in a steamboat accident is saturated with pietism and sentimentalism alike. Yet he could not make a vital connection somehow. He knew there was something he needed beyond material satisfactions to make him happy, but what he knew as religion, and what his neighbors knew, satisfied neither his mind nor his heart, and there was nobody around to tell him that, as yet, he had savored religious belief and religious experi-ence only in one of its harshest and unloveliest forms. At times it seemed as though there was nothing to do save throw it over altogether. "What a man wants with religion in these breadless times," he writes Orion in 1860, "surpasses my comprehension."

Moreover the man was a humorist by profession, a dissenter by the natural bent of his temperament. He cannot accept truth on authority. It is his business to find, if he can, the weak place in the armor, to ridicule, to "show up" whatever is susceptible of such handling. How strong, at this point, is the contrast be-tween him and his great British contemporary, Thomas Hardy. Hardy, too, found it impossible to accept the religious beliefs of his contemporaries. But Hardy has always a fine reverence for belief, whether he can share it or not. His background, his early associations, his training in ecclesiastical architecture—all these things tie him up with the past, give him an understanding of how the Church and the Christian faith have been intimately associated with the highest aspirations of his race. There is nothing of the iconoclast in him.

Mark Twain knows no Church, in the sense in which Hardy knows it—and how can he, coming as he does out of the religious anarchy of his intensely negative Protestant America? All he knows is a succession of clergymen, mostly of the ranting persuasion, not too intelligent most of them, each one contradicting half of what all the others stand for, yet all agreed on one thing—that this world is a vale of tears in which God intends us to be thoroughly miserable, and that He will roast us all in hell if we manage somehow to evade here the miseries which, in His merciful wisdom, He designed for us. Church services, as he knew them—devoid of beauty and feeling, always tended strongly to bore him. He was brought up to hate Catholicism, and when he went to Italy, he was shocked by the spectacle of luxurious churches set down in the midst of reeking slums. But Protestantism was no better, for if the contributors were in general more prosperous than the Catholics, what did that mean save that the church was tied up with big business, and so learning to oppress mankind in new and devious ways? Furthermore, the Church—Catholic and Protestant alike—was lacking altogether in the progressive spirit. Others pioneered in behalf of good causes; then when the fight had been won, she fell in at the end of the procession to claim credit for whatever good had been achieved by the change. "The Church has opposed every innovation and discovery from the day of Galileo down to our own time, when the use of anesthetics in childbirth was regarded as a sin because it avoided the biblical curse pronounced against Eve. And every step in astronomy and geology ever taken has been opposed by bigotry and superstition."

Even aside from all these things, both Van Wyck Brooks and Gamaliel Bradford feel very strongly that Mark Twain was essentially lacking in reverence.

". . . If Mark made the world better," writes Bradford, "he also made it worse; at any rate, many individuals in it. For,

with the wholesale destruction of shams, went, as so often, the destruction of reverence, 'that angel of the world,' as Shake-speare calls it. When Mark had fairly got through with the shams, the trouble was that there was nothing left. . . .

"Mark himself frequently recognizes this charge of being a demolisher of reverence and tries to rebut it. I never assault real reverence, he says. To pretend to revere things because others revere them, or say they do, to cherish established superstitions of art, or of morals, or of religion, is to betray and to deceive and to corrupt. But I never mock those things that I really revere myself. And one is driven to ask, What does he really revere himself? His instinctive reverence for humanity in individual cases is doubtless delicate and exquisite. But in theory he tears the veil from God and man alike."

Mr. Brooks is even more emphatic when he declares that Mark Twain's humor "degrades, 'takes down,' punctures, ridicules as pretentious and absurd everything of a spiritual, aesthetic and intellectual nature the recognition of which, the participation in which, would retard the smooth and simple operation of the business man's mind. Mark Twain, as we shall presently see, enables the business man to laugh at art, at antiquity, at chivalry, at beauty and return to his desk with an infinitely intensified conceit in his own worthiness and well-being. That is one aspect of his humor. In another aspect, he releases, in a hundred murderous fantasies . . . all the spleen which the business life, with its repression of individuality, involves. Finally, in his books about childhood, he enables the reader to become 'a boy again, just for a day,' to escape from the emotional stress of maturity to a simpler and more primitive moral plane."

All readers of Mark Twain will, I believe, recognize the fundamental justice of these judgments, in so far, at least, as they apply to one aspect of his personality and his work.

His attitude toward the Church being what it is, one is a little surprised, on first consideration, by his close association with clergymen. As a small boy he made up his mind that he would be a clergyman himself, for the prudent if unedifying reason that he believed it impossible that a clergyman could be damned. In 1866, he writes: "I am thick as thieves with the Rev. Stebbings, and I am laying for the Rev. Scudder and the Rev. Dr. Stone. I am running on preachers now, altogether. I find them gay. . . . Whenever anybody offers me a letter to a preacher, now I snaffle it on the spot." In Hartford, he was associated with the Monday Evening Club, whose membership was largely clerical. Henry Ward Beecher was kind to him, soon after he came East. Above all, there was the Rev. Joseph H. Twichell, after William Dean Howells probably his closest friend.

He denounced the missionaries in China, of course, but this has nothing to do with the case, for his strictures were not inspired by any dislike of the missionary movement as such. He had whole-heartedly admired the work of the missionaries in the Sandwich Islands, and in the pages of Parkman he had thrilled to the story of Jesuit heroism in North America. As for China, he did express some doubts as to the wisdom of trying to impose an alien world-view upon a country which had an ancient civilization of its own: it seemed a good deal like trying to teach your grandmother to suck eggs. But the real cause for his anger was something very different—the connection between the missionary enterprise and imperialism, and there are few sensible churchmen today who could fail to admit that the protest was salutary as well as justified.

Since Joseph H. Twichell was, however, the clergyman Mark Twain knew best, and the one who might reasonably be supposed to have exercised an influence upon him, Twichell's personality becomes of considerable interest in this connection. For, in his professional capacity, Twichell was, as regards Mark Twain, an utter failure. He did not convince him of the truth of the Christian revelation, nor, after the early years, would Mark any longer attend his church.

We have none of Twichell's sermons, save a few of his remarks at the funeral of Mrs. Clemens, plus whatever we wish to make of Howells' opinion that his discourses were "sane and beautiful." Concerning the theology he preached, no information has been recorded; concerning his personality, much less than we could desire. He was a large, personable man, if his portraits may be trusted, of rather a florid type, and distinctly of the "man's man" variety. He had taken both his liberal arts and his theological training at Yale, where—in his undergraduate days—he was an active athlete, and he went through four years of chaplaincy in the Civil War. The Asylum Hill Congregational Church, of Hartford, where Mark Twain knew him, was the only pulpit he ever held, and it is clear that his congregation exemplified, in an extreme form, the connection between Protestantism and capitalism which has created such embarrassing problems in our own day. "The Church of the Holy Speculators," Mark Twain called it, and declared that wherever Twichell opened a church, the value of the adjoining real estate would promptly go up. Twichell had a big heart and a hunger for life; he was not easily repelled by those whose acquaintance he sought, either personally or professionally. He did not preach a social gospel; his parishioners would not have tolerated any political or economic heresies on his part. Early in his career, he shocked them terribly by bolting the Republican party to vote for Cleveland, and if we may trust Mark's account, his act nearly cost him his church, and he was careful not to make a similar mistake again. There can be no doubt of the sincerity of Twichell's religion as far as it went, but there was nothing of the saint about him, and one is not inclined to credit him with any particular depth. He drank. He smoked. He adored the *Rubáiyát*. He read "1601" with relish. He enjoyed Mark's profanity, and was not incapable of a bit of strong language himself, when he thought it would commend him to the group in which he found himself. Unless Mark belies him in his portrait of him as Harris in *A Tramp Abroad,* he was bigoted in his attitude toward Catholicism. In short, he was the kind of clergyman who tries not to act like a clergyman, with the usual, inevitable, pitiful result of falling between two stools. As a genial companion for Mark Twain, he was, no doubt, ideal; as a spiritual guide he left a good deal to be desired.

Yet it was during his early married life, when he was strongly under the influence of Twichell, that Mark Twain came closer to being an orthodox Christian than was ever the case again. For this, however, probably Mrs. Clemens rather than Twichell was responsible. Falling in love is, after all, a form of religious experience, and so it was with Mark Twain. There are some rather astonishing passages in the letters he wrote to Livy: "But I shall so strive all the days of my life to make you happy, and shall try so hard to walk as you do, in the light and the love of God, that some of the bitterness of your exile shall be spared you." And "Don't be sad, Livy, we'll model our home after the old home, and make the Spirit of Love lord over all the realm. Smile again, Livy, and be of good heart. Turn towards the Cross and be comforted—I turn with you—What would you more? The peace of God shall rest upon us, and all will be well."

He did try to walk as she walked; they read the Bible together, and visitors to the Hartford house were astonished to see him sit down at the head of the table and ask a blessing. But it did not work for long. The time came when he could not do it; he felt that he was living a lie. To Twichell he explained his attitude as they were tramping together in the Black Forest, and the subject did not come up between them again. "Joe," he said, "I'm going to make a confession. I don't believe in your religion at all. I've been living a lie straight along whenever I pretended to. For a moment, sometimes, I have been almost a believer, but it immediately drifts away from me again. I don't believe one word of your Bible was inspired by God any more than any other book. I believe it is entirely the work of man from beginning to end—atonement and all. The problem of life and death and eternity and the true conception of God is a bigger thing than is contained in that book."

Livy understood long before Twichell did, and when Mark decided to give up formal religious exercises, she gave them up

too, telling him that if he must be lost, she wished to be lost
with him. The truth is that she herself was growing less orthodox until once, in a time of bereavement when he said, "Livy,
if it comforts you to lean on the Christian faith do so," she replied, "I can't, Youth. I haven't any." How could he with that
hypersensitive conscience of his, fail to upbraid himself afresh, to
count this as another wrong he had put upon her, another dep-
rivation he had brought her to suffer? It is Howells who gives
us much of our information at this point,[2] yet I think he over-
stresses Mark's apostasy somewhat; the *Letters* and Mr. Paine's
biography, made available since he wrote, show that his friend
was much less settled in his apostasy than Howells believed. But
he might just as well have been, for all the comfort he derived
from religion. His continued gropings, his alternate hope and
despair—these are precious as testifying to the presence in him
of something that could not be satisfied by mere negation, yet
after all religion has little to give to those who must be so uncertain in their attitude toward it as was Mark Twain. "It is
sweet to believe, even in hell."

II

IN spite of his religious skepticism, however, Mark Twain is by
no means free from superstition. The voodoo magic of the negroes hovered about his childhood, and he never altogether
threw off its spell. He was personally acquainted with an old,
bedridden, whiteheaded slave woman who was believed to be
more than a thousand years old. She had come out of Egypt
with Moses, and there was a bald spot on the top of her head
which had been caused by fright at seeing Pharaoh's army
drowned. "Whenever witches were around she tied up the
remnant of her wool in little tufts, with white thread, and this
promptly made the witches impotent." The negroes told marvelous ghost stories, and to hear them told, to thrill to them
afterwards was probably the intensest form of emotional stimu-
lation that young Sam Clemens ever received.

All this was fortunate from the standpoint of the artist he was to be: negro folklore is no small element in the charm of his books. But the man was affected as well as the artist. To get out of bed on the wrong side was a bad omen for the day;[3] he would not speak or write of an improvement in his wife's health without adding "unberufen"; in leaving Quarry Farm at the end of a happy summer, he must leave some article behind him to insure his safe return. Thrice in his life, he saw a lunar rainbow, which he took as a sign of good fortune, and since he had come into the world with Halley's Comet in 1835, he was sure he would go out again upon its reappearance in 1910— which he did. His cousin, J. R. Clemens, tells an interesting story of what happened one night when he went with Mark Twain to see William Gillette in *Secret Service*. When a black cat walked across the stage in the second act, Mark was greatly agitated. "Mark my words, Dr. Jim, poor Gillette is in for some misfortune or other this evening." And, sure enough, when they went back stage to see him afterwards, they found the actor binding up a finger he had cut badly on the telegraph key.[4]

Mark Twain believed profoundly in luck. When the business crash came upon him, it found him bewildered. "There's one thing which makes it difficult for me to soberly realize that my ten year dream is actually dissolved; and that is, that it re- verses my horoscope. This proverb says, 'Born lucky, *always* lucky,' and I am very superstitious. . . . I am so superstitious that I have always been afraid to have business dealings with certain relatives and friends of mine because they were unlucky people. All my life I have stumbled upon lucky chances of large size, and whenever they were wasted it was because of my own stupidity and carelessness. And so I have felt entirely certain that that machine would turn up trumps eventually. It disap- pointed me lots of times, but I couldn't shake off the confidence of a life-time in my luck." It is a suggestive, possibly significant, passage. One wonders whether Mark Twain was, at this time, permanently disillusioned concerning his luck, and whether this circumstance may not have had some influence on the de- velopment of his pessimism.

Just where the line is to be drawn between superstition and sensitiveness to psychic influences is, in the present state of human knowledge, a very difficult thing to determine. But there is no doubt that psychic phenomena always greatly interested Mark Twain.

To begin with, there is his interest in dreams. He was always dreaming; recurrent dreams came to him through the years; unless we are to throw out "My Platonic Sweetheart" altogether, we shall have to believe that he lived an actual dream-life, independent of and quite as interesting as the life that he lived in the body. Categorically he affirms his faith: "In our dreams—I know it!—we do make the journeys we seem to make; we do see the things we seem to see; the people, the horses, the cats, the dogs, the birds, the whales, are real, not chimeras; they are living spirits, not shadows; and they are immortal and indestructible." "My Platonic Sweetheart" is perhaps the most beautiful thing he ever wrote; certainly he never created a lovelier heroine than this girl he met through the years in his dreams and whom he seems so devotedly to have loved. In any event, no believer in the "astral world" could ask him to go further than he goes here.

He had interesting experiences too—though he often ridiculed fortune tellers—with palmistry. Like many of the prominent writers and artists of his time, he consulted Cheiro and talked to him at some length about the possibility of our histories being written in our hands. In 1895, when he was wallowing in bankruptcy, Cheiro told him that in his sixty-eighth year he would become rich. Two years later, the prediction was repeated. On October 22, 1903, when there was but a little time to spare, Mark Twain signed the contract which placed all his books in the hands of Harper and Brothers, guaranteeing him an income of $25,000 a year.

He was much more interested in telepathy, which he regarded as his own discovery, and concerning which he worked out his ideas independently of other investigators. His views are set forth in some detail in the two essays he wrote on the subject, and he speaks of it incidentally elsewhere. Some of his evidence is impressive, but his zeal weakens his argument through overemphasis. Dr. Still in a Kansas village in 1874 began the same series of experiments that Dr. Kellgren had been working on for five years in Germany. "Dr. Still seems to be an honest man; therefore I am persuaded that Kellgren moved him to his experiments by Mental Telegraphy across six hours of longitude, without need of a wire." Credulity could hardly go further. "I imagine we get most of our thoughts out of somebody else's head, by mental telegraphy—and not always out of heads of acquaintances, but, in the majority of cases, out of the heads of strangers; strangers far removed—Chinamen, Hindus, and all manner of remote foreigners whose language we should not be able to understand, but whose thoughts we can read without difficulty." Some day, he was sure, this great power would be brought under control, and we should be able at all times to call up whomever we wanted in any part of the earth and talk with him freely.

Faith healing was another interest. It would have been strange indeed if the Clemens family had not been interested in faith healing, for when Mrs. Clemens, as a girl, was a helpless invalid, it was a faith healer, a Doctor Newton, who restored her, if not to health, to activity. Observing oriental fakirs upon his travels, Mark Twain would sometimes commit himself to the thesis that the power of the mind over the body is absolute. At one time, as has already been pointed out, he tried to apply the faith healing principle to the matter of defective sight. Susy, always strongly attracted by the psychic, found her nearsightedness improving, and Baby Jean, not to be outdone, tried faith healing on the stomach-ache. From this extreme position, they all later fell back, and Mark Twain attempted to formulate his final conclusions: "The mind cannot heal broken bones, and doubtless there are other physical ills which it cannot heal, but it can greatly help to modify the severities of all of them without exception, and there are mental and nervous ailments which it can wholly heal without the help of physician or surgeon."

This will be surprising to some readers in view of Mark Twain's attack on Christian Science, but he never opposed Christian Science as a religion, either because of its stress on mental healing or on account of the element of philosophical idealism involved. He has plenty of philosophical idealism of his own in *The Mysterious Stranger,* though it would be too much to seek to describe it as definitely an article in his own creed. What he objected to in Christian Science was what seemed to him Mrs. Eddy's personal duplicity—an opinion in which recent investigation has certainly tended to sustain him —and the fact that he saw her building up a powerful machine which he naïvely believed would control America by the year 1940. "It was out of powers approaching Mrs. Eddy's—though not equaling them—that the Inquisition and the devastations of the Interdict grew. She will transmit hers. The man born two centuries from now will think he has arrived in hell; and all in good time he will think he knows it."

The book on Christian Science itself recognizes the reality of mental healing. Mrs. Eddy did not invent it or discover it; it has appeared among all peoples and in every period. What, then, is Mrs. Eddy's achievement? Simply that she has organized this force and made it available. In this aspect "she is the benefactor of the age." Suppose she is able to help nobody except fools? "The fools, the idiots, the pudd'nheads" make up the bulk of the race anyway; her title still stands. But her services are not confined to these classes. Four-fifths of the ills from which mankind suffers are kept alive in the imagination; Christian Science can banish that four-fifths. It can destroy all fretting and anxiety, and this is a boon that "outvalues any price that can be put upon it."

Mark Twain, however, goes further than this; indeed I cannot imagine how any Christian Scientist could ask for a higher tribute to his religion than Mark Twain pays it:

"The Christian Scientist believes that the Spirit of God (life and love) pervades the universe like an atmosphere; that whoso will study *Science and Health* can get from it the secret of how to inhale that transforming air; that to breathe it is to be made new; that from the new man all sorrow, all care, all miseries of the mind vanish away, for that only peace, contentment, and measureless joy can live in that divine fluid; that it purifies the body from disease, which is a vicious creation of the gross human mind, and cannot continue to exist in the presence of the Immortal Mind, the renewing Spirit of God.

"The Scientist finds this reasonable, natural, and not harder to believe than that the disease-germ, a creature of darkness, perishes when exposed to the light of the great sun—a new revelation of profane science which no one doubts. He reminds us that the actinic ray, shining upon lupus, cures it—a horrible disease, which was incurable fifteen years ago, and had been incurable ten million years before; that this wonder, unbelievable by the physicians at first, is believed by them now; and so he is tranquilly confident that the time is coming when the world will be educated up to a point where it will comprehend and grant that the light of the Spirit of God, shining unobstructed upon the soul, is an actinic ray which can purge both mind and body from disease and set them free and make them whole."

It would be pretty difficult to show that the writer of these lines did not understand Christian Science. It would be still more difficult to show that he did not understand the spirit of true religion.

We must pass on to the subject of spiritism. There are many scornful references to spiritism in Mark Twain. He finds it difficult to realize that people in modern times have believed in ghosts, and in *The American Claimant,* Sellers' interest in "materialization" becomes an element—a very ineffective element, too—of comedy. Yet psychic phenomena pursued him all his life. When he was four years old, his sister Margaret died: the village shoemaker claimed that weeks before, while the little girl was still strong and well, he had seen in a vision the funeral procession pass by his door, exactly as it afterwards did. One night in 1858, Sam himself had a dream. He saw his brother Henry, dead, lying in a metallic casket, supported by two chairs.

On his breast was a bouquet of white flowers with a single crimson bloom in the center. The dream was so vivid that he woke up the next morning believing his brother to be dead, and it was not until after he had dressed and got out into the street that he realized the truth. In June Henry was blown up with the *Pennsylvania*. After the body had been prepared for burial, Sam found his brother in a leaden casket exactly like the one he had seen in his dream, and while he stood rapt in the wonder of it, an elderly lady entered the room bringing a floral offering. The flowers were pure white and there was a single red rose in the center.

Many years later, during one of his skeptical moods, Mark Twain denied the reality of all psychic manifestations. When Paine reminded him of this experience, he replied, "I ask nobody to believe that it ever happened. To me it is true; but it has no logical right to be true, and I do not expect belief in it." Logic abdicates in such an answer. It was as if he knew that the "philosophy" he had developed was not big enough to satisfy all the needs of his personality, to cover all the experiences of his life.

This was not the only strange experience he had in the psychic world. I will not spoil by a paraphrase Mr. Paine's wonderfully told story of the billiard balls—a phenomenon to be explained on the hypothesis of dematerialization or else left simply unexplained.[5] Once a distracted husband came to Mark, fearing that his wife had met with some disaster. Mark led him straight to the ascending elevator of the hotel, confident that when it stopped the wife would step out of it, and she did. To Paine himself this power was one day curiously exemplified when Mark Twain sent him a message: "Tell Paine I am sorry he fell and skinned his shin at five o'clock yesterday afternoon." And Paine replied: "I did fall and skin my shin at five o'clock yesterday afternoon, but how did you find it out?"

One day in Montreal at an afternoon reception, he glimpsed across the room an old friend, a lady whom he had not seen for twenty years. He wondered why she did not come forward to speak to him, but she kept her distance, and at last he lost sight of her altogether. That night she turned up at his lecture, dressed exactly as he had seen her some hours before. "I knew you," he said to her, "I knew you the moment you appeared at the reception this afternoon." And to his utter astonishment she replied, "But I was not at the reception. I have just arrived from Quebec, and have not been in town an hour."

Most interesting of all was the bathroom experience, just after the death of Jean. This may best be told in his own words to Paine:

"For one who does not believe in spirits I have had a most peculiar experience. I went into the bath-room just now and closed the door. You know how warm it always is in there, and there are no draughts. All at once I felt a cold current of air about me. I thought the door must be open; but it was closed. I said, 'Jean is this you trying to let me know you have found the others?' Then the cold air was gone."

He did not formulate his opinions on these subjects, or rather he formulated them only to depart immediately from whatever formula he had adopted. When he came to tell the story of Joan of Arc, the psychic element puzzled him considerably, though the naïveté of the assumed narrator was a great help to him here. He was always interested in the work of the Society for Psychical Research, and when Mrs. Clemens became interested in spiritualism, he accompanied her willingly to séances. "I have never had an experience which moved me to believe the living can communicate with the dead," he wrote a correspondent in 1901, "but my wife and I have experimented in the matter when opportunity offered and shall continue to do so." He was willing to consider the testimony of persons he considered truthful, even when it carried him beyond the bounds within which he traveled habitually, and Madame Gabrilowitsch prints a late note to her mother "because it is interesting to see that he never shut up his mind so tight that it would not unfold to the possible mysteries of an invisible world." He wrote:

"Livy, darling: Here is Rev. Dr. X. furnishing some spiritual-

ism of a most unaccountable and interesting character. This is
the kind of episode that puzzles a body entirely. It isn't telepathy and it isn't clairvoyance; they can explain many, if not
most of the spiritualistic wonders, but they are out of court this
time. This is an altogether startling and marvelous case. Love."

It is clear, for he tells us specifically, that his interest in me-
tempsychosis was one of the things that made *The Master of
Palmyra* so fascinating to him, and recently Miss Annella
Smith has shown that several features of the Stormfield skit are
in complete harmony with occult teaching, though I find no
evidence to support her conclusion that Mark Twain was himself well versed in occult lore.

III

It is time now to try to sum up, as completely as the evidence
will allow, what Mark Twain actually did believe on religious
subjects, and it may be well to begin with the idea of God.

Emotionally, as we shall see later, Mark Twain never freed
himself from the anthropomorphic God of his early teaching.
Intellectually, however, he made considerable advance. Early
in his married life, he tried to state, in a paper that Mrs. Clemens would not let him print, the differences, as he saw them, between the God of the Bible and the God of his own day:

"The difference in importance, between the God of the Bible
and the God of the present day, cannot be described, it can only
be vaguely and inadequately figured to the mind. . . .

". . . His sole solicitude was about a handful of truculent
nomads. He worried and fretted over them in a peculiarly and
distractingly human way. One day he coaxed and petted them
beyond their deserts. He sulked, he cursed, he raged, he grieved,
according to the mood and the circumstances, but all to no purpose; his efforts were all vain, he could not govern them. When
the fury was on him he was blind to all reason—he not only
slaughtered the offender, but even his harmless little children
and dumb cattle.

"To trust the God of the Bible is to trust an irascible, vindic-

tive, fierce and ever fickle and changeful master; to trust the
true God is to trust a Being who has uttered no promises, but
whose beneficent, exact, and changeless ordering of the machinery of his colossal universe is proof that he is at least steadfast to his purposes; whose unwritten laws, so far as they affect
man, being equal and impartial, show that he is just and fair;
these things, taken together, suggest that if he shall ordain us
to live hereafter, he will still be steadfast, just, and fair toward
us. We shall not need to require anything more."

This was a vast conception, infinitely more rational than the
one presented in the Bible, but not so satisfying emotionally.
"For that Supreme One is not a God of pity or mercy—not as
we recognize these qualities." Mark Twain accepted always the
argument from design—it was one of the things that kept him
from being an atheist—and so he had to account somehow for
the typhus germ, the tsetse fly, and the rattlesnake. "Two
things," therefore, "are quite certain: one is that God, the limit-
less God, manufactured those things, for no man could have
done it. . . . The other conclusion is that God has no special
consideration for man's welfare or comfort, or He wouldn't
have created those things to disturb and destroy him. The human conception of pity and morality must be entirely unknown
to that Infinite God, as much unknown as the conceptions of a
microbe to man, or at least as little regarded." It was the old,
old problem of evil, always the great obstacle in the way of religious faith, from the Book of Job to *The Bridge of San Luis
Rey.*

Such speculations led him at last to a kind of vast, materi-
alistic pantheism, suggestive, here and there, of Robert Fludd.
There occurred to him "the possibility, and substantially the
certainty, that man is himself a microbe, and his globe a blood-
corpuscle drifting with its shining brethren of the Milky Way
down a vein of the Master and Maker of all things, whose body,
mayhap—glimpsed part-wise from the earth by night, and re-
ceding and lost to view in the measureless remotenesses of space
—is what men name the Universe." Or, more elaborately:

"The suns and planets that form the constellations of a billion billion solar systems and go pouring, a tossing flood of shining globes, through the viewless arteries of space are the blood-corpuscles in the veins of God; and the nations are the microbes that swarm and wiggle and brag in each, and think God can tell them apart at that distance and has nothing better to do than try. *This*—the entertainment of an eternity. Who so poor in his ambitions as to consent to be God on those terms? Blasphemy? No, it is not blasphemy. If God is as vast as that, He is above blasphemy; if He is as little as that, He is beneath it."

What, now, of Jesus? Mark Twain never fails in reverence toward him. "All that is great and good in our particular civilization," he wrote in 1871, "came straight from the hand of Jesus Christ." When he went to Palestine in the 'sixties, he was still fairly orthodox in his religious beliefs; it was natural that he should gaze upon the site of the Crucifixion "with a far more absorbing interest than I had ever felt in anything earthly before." He is already trying to differentiate, to distinguish between traditions which, by their own inherent reasonableness, are plainly worthy of credence and those which are mere pious fictions of monks and the impostures of churchmen. But this does not keep him from being impressed by the idea that he is now traversing ground once pressed by the feet of a god.

Such a view would have seemed utterly absurd to him in later years, yet when Orion sent him a manuscript in 1878, he objected to what he considered the irreverent attitude toward Jesus expressed in it. Though taking pains to explain that "neither Howells nor I believe in . . . the divinity of the Savior," he insists that nevertheless "the Savior is . . . a sacred Personage, and a man should have no desire or disposition to refer to him lightly, profanely, or otherwise than with the profoundest reverence." One late conversation with Mr. Paine implies doubt of the historicity of Jesus, and the same point of view seems involved in a 1908 statement to an unknown correspondent that between A.D. 350 and A.D. 1850, Jesus and Satan "exercised a vaster influence over a fifth part of the human race than was exercised over that fraction of the race by all other influences combined." But Mark Twain was so volatile in his thinking that I should not dare to take such utterances as expressing a settled conviction.

In any case he remained reverential toward the ideal presented in the gospel narrative. In his youth he was shocked, when he went to Italy, to find Christ subordinated in favor of "some twelve or fifteen canonized Popes and martyrs"; in his old age, he was equally shocked when he found some of his contemporaries disposed to raise Mrs. Eddy to a level of equality with him. He himself wrote one book that he feared might be taken as irreverent, and he kept it by him unpublished for many years. Yet this very book contains one of the most beautiful tributes ever paid to Christ in modern literature. When Captain Stormfield arrives in a section of heaven where the denizens of our particular earth are unknown, it finally occurs to him that there is one infallible way of identifying himself:

" 'Well, sir,' I says, pretty humble, 'I don't seem to make out which world it is I'm from. But you may know it from this— it's the one the Saviour saved.'

"He bent his head at the Name. Then he says, gently—

" 'The worlds He has saved are like to the gates of heaven in number—none can count them.' "

Many of Mark Twain's contemporaries actually believed in the veritable existence of Satan. That Mark Twain himself shared this belief, I very much doubt, but of all the figures in the Christian mythology, Satan was the one that interested him most. His interest began as a boy—he was disappointed when he found that his Sunday School teacher did not care to encourage it—and it grew apace with the years. I do not find that he ever made any special study of diabolical literature, but he would certainly have enjoyed such books as, of late years, the Rev. Montague Summers and Maximilian J. Rudwin have been publishing. Satan is, after all, the principle of rebellion, the champion of the outcast, and not even Milton could quite resist his fascination. How then could Mark Twain? The classical passage, one of the brightest examples of his humor, appears in the essay, "Concerning the Jews":

"I have no special regard for Satan; but I can at least claim that I have no prejudice against him. It may even be that I lean a little his way, on account of his not having a fair show. All religions issue bibles against him, but we never hear *his* side. . . . A person who has for untold centuries maintained the imposing position of spiritual head of four-fifths of the human race, and political head of the whole of it, must be granted the possession of executive abilities of the loftiest order. . . . I would like to see him. I would rather see him and shake him by the tail than any other member of the European Concert."

Prayer was definitely a part of the background of Mark Twain's youth: when Tom Sawyer and his comrades were alone on the island, they omitted the ceremony of kneeling, indeed considered omitting their prayers altogether, "but they were afraid to proceed to such lengths as that, lest they might call down a sudden and special thunderbolt from Heaven." When Tom, bored in school, unexpectedly found something in his pocket that he could play with, "his face lit up with a glow of gratitude that was prayer, though he did not know it." Mr. Paine tells a delightful story of how little Sam was disillusioned when he tried praying for gingerbread—perhaps the first skeptical note.

He came early to distinguish between the conventional set prayer—which was of no value—and the prayer which is the sincere, spontaneous overflow of powerful feelings. As early as 1865, he ventures a suggestion: "How would it answer to adopt the simplicity and the beauty and the brevity and the comprehensiveness of the Lord's Prayer as a model? But perhaps I am wandering out of my jurisdiction." At a later date he was shocked by prayers for rain and all kindred petitions demanding that the Deity upset the natural order of creation to accommodate the individual needs of the petitioner, regardless of the needs and the rights of others, and I shall have something to say later of his horror over the appalling blasphemy of prayers offered up for success in war. Huckleberry Finn is, as ever, the skeptic, making a determined effort to be fair, to consider all sides of the question, and it comes to Huck finally that possibly "there's something in it when a body like the widow or the parson prays, but it don't work for me, and I reckon it don't work for only just the right kind." Perhaps Mark Twain came to accept Huck's opinion. It is difficult to think of him as employing private prayer—at least in any systematic way—during his later years, but when, shortly before his death, he was told that a company of nuns were praying for him, he was vastly pleased: "I am grateful for the prayers of those good nuns, and for yours; they have already answered themselves in giving me deep pleasure."

On one occasion, Mark Twain plays, discriminatingly enough, the rôle of biblical critic. This is when he discusses Herod's slaughter of the innocents, as reported in the Gospel According to St. Matthew. "Tacitus makes no mention of it," he says, "and he would hardly have overlooked a sweeping order like that, issued by a petty ruler like Herod. Just consider a little king of a corner of the Roman Empire ordering the slaughter of the firstborn of a lot of Roman subjects. Why, the Emperor would have reached out that long arm of his and dismissed Herod." His opinions on the question of biblical inspiration have already been suggested. In the creed printed in Paine's last volume, he declares that the Bible was written wholly by man, and that the world's moral laws are wholly the result of the world's experience, not the outcome of special revelations.

There was probably no phase of religious aspiration that interested Mark Twain more than the thought of life after death. Leaving Egypt as a *Quaker City* pilgrim, he says: "We were glad to have seen that land which had an enlightened religion with future eternal rewards and punishment in it, while even Israel's religion contained no promise of a hereafter." He did not himself care much for the punishment part of it; he would not roast his enemies through eternity, and he found it difficult to believe that God was less humane than Samuel L. Clemens.

Heaven, too, was going to be something radically different from
what the average Christian expected. Harps and halos might
appear, but nobody would have much regard for them, and
there would be plenty of work and pain and growth and progress. But like all men who have loved deeply, he could not endure the thought that death was the end. Like T. T. Munger,
he knew that love cannot tolerate the thought of its own end.
"It has but one word—forever. Its language is 'there is no
death.'" Only once in his writings is it even transiently suggested that a life lived here on this planet alone, without
thought or hope of anything afterwards, might be the nobler
ideal.

When he lost the Christian faith of his earlier years, he naturally lost immortality too as a dogma, but he clung to it as a
hope. For as the sorrows of life piled thick and fast upon him,
he believed more and more, despite all his skepticism, that there
is no sense to the universe if death must end all, and the thought
of what lay beyond was increasingly on his mind. "As to a hereafter," he told his biographer, "we have not the slightest evidence that there is any—*no* evidence that appeals to logic and
reason. I have never seen what to me seemed an atom of proof
that there is a future life." And then, after waiting a long time,
he added: "And yet—I am strongly inclined to expect one."

As those he loved slipped away from him, he needed immortality more than ever. "Let us believe it!" he writes his wife,
following the death of Susy. "I will believe in it with you. It
has been the belief of the wise and thoughtful of many countries for three thousand years; let us accept their verdict; we
cannot frame one that is more reasonable or probable. I will try
never to doubt it again." When Jean died, Katy Leary was sure
he said to her: "Oh, Katy! She's in heaven with her mother."
Madame Gabrilowitsch writes: "Father had often said he hoped
he might die by a stroke of lightning without any warning of
change from this life to the other. Sometimes he believed that
death ended everything, but most of the time he felt sure of a
life beyond."

So, making due allowance for buffoonery, annoyance, and exaggeration, there is less positive irreverence in Mark Twain than many persons believe. He recognizes the power of religion, and consistently maintains that he never wishes to interfere with another man's faith. There might be nothing in it, but if it served to comfort him who held it, it had still justified itself.

At one point, he understands true reverence better than many of the devout Christians of his time: he recognizes and respects the religious instinct even when it manifests itself in forms that are utterly strange to him. To be sure, he was assisted here by the fact that he did not regard Christianity as embodying a unique revelation, in the sense in which most of his contemporaries did. In fact, it sometimes seemed to him that the heathen were in many ways more civilized than the Christians. "When he looked at the hosts of men and women kneeling in worship before the sun, by the shores of the Holy river of Ganges, in the town of Benares," writes his daughter, "he exclaimed: 'They spend hours like this while we in America are robbing and murdering.'" But in any case, the principle he lays down is perfectly sound: "True irreverence is disrespect for another man's god." For the European who treads rudely on the Arab's praying carpets, he has only contempt.

The same tendency in him comes out in his comments on Roman Catholic practices. As we have already seen, he was brought up to dislike Catholicism, and there are many passages in *The Innocents Abroad* which make unpleasant reading for the devout Catholic reader. Yet the very frankness with which he avows his prejudice proves that he was not wholly enslaved to it. Even that bigoted Protestant, the Connecticut Yankee, admits that "the great majority" of the parish priests "were sincere and right-hearted, and devoted to the alleviation of human troubles and sufferings." The good priest who taught Tom comes in for nothing but praise in *The Prince and the Pauper,* and Clemens himself became intimate with two priests, one in Italy, and one whom he met on his trip around the world. It was his old habit of recognizing merit wherever he found it.

When he was asked to contribute to a Catholic magazine he replied, "I wish I were not so hard driven; then nothing could give
me more contentment than to try to write something in your
periodical, 'Christ's Poor'; indeed you pay me a compliment
which I highly value when you invite me to do it, as holding
me not unworthy to appear in its pages." But most interesting
of all is a letter to his wife which has only recently been
printed: "I am very, very glad Jean is in a convent. . . . And
away deep down in my heart I feel that if they make a good
strong unshakable Catholic of her I shan't be the least bit sorry.
It is doubtless the most peace-giving and restful of all the religions. If I had it I would not trade it for anything in the earth."

Finally, we must recognize that though Mark Twain may
have rejected the theology of Christianity, he never rejected the
Christian ethic. All Americans, he says, whatever their religious
beliefs, have the moral constitution of Christians—surely a statement that should forever silence all accusations of pessimism!
Perhaps that is why bad conduct on the part of Americans
shocked him so much: it was so blatantly inconsistent with the
principles they professed. In 1880, petitioning Congress to enact
a copyright law, he declares that he acts in the conviction that
"the infusing of the spirit of God into our laws will be something better than the empty honor of putting His name in the
Constitution." He is in favor of protecting foreign authors in
America even without insisting on similar treatment for American authors abroad, "there being nothing in the Christian code
of morals which justifies a man in requiring that another man
shall promise to stop stealing from him before he will consent
to stop stealing from said other man." If there were one nation
on the face of the earth today that had the courage to go into a
disarmament conference in the same spirit, perhaps we might
still be able to avoid destruction.

Unchristian conduct on the part of professing Christians was
always shocking to Mark Twain. Once more let us give the
final word to Huckleberry Finn, this time disgusted and horrified over the Grangerford-Shepherdson feud:

"Next Sunday we all went to church, about three mile, everybody a-horseback. The men took their guns along, so did Buck, and kept them between their knees or stood them handy against the wall. The Shepherdsons done the same. It was pretty ornery preaching—all about brotherly love, and such-like tiresomeness; but everybody said it was a good sermon, and they all talked it over going home, and had such a powerful lot to say about faith and good works and free grace and predestination, and I don't know what all, that it did seem to me to be one of the roughest Sundays I had run across yet."

IV

THIS chapter opened with the consideration of Mark Twain's relationship to Calvinism; it must end on the same note. Intellectually, as we have seen, he was able to throw off the stamp of his early environment; emotionally, he retained his scars as long as he lived. He thinks, he jokes in terms of Calvinism; no illustrations come so readily to his mind as those involving the old orthodox interpretations of religion. The "jackass rabbit" sits quietly "thinking about his sins." He cannot see Victoria's Diamond Jubilee procession without being reminded of the Last Judgment—"and some of us who live to see that day will probably recall this one—if we are not too much disturbed in mind at the time." How fierce is his rebellion against a rule-of-thumb morality at the end of his touching story, "Was It Heaven? or Hell?" and how much of its power this narrative has lost by the fact that we can no longer conceive the possibility of any sane person wishing to debate the subject against him. Shortly before his death he wrote a series of directions designed to assist Mr. Paine in learning how to comport himself in the life to come. "You will be wanting to slip down at night, and smuggle water to those poor little chaps [the infant damned], but don't you try it. You would be caught, and nobody in heaven would respect you after that." Humorous? Yes. But without Calvinism, without vividly remembered Calvinism, without a Calvinism that had sunk into the very marrow of his bones, such a passage could never have been written.

There are other utterances where no striving for humorous effect can possibly enter in. "God does not willingly punish us," a correspondent writes him. And he comments, "Well, why does He do it then? We don't invite it. Why does He give Himself the trouble?" The missionaries in the Congo labor to stamp out a hideous and loathsome disease: "Evidently those missionaries are pitying, compassionate, kind. How it would improve God to take a lesson from them! He invented and distributed the germ of that awful disease among those helpless, poor savages, and now He sits with His elbows on the balusters and looks down and enjoys this wanton crime. Confidently, and between you and me—well, never mind, I might get struck by lightning if I said it." The blasphemy would be shocking if it were not so crude; it would be naïve if it were not so pitiful. "I wish the Lord would disguise Himself in citizen's clothing and make a personal examination of the sufferings of the poor in London. He would be moved and would do something for them Himself." Even in his reading the problem pursued him, as when he penciled on the margin of Saint-Simon's account of Louis XIV: "We have to grant that God made this royal hog; we may also be permitted to believe that it was a crime to do so." No wonder he thought that in a heaven presided over by such a God society would consist mainly of undesirable persons. But the thing comes home in the closest possible way in Grace King's story of how he told her he was afraid he was going to hell. "But you don't believe in hell!" was her reply. "Nobody believes in hell any longer!" The whole history of Mark Twain's religious life is in his answer: "I don't believe in it, but I'm afraid of it. It makes me afraid to die!"

In short, he could enlarge his God along the lines suggested and made necessary by the new astronomical speculations and discoveries, but he could not fundamentally alter his inherited conception of what we may call the human side of God, of God in His relations with humanity. Such speculations as, during

the War, occurred to Mr. H. G. Wells, to be expressed in his
God, the Invisible King, such ideas as, in quite a different
form, have recently been set forth by Professor Brightman, of
Boston University, might have solved his problem, but they
never occurred to him. Nor did he catch even a far-off glimpse
of the God of Lyman or of Wieman.

In this particular, there is, I think, an interesting comparison
to be made between Mark Twain and one of his staunchest
American admirers of these latter days, Mr. H. L. Mencken.
More than any other critic of our time, Mr. Mencken has the
temperament of the popular evangelist of a generation ago.
Bliss Perry was not trying to be funny when he compared Mr.
Mencken to a Salvation Army captain; there is a point here that
has escaped many of his critics. The principal difference is that
the evangelist and the Salvation Army captain are generally engaged in asserting something, while Mr. Mencken's principal
business is to be forever denying something. This difference is
less fundamental, however, than it might appear, for the apostle
of unbelief has his definite convictions and must be as zealous
in urging them as the prophet of faith. It is only the man to
whom all things alike are possible, the good as well as the bad,
only the man who is sure of nothing, who is the true skeptic.
Mencken has not the same sensitiveness as Mark Twain, and
none of what, in the highest sense of that much misused word
may be called Mark Twain's "sweetness." Furthermore he has
gone at the religious problem from a rather different angle;
that is to say, he has assumed that the way to solve the problem
is to "squelch" religion. Unfortunately, religion has a way of refusing to be "squelched." Unless a man is completely animal, he
cannot "squelch" it even in himself, and if he does succeed in
this, it still remains a factor in the society in which he must live
and in the lives of other men with whom he is brought in
touch. Now when a man does succeed completely in emancipat-
ing himself from religion, he thereafter ignores it, but Mr.
Mencken, as any of his books will testify, is instead fairly obsessed by it. His world swarms with fearful creatures called

"Puritans," "Baptists," and "Methodists." He has created them
after a pattern of his own; they bear only the remotest resemblance to anything that has ever existed in life; it is no wonder
they invade even his dreams. He is forever thinking about
them, forever talking about them; Falstaff-like, he finds his
mind ever centered on the things he has repudiated, the things
that he hates. The religious history of Mr. Mencken's mind
would be a strange document indeed, for the most bigoted zealot
does not live, think, and move with religion as a background
more consistently than he. This is no doubt the reason why his
influence has declined so notably during recent years. There is
nothing quite so out-of-date as yesterday's newspaper, and Mr.
Mencken, who only a few years ago was quite "the latest
thing," now seems a curious, almost a precious antique. His
contemporaries have either learned that religion is not, never
has been, in this day and age, what he imagines it to be, or else
they have gone on to other things and forgotten religion altogether.

Mark Twain himself would, I believe, accept what I have
written here about his Calvinism, for he was fully aware that
early impressions, along this line, are not to be lightly eradi-
cated. "The religious folly you are born in you will *die* in," he
wrote, "no matter what apparently reasonabler religious folly
may seem to have taken its place meanwhile, and abolished and
obliterated it." What was his "apparently reasonabler religious
folly" but his "Gospel" of determinism? And what is this
"Gospel" but an inverted Calvinism? How close he himself
came to seeing this, yet how completely he escaped the logical
conclusion to be drawn, we may see very clearly in the amazing
letter he wrote to Twichell after the latter had given him a volume of Jonathan Edwards to read. He took it home and "wal-
lowed and reeked" in it until midnight; he went "on a three
days' tear with a drunken lunatic." Then he wrote:

"Jonathan seems to hold (as against the Arminian position)
that the Man (or his Soul or his Will) never creates an impulse

itself, but is moved to action by an impulse back of it. That's sound!

"Also, that of two or more things offered it, it infallibly chooses the one which for the moment is most pleasing to IT-SELF. *Perfectly* correct! An immense admission for a man not otherwise sane.

"Up to that point he could have written chapters III and IV of my suppressed 'Gospel.' But there we seem to separate. He seems to concede the indisputable and unshakable dominion of Motive and Necessity (call them what he may, these are *exterior* forces and not under the man's authority, guidance or even suggestion)—then he suddenly flies the logic track and (to all seeming) makes the *man* and not these exterior forces responsible to God for the man's thoughts, words, and acts. It is frank insanity."

So much for his philosophy. On his pessimism, too, Calvinism may well have exercised an influence. The thought that God has chosen a large share of the race to roast in everlasting torment through no fault of their own cannot be called particularly cheerful, yet this was the decree of the first God to whom Mark Twain was ever introduced. It is not wonderful that he rebelled, that he expressed himself wildly and "irreverently," that he sprang at the loathsome image like Shaw's Black Girl with her knobkerrie.

We know he considered this aspect of the problem, for he once declared that to beget a child in a world like this, to thrust the uninvited burden of life upon an innocent creature was a crime, as if one should insist upon building a village on the slope of a volcano, directly in the path of the lava flow. "Formerly," he observed significantly, "it was much worse than now, for before the ministers abolished hell a man knew, when he was begetting a child, that he was begetting a soul that had only one chance in a hundred of escaping the eternal fires of damnation. He knew that in all probability that child would be brought to damnation—one of the ninety-nine black sheep."

Here is a phase of the psychology of our ancestors that deserves more careful consideration than it has received. "What is humanity made of," asks Gamaliel Bradford in another connection, "that it can support such pangs as these and survive?" How could men and women who were not insane go on bringing children into such a world, a world which, as they believed, was ruled by the Monster-God of *The Mysterious Stranger?* Or did they only believe such things with their minds, and did the vital Life Force in them—the True God—insist on going on in spite of their barbarous creeds? And, after all, were they much crazier than the men and women of today who go on bringing innocent lives into a world brooded over by the fear of such horror and destruction as mankind has never known, and then sit supinely by and allow knaves and fools to dictate such policies to the nations as must surely lead at last to utter, irretrievable ruin?

At the close of *Paradise Lost,* Milton, reversing his source in the *Adamus Exul* of Hugo Grotius, gives to Eve, not Adam, the suggestion of racial and personal suicide; since mankind has been defeated there is no use going on, no sense in bringing a doomed race into a repudiated world. He would not have made this mistake had he had access to modern statistics which show that, possibly because they have more imagination, certainly because they have less endurance, many more men commit suicide than women. But the modern reader finds it impossible to avoid agreeing with Eve. Granted her premises, her conclusion seems perfectly logical. It was not the pangs of childbirth that she feared; she simply does not wish to be party to a crime.

Was there ever a man who had better reason than Mark Twain to curse the name of that cold-blooded reptile among theologians, that prophet of the wrath of God—John Calvin?

CHAPTER II

Hymn to Death

"As for me, I see no such great reason why I should either be fond to live or fear to die. I have had good experience of this world, I have known what it is to be a subject, and I now know what it is to be a sovereign. Good neighbors I have had, and I have met with bad; and in trust I have found treason. I have bestowed benefits on ill-deservers; and where I have done well, I have been ill-requited, and spoken of. While I call to mind things past, behold things present, I count them happiest that go hence soonest."

QUEEN ELIZABETH.

I

MARK TWAIN'S biographer is rather inclined to minimize his pessimism. "Mark Twain," he writes, "was not a pessimist in his heart, but only by premeditation. It was his observation and his logic that led him to write those things that, even in their bitterness, somehow conveyed the spirit of human sympathy which is so closely linked to hope." Later writers have taken it more seriously, finding in his pessimism, indeed, the key to his whole life. Mr. Paine, they allege, did not fairly face the facts. Enamored of his hero and mindful of the conventional American optimisms, he shrank from depicting the history of the great humorist in terms of the desolate tragedy it really became. It is time, then, for a fresh examination of the evidence.[1]

No man could travel farther into the Waste Land than Mark Twain goes in many considered utterances of his later years. "A myriad of men are born; they labor and sweat and struggle for bread; they squabble and scold and fight; they scramble for little mean advantages over each other; age creeps upon them; infirmities follow; shames and humiliations bring down their prides and their vanities; those they love are taken from them and the joy of life is turned to aching grief. The burden of pain,

care, misery grows heavier year by year; at length ambition is
dead; pride is dead; vanity is dead; longing for release is in
their place. It comes at last—the only unpoisoned gift earth ever
had for them—and they vanish from a world where they were
of no consequence, where they have achieved nothing, where
they were a mistake and a failure and a foolishness; where
they have left no sign that they have existed—a world which
will lament them a day and forget them forever."[2]

Here despair is wrought into literary beauty. He can make it
snap the whip of an epigram too: "Each person is born to one
possession which outvalues all his others—his last breath." And
again: "Whoever has lived long enough to find out what life is,
knows how deep a debt of gratitude we owe to Adam, the first
great benefactor of our race. He brought death into the world."
And we get the same effect exactly in private letters and memoranda, where no literary influence can possibly enter. Like the
mad priest in "John Bull's Other Island," he thinks that this
world is hell—"The true one, not the lying invention of the superstitious; and we have come to it from elsewhere to expiate
our sins." It would be somewhat difficult to find bitterer words
than these in which to sum up your impression of the human
adventure: "Anybody that knows anything knows that there
was not a single life that was ever lived that was worth living.
Not a single child was ever begotten that the begetting of it was
not a crime."

So much for generalization. He takes the same tone as he
faces the individual, the unspeakably direct fact of death. Irving
goes. "It is another reminder. My section of the procession has
but a little way to go. I could not be very sorry if I tried." Hale
goes. "I am as grieved to hear of his death as I can ever be to
hear of the death of any friend, though my grief is always tem-
pered with the satisfaction of knowing that for the one that
goes, the hard, bitter struggle of life is ended." Gilder goes. He
attends the funeral, and as he enters the church, he is heard to
whisper, "I wish that I were that man lying in there."

Death strikes closer home. His brother, his daughters, his beloved wife. . . . Life crumbles in his hands, but he does not falter. He lives on himself, unfortunately. Why didn't they let him drown when he went swimming in his boyhood? Why did they have to pull him out of the water, not once but several times? They "interfered with the intentions of a Providence wiser than themselves," and it is difficult for him to forgive them. "He was good—" he writes his sister-in-law, when Orion is taken, "all good, and sound; there was nothing bad in him, nothing base, nor any unkindness. It was unjust that such a man . . . should have been sentenced to live 72 years. It was beautiful, the patience with which he bore it." Susy? Death knew what was best for Susy. "Susy died at the right time, the fortunate time of life, the happy age—twenty-four years. At twenty-four, such a girl has seen the best of life—life as a happy dream. After that age the risks begin; responsibility comes, and with it the cares, the sorrows, and the inevitable tragedy. For her mother's sake, I would have brought her back from the grave if I could, but not for my own." As Jean's body lies before him, that last lonely Christmas of his life, he sums it all up: "Would I bring her back to life if I could do it? I would not. If a word would do it, I would beg for strength to withhold the word. . . . In her loss I am almost bankrupt, and my life a bitterness, but I am content: for she has been enriched with the most precious of all gifts—that gift which makes all other gifts mean and poor—death. I have never wanted any released friend of mine restored to life since I reached manhood. I felt in this way when Susy passed away; and later my wife, and later Mr. Rogers. When Clara met me at the station in New York and told me Mr. Rogers had died suddenly that morning, my thought was, Oh, favorite of fortune—fortunate all his long and lovely life—fortunate to his latest moment! The reporters said there were tears of sorrow in my eyes. True—but they were for *me,* not for him. He had suffered no loss. All the fortunes he had ever made before were poverty compared with this one."

II

But now let us turn to the other side.

It will be noted that all these expressions of extreme despair date from the last years of Mark Twain's life. Is there anything at all similar that turns up during the earlier periods?

Comparatively little, I think—very little indeed that could be noted except our eyes had sharpened by what we have already seen of the end. He is sensitive to the sorrows and tragedies of life, to be sure, but there are plenty of high spirits in piloting days, and surely nobody could call the Hartford years as a whole unhappy. "Indeed I *am* thankful for the wife and the child—" he writes in 1874, "and if there is one individual creature on this footstool who is more thoroughly and uniformly and unceasingly *happy* than I am I defy the world to produce him and *prove* him. In my opinion, he doesn't exist." As late as 1888, he adds a postscript to a perfectly furious letter to Orion: "Don't imagine . . . that I am uncomfortable or unhappy—for *I never am*. I don't know what it is to be unhappy or uneasy; and I am not going to try to learn how, at this late day." When we compare such words as these with the utterances already quoted, it would seem that Mark Twain had illustrated his own aphorism: "When a man is a pessimist before forty-eight he knows too much; if he is an optimist after, he knows too little."

And even in the final period itself. . . . The Old Man in his "Gospel"—confessedly a mask for Mark Twain—claims a happy temperament, and those who lived with him during his last years make it clear that he did not go about like a professional mourner. "I am old;" he writes in 1906, "I recognize it but I don't realize it. I wonder if a person ever really ceases to feel young—I mean, for a whole day at a time." In his paper on the death of Jean, he tells us he knows his temperament too well to suppose that he will be depressed permanently by even such a calamity as that, and Miss Elizabeth Wallace has written engagingly of his gayety in Bermuda: "Often, when the long corridor of the second floor of the hotel presented a temptingly empty avenue, he hopped, skipped, and ran, and then gave a delicious suggestion of a cakewalk. As soon as a door opened, however, he stopped and assumed a supernaturally grave aspect." This is hardly the behavior of a despairing man, and the suggestion of *Galgenhumor* will hardly cover the case. Even on January 26, 1910, a month after the death of Jean, he writes, "I am happy—few are so happy."

This does not mean that he was insincere when he uttered grave counsels of despair, nor does it at all imply that he did not suffer deeply at such times. It does mean that he was a mercurial person; he did not live long on the heights nor did he wallow for any considerable period in the Slough of Despond. Readers of *Tom Sawyer* will remember that it is their hero's habit, every now and then, to go off by himself to meditate and wish he were dead, but they will remember too that a very slight change of stimulus will often banish this mood altogether. In this respect, as in many others, we may be sure that Tom Sawyer is a true image of young Sam Clemens, and the boy Sam Clemens was the father of the man Mark Twain. "I can suck melancholy out of a song," says Jaques, "as a weasel sucks eggs." In the last analysis, there probably are no consistent pessimists save those who fill our suicides' graves. Or, as Mark Twain himself puts it: "Pessimists are born not made; optimists are born not made; but no man is born either pessimist wholly or optimist wholly, perhaps; he is pessimistic along certain lines and optimistic along certain others. That is my case."

It is interesting to look at Mark Twain's references to suicide. They are less numerous than might be expected in a man who speaks so often in praise of death. He tells us that in the unsettled days following his return from Hawaii, before the world had ever heard of him, he was so depressed one morning that he placed a loaded pistol against his head but found that he lacked courage to pull the trigger; and toward the end of his life he told Paine, one day, that he had made up his mind that if he lived two years longer he must put an end to it. After Mrs. Clemens' death in Italy, he one day, by the merest chance, saved himself from a fall through a window which would probably have resulted in his death. He seems glad that he escaped it; he would not have the world think he had taken his own life. "You see the lightning refuses to strike me—" he once remarked, "there is where the defect is. We have to do our own striking as Barney Barnato did. But nobody ever gets the courage until he goes crazy." All in all, one cannot think of him as a very promising subject for suicide. He never went crazy, and he had a great deal of endurance. He could play with the idea —as he did in that rather histrionic moment in his early life— he could play with anything that was human. But suicides do not kill themselves two years hence; they do it now. He waited, waited through all calamities for the natural end.

I think our conclusion must be that in analyzing Mark Twain's pessimism, Albert Bigelow Paine was nearer right than any of his critics. We may grant freely that he was seeking to make the best case possible; it would be rather difficult to show that this is not a biographer's duty, especially that of a first biographer, who gathers together the materials on which later interpretations must so largely depend. Essentially, however, Mr. Paine's interpretation of Mark Twain's pessimism is not due to this cause. It is due to the fact that he knew Mark Twain very much better than any of the people who have more recently studied him; he was, therefore, in a better position to elucidate his extreme, often contradictory statements.

III

WHEN all exaggerations have been allowed for, however, Mark Twain's pessimism still remains a sufficiently marked feature of his thought in later years to make it necessary for us to try to sum up its genesis and its growth. I will say nothing here of purely literary influences: Schönemann, for example, suggests that *The Citizen of the World* may have been important. I will pass by, also, any suggestions which may have been made to him by the Scotchman, Macfarlane. Undoubtedly Macfarlane planted a seed in the mind of young Sam Clemens. But many seeds are planted in a man's mind; only a few of them can sprout. The problem, then, is to determine what it was in Mark Twain's temperament or in his experience of life that encouraged the development of a pessimistic outlook.

First, and most obviously, the personal griefs and misfortunes under which he suffered. His financial failure was undoubtedly a great disappointment to him, for though he ultimately recovered from it—though, indeed, at the end, it probably widened and deepened his consciousness of humanity's good will toward him—it was, for many years, a great strain; it left its mark upon him; he could not help being dashed by the thought that the thing to which he had devoted so much of his mature energies had turned out finally a chase after wind. But a much stronger influence—so much stronger, in fact, that it can hardly be mentioned in the same breath—is that of the long series of crushing personal losses. As he himself puts it, in 1906: "Life was a fairy-tale, then, it is a tragedy now. When I was 43 and John Hay was 41, he said life was a tragedy after 40, and I disputed it. Three years ago he asked me to testify again: I counted my graves, and there was nothing for me to say."

Earliest in point of time, was the death of his brother Henry in the frightful steamboat accident of 1858. Mark Twain held himself responsible for Henry's presence on the fated steamer, and life was never quite the same again. With more reason, he blamed himself, as we have seen, for the death of his son Langdon. I must not at this point be misunderstood. Such sorrows as these did not and could not, by themselves, have made Mark Twain a pessimist, but they spoiled the taste of life in his mouth, they inclined his mind toward counsels of despair. After all, as Gertrude points out, Hamlet had always known that fathers die, he had always known—she might have added—that women are false. But since he had never before personally experienced either of these things, he had only a theoretical kind of knowledge which did not prevent his entering with full zeal into the battle of life. Now he knows; his eyes are open; he will never be the old Hamlet any more. And having the imaginative temperament, he will not stop with his own sorrows, though they are crushing enough. Instead, he will use those very sorrows as a key to unlock the heart of humanity; through his own sympathetic imagination, he enters into the woes of all mankind, and it actually comes to seem to him as if the full weight of the griefs of all the world were resting on his single pair of shoulders.

It is so with all men of imagination; it was so with Tennyson after the death of Hallam, as he specifically tells us in one of the many passages in *In Memoriam* that so closely echo *Hamlet;* it was so, too, with Mark Twain. "Once Twichell heard me cussing the human race, and he said, 'Why, Mark, you are the last person in the world to do that—one selected and set apart as you are.' I said, 'Joe, you don't know what you are talking about. I am not cussing altogether about my own little troubles. Any one can stand his own misfortunes; but when I read in the papers all about the rascalities and outrages going on I realize what a creature the human animal is. Don't you care more about the wretchedness of others than anything that happens to you?' Joe said he did, and shut up."

Mark Twain had not lived long before he discovered that life is a terrible thing. Indeed he did not even have an opportunity to grow out of childhood first, which is a privilege the world owes to all her children and pays so few. There were horrible sights to be seen in Hannibal, and he seems to have had a perfect genius for running into them. Here is just one paragraph on the subject from the *Autobiography:*

"All within the space of a couple of years we had two or three other tragedies, and I had the ill luck to be too near by, on each occasion. There was the slave man who was struck down with a chunk of slag for some small offense; I saw him die. And the young Californian emigrant who was stabbed with a bowie knife by a drunken comrade; I saw the red life gush from his breast. And the case of the rowdy young brothers and their harmless old uncle: one of them held the old man down with his knees on his breast while the other one tried repeatedly to kill him with an Allen revolver which wouldn't go off. I happened along just then, of course."

One can imagine something of the effect such things must have had on the mind of a nervous, hypersensitive, highly imaginative boy. Worst of all was the tramp confined in the village jail, to whom, in the kindness of his heart, young Sam Clemens smuggled some matches, only to see the fool burn himself to death.

Then he grew up and went to the River—the River and the Far West. In the mining camps, he saw how the human animal behaves when the lust for gold takes possession of him and drives all other thoughts and emotions out. On the River, he met a wide variety of human types, and they did not all tend to raise his opinion of the merits of his kind. He stood up well under it, however, for he was young, he was ambitious, he had his way to make in the world. The time came later when he had made it, when his vitality did not surge so high, when his sensitiveness had grown with the years. Then he could no longer bear the thought of such things. "I have been reading the morning paper. I do it every morning—well knowing that I shall find in it the usual depravities and basenesses and hypocrisies and cruelties that make up civilization, and cause me to put in the rest of the day pleading for the damnation of the human race. I cannot seem to get my prayers answered, yet I do not despair." Paine suggested that he disregard the papers, but that was no solution. His horizon was wider now. He found the same damnable cruelties in books, and the fact that the rascals were all dead and done with did not make their rascalities hurt him less. Moreover, he knew something of science, and science taught him that every quiet meadow is, in reality, a hideous battlefield—how could he help feeling that there was something rotten at the heart of life?

Let us make no mistake about it: it was the man's tenderness that impelled him toward despair—his tenderness and his idealism and the great dreams that he had dreamed. His pessimism may not have been the best way to meet the problem; neither was it, by any means, the worst. And it was because he was good, not because he was bad, that he took that unhappy turning. Listen to the terrible cry of the young prince in *The Prince and the Pauper,* when he sees a girl burned at the stake: "That which I have seen, in that one little moment, will never go out from my memory, but will abide there; and I shall see it all the days, and dream of it all the nights, till I die. Would God I had been blind!"

The body of Jonathan Swift lies in Dublin Cathedral under this inscription, written by himself: "Here lies the body of Jonathan Swift, D.D., dean of this cathedral, where burning indignation can no longer tear his heart. Go, traveler, and imitate if you can a man who was an undaunted champion of liberty." The great idealists ask too much of mankind, too much of themselves. The Swifts, the Leopardis, the Byrons, the Mark Twains—their vision of what life could be is so high that the thought of what it is becomes unendurable. Sometimes they take refuge in cynicism; they wear indifference like a piece of armor over their hearts; they tell themselves and others that they do not care. Mark Twain never got very far along that road. He could rail; he could denounce; he could curse mankind—for what? Ever and always, for its cruelty to mankind. He had been born with his feet on the edge of Utopia; no thoughtful reader of his much-misunderstood book about the Yankee at the court of King Arthur can doubt the earnestness and the sincerity of his faith in the democratic experiment. And he saw—well, he saw what all men saw in America, in the 'seventies and the 'eighties and the 'nineties. Or, rather, he saw what many men did not see—though it was there before their eyes. Mark Twain himself did not comprehend the full significance of it. He never knew just what it was that the robber barons were doing—some of them he counted among his personal friends—but he did know that something had happened to America. The hopes of the Enlightenment had faded. The world into which he had been born was dead, and he was roaming about in a strange new world, a world that he did not understand, that he could not love. You must not be discouraged, they told him: the Kingdom of God marches on, it progresses steadily from age to age. " 'From age to age,'—" he cries, "yes, it describes that giddy gait. I (and the rocks) will not live to see it arrive, but that is all right—it will arrive, it surely will."

The griefs and sorrows of Mark Twain's personal life pass over then, as by a natural transition, into his sympathy for humanity, impelling him powerfully in the direction of pessimism as he contemplates the wrongs that humanity has to bear. And since men are oppressed by men, we tie up again with the third cause, which I find in his own natural tendency to rage, violence, and exaggeration. His temper, as we know, had never been of the best, and though he might have helped himself along this line, it would have called for more heroic self-discipline than he was ever disposed to exercise upon himself. This was, indeed, his Achilles heel, the place where the lime leaf clung, and it was through this tragic flaw that life struck at him in the end. Anyone who possesses this tendency, in however mild a form, knows how easy self-indulgence is and how rapidly it grows upon him. Add to this the artist's natural love of sensation, and it is easy to understand how the rage, the impatience which appears so often in the letters of Mark Twain's middle period passes over, as by a natural development, into the pessimism of the final years.

Finally, there is the influence of his own mechanistic determinism, his personal philosophy of life. Oh, I know many men can live happily—or think they can—under determinism. We are not talking of many men. We are talking of Samuel L. Clemens. He was the child of an age of faith—faith in God, faith in democracy, faith in mankind—and he could not breathe the thin air of the modern self-styled intellectual. We may grant that the ideas he set forth in *What Is Man?* were in his mind long before he ever put pen to paper. Mrs. Clemens could keep him from publishing; she could not keep him from writing; least of all could she keep him from thinking. The actual formulation of his doctrine into what he himself regarded as a water-tight system, a bleak, bare nihilism that he was thenceforward committed to stand by whether or no, was not a good thing for him. Mark Twain was human; he did not altogether escape the common tendency to define orthodoxy as "my doxy" and heterodoxy as "the other fellow's doxy." He himself admits it frankly. I have found the Truth, he says, and "the rest of my days will be spent in patching and painting and puttying and caulking my priceless possession and in looking the other way when an imploring argument or a damning fact approaches." The very frankness of his admission is the best testimony we could have to his fundamental sincerity, and there were many ways in which he remained extraordinarily open-minded to the end. Nevertheless, so far as his fundamental world-view was concerned, the writing of *What Is Man?* did deliver him over, bound and gagged to the futilitarians, and I have already quoted passages which make it clear that he himself recognized that there had been a change. All students of Mark Twain's pessimism, from Paine to Brooks, agree that it was not basically temperamental. I think we shall come as close to the truth of the matter as we can hope to get, if we assume that after the death of Susy, he reasoned himself into despair.

Intellectual honesty! What curious tricks it plays on us, after all! Milton laid aside his poetic ambitions for years, and finally sacrificed his eyesight, to write scurrilous pamphlets which accomplished considerably less than he had hoped for even in his own day and which have considerably shrunken his stature in the eyes of posterity. Yet for Milton to leave them unwritten, would have been, in his own eyes, to betray the cause of truth and duty. Mark Twain gave up his happiness to develop a "Gospel" of despair, because a man must be ready to face the truth wherever it leads. With what result? The orthodox have refused to read it or be influenced by it, and the unwashed heathen are already quite indifferent to it, having long since gone on to graze in other pastures.

IV

But, after all, why this to-do over the question of Mark Twain's pessimism? Doubtless it throws some light on the America of his day, but we are studying him. Suppose we accept the most serious analysis of all; suppose we agree that his despair destroyed him as an artist. Nijinsky's madness destroyed him as an artist, but it does not therefore become an absorbing subject for study. The important thing about Nijinsky will always be the art that possessed him before he lost his mind.

With Mark Twain's pessimism it is different. It is a part of his character, closely bound up with his weakness and with his strength. We must not forget that he died in the first full flush of the Pollyanna optimism of our Western world. Mechanical civilization had triumphed; democracy was successful and unassailed; war was definitely a thing of the past. The churches had stopped preaching the fatherhood of God; it was the grandfatherhood of God that concerned them. To be sure, there was a great deal that was not just as it should be, but there was nothing that, under the inspiration of our Rooseveltian idealism, might not easily be made right. There had not yet entered into many minds the dark suspicion that some of our problems, rooted in the essential deficiencies of human nature, might turn out to be insoluble in the end.

To Mark Twain all this was a bit unconvincing. Things were happening all about him that did not quite square with the assumption that this was the best of all possible worlds. There were times when he feared that civilization was taking the trail of the Gadarene swine down to the sea.

In such a world, happiness is impossible without faith, and we have already traced the history of Mark Twain's spiritual pilgrimage. After he had formulated his "Gospel," he gave himself to what might not unfairly be described as an "unfaith"; his god became a kind of *Ab-Gott*. The subject of the relationship between Christianity and pessimism is far too vast to enter upon here. I must say this much, however, that despite all the tre-

mendous dynamic of Christianity, it would be almost as unfair
to speak of Christianity as optimistic—in the usual, American,
cheerful-idiot sense of the word—as it would be to speak of it as
pessimistic. Christianity sees all the ills of life as keenly as Mark
Twain saw them. Its vision is as keen, its sympathies as deep; it
experiences the same profound sorrow over the vast moral dis-
crepancies of human experience. Only, Christianity does not
stop there: it goes on from the wreck of all things human to lay
hold upon a supernatural faith and hope. The modern world
has no greater Christian hero than Albert Schweitzer. "I am
pessimistic," says Schweitzer, "in that I experience in its full
weight what we conceive to be the absence of purpose in the
course of world-happenings. Only at quite rare moments have I
felt really glad to be alive. I could not but feel with a sympathy
full of regret all the pain that I saw around me, not only that of
men but that of the whole creation. From this community of
suffering I have never tried to withdraw myself. It seemed to
me a matter of course that we should all take our share of the
burden of pain which lies upon the world." Yet Schweitzer does
not stop there, for his horizon is not bounded by the limitations
of mere human vision. In almost the same breath he can speak
of himself among those "who have won their way through to
the peace which passeth all understanding," and it is this
strength that sustains him, that has carried him through the
herculean tasks he has required of himself.[3] Comparing Albert
Schweitzer with Samuel L. Clemens is to bring into juxtaposi-
tion the sacred and the secular, and we need not be frightened
by the fact that "supernaturalism" is at present a very unpopular term. It has happened before this that a whole generation has
missed the truth of life; it can happen again. Those who set out
to take the so-called supernatural element out of life may discover in the end that they have destroyed the very thing that
makes men, in the highest sense, human. Some, like Mr. Krutch,
have already discovered it; others are likely to stumble across
the discovery a good deal sooner than present indications might
suggest. The best that any of them are going to be able to do

will be to hold on to life on some such terms of despair and discouragement as are indicated in the final nihilism of Mark Twain.

Only, not many of them, I fear, will have the sweetness, the essential goodness, the inherent fineness of spirit that was his, and not many of them will be such good company. I have already admitted that many men live happily under determinism, but these men do not count; one cannot discuss the life of the spirit with special reference to those whose souls are dead.

> Men moste axe at seyntes if it is
> Aught fair in hevene; why? for they conne telle;
> And axen fendes, is it foul in helle.

Mark Twain's soul never quite found its way into harbor, but it did not die, it went on seeking always. There are millions of men among those who never find the answer to the riddle of human life who yet see life's evils quite as clearly as Mark Twain saw them. They do not all become pessimists. What, then, do they do? One of two things, I believe. Either they accept the situation, embrace the sin, make themselves a part of the bitter struggle—"Every man for himself and the devil take the hindmost"—or else they shrug their shoulders, repudiate personal responsibility, forget or try to forget, and go off

> To sport with Amaryllis in the shade,
> Or with the tangles of Neæra's hair.

Mark Twain chose neither alternative, but what he did was more noble. He could not find the supernatural solution of life's problem. He tried his best to solve it on the secular level and failed, for the simple reason that there is no secular solution. But because he was a great man, he could not rest content with that. He went about brooding over the question of human days, and he was profoundly unhappy because he could not find the answer.

Testament

I

MARK TWAIN was a born reformer; nothing could be further from the truth than to imagine that he was a humorist pure and simple in the early days and became interested in more serious matters only toward the end when personal sorrows had hurt him and bitter reflection imposed the feeling that all was wrong with the world. Gamaliel Bradford complains that "much of the jesting of Mark's early days is so trivial that it distinctly implies the absence of steady thinking on any subject." This is true so far as mere thinking is concerned. But, as Bradford himself fully realized, there never was a time when he was indifferent to corruption and cruelty, when he was not ready to smite the serpent wherever it should raise its ugly head.

In Hannibal days, to be sure, he tells us he felt no particular aversion to slavery as an institution, though we know that he did react strongly to individual instances of ill treatment. His abstract speculative turn had not yet developed. When he gets to Carson City, we find him, for the only time in his career, wielding political influence, directly through his pen, indirectly as the brother of Orion Clemens, Secretary of the Territory. Later he becomes a Comstock journalist and frankly casts himself as Childe Roland. In San Francisco he is shocked by political corruption, and since the *Call* will not print his articles he sends them back to Joe Goodman's *Enterprise*. It is not long before he is being called the "Moralist of the Main," and political corruptionists, no doubt, are calling him other names as well. I know nothing in Mark Twain's career that is more disinterested or more creditable to him than his exposé of the wanton cruelties to which Orientals were subjected in California. Even the notorious Empire City hoax[1] had a serious purpose, being intended to expose the habit of "cooking dividends" among California speculators, though it must be admitted that Mark's zeal was not wholly disinterested in this connection.

He brought the habits he had formed on the Comstock with him to the east coast. He had caricatures of the leaders of the Erie Railroad Ring running through his *Burlesque Biography,* published in 1870, and the sketch, "A Curious Dream," called the attention of the public to the disreputable condition of one of the city's cemeteries, thus inspiring directly a movement for reform. Other sketches of the period attack the growing use of the insanity plea as a means of making it possible for murderers to escape the just reward of their crimes, the mounting expenses of government, and the dishonest habit of making out fraudulent tax returns.

It is not necessary to trace this tendency in any detail through Mark Twain's later writings: the shortcomings of the jury system are attacked in *Roughing It;* *Life on the Mississippi* contains a strong plea for cremation; the feud as an institution is attacked in *Huckleberry Finn;* and the monstrous wickedness of war is abundantly excoriated in *The Mysterious Stranger.* To this we must add the letters and the speeches. Woman suffrage, justice to negroes and Indians, more careful supervision of our railways—this by no means exhausts the list of causes that Mark Twain espoused in the course of his life. Undoubtedly his most spectacular public service came in connection with his assault against Tammany; and that he did not shrink from incurring personal discomfort in the interest of the public welfare is sufficiently shown in the pains he took to prosecute a cabman who had overcharged his servant, Katy Leary.

The two great satires are, however, *The Gilded Age* and *A Connecticut Yankee.* The former is poor stuff indeed from a literary point of view, but it will always remain a significant social document, and Mr. DeVoto is entirely just when he remarks of its author: "Alone among the novelists of the time he concerns himself with the national muck. In him only exist the

boom towns, the railroad builders, the Dilworthies, the lobby-
ists, the gallicized Irish, society swelling to a gimcrack pretension with the manure of empire under its finger nails, the monster fungus of the gilded age." Parrington complains that his
criticism never gets to the root of the matter, that he never realized that the kind of thing that so disgusted him in Washington "was only the backwash of the spirit of exploitation" with
which he himself was connected as speculator and as business
man, and he goes on to observe that "with the innocence of his
generation," Mark Twain "damned the agent and overlooked
the principal." This is no doubt true, yet it is something to have
seen even as far as he saw—and to have spoken out concerning
it. It was more than the others could do.

The *Yankee* is, however, a much greater book than *The
Gilded Age,* and that criticism is particularly obtuse which sees
Mark Twain, in the *Yankee,* deserting the problems of his own
time to take refuge in the past, and relieving his *saevo indig-
natio* by blowing off steam on the very "safe" subject of the
iniquities of sixth-century England. There are passages in the
book which mislead the careless reader, and there is much
fumbling of materials, but there is nothing to excuse such a verdict. It is the crimes of the Gilded Age against which Mark
Twain turns his most gallant lances in the *Yankee,* and the fact
that he has chosen to make a romance out of his parable does
not prove that he was a coward; it simply shows that he was an
artist and no mere pamphleteer.

The artist has an advantage over the pamphleteer also, even
from the mere practical point of view of securing a hearing,
and of course the humorist has an advantage even over the serious artist. Men will often tolerate in jest what they cannot bear
to have said in earnest, and when the process has been repeated
over a considerable period, there is always the chance that somebody may discover the virtue of the jest. Mr. Paine glances at
this circumstance in his commentary on Mark Twain's service
to the cause of Grover Cleveland in 1884, when he tells us that
he "made political speeches which invited the laughter of both

parties, and were universally quoted and printed without regard to the paper's convictions." As we shall see a little later, many of Mark Twain's best pronouncements on international questions are in this class.

In observing Mark Twain's record as a reformer, it is impossible to avoid being impressed by the strong note of chivalry running through it; temperamentally he was always on the side of the underdog. He might or he might not believe in the cause, he might or might not admire the people involved, but let him once be convinced that an injustice was being practiced, and he would immediately constitute himself counsel for the defense. He had a particular interest in osteopathy, for example, and when the Bell bill proposed to drive the osteopaths out of the state of New York, he urged that they might be allowed to continue to practice. He had no love for the Mormons and no sympathy with their peculiar tenets, but this did not prevent him from denouncing the oppression under which they had suffered. The Jews he did consistently admire as a people and considered the most gifted race in the world. Some of us have had to wait until very recent times to have our eyes opened to the shameful exploitation of the colored races of the world that has been carried on by men of our own complexion under the pretense that we were sharing the blessings of civilization with our less fortunate brothers. Mark Twain saw through the hollow hypocrisy of such tommyrot as far back as the 'seventies, and he did not hesitate to express his views.

This was, perhaps, a bit easier for him than it has been for many white persons, for the reason that he did not, like many whites, regard the dark-skinned races as invariably ugly. He was, in fact, remarkably free from race prejudice in general: his record in this respect is marred only by a dislike—to which he freely confesses—of the French. "I am quite sure that (bar one) I have no race prejudices, and I think I have no color prejudices nor caste prejudices nor creed prejudices. Indeed, I know it. I can stand any society. All that I care to know is that a man is a human being—that is enough for me; he can't be any worse."

This was undoubtedly due, in the first place, to his having been brought up among negroes, for—all unfair discriminations notwithstanding—the Southerner did, even in slavery days, often understand the negro better and love him more than the Northern abolitionists who were so untiring and so vociferous in his defense. It is always a comparatively easy thing to become enthusiastic about the rights of a race we do not have to live with. It was not the black skin, it was the brown, that Mark Twain finally chose as "the most beautiful and satisfying of all the complexions that have been vouchsafed to man."[2] Nevertheless he loved the negro, and probably no white man ever dealt more justly with that race than Mark Twain did in *Pudd'nhead Wilson*, where all its faults are so mercilessly revealed, yet so tenderly and understandingly, so utterly without any sense of racial superiority. In life, too, he had an infinite charity for the negro's shortcomings, and Mrs. Clemens once suggested that he might save himself a good deal of trouble if he would only consider every man colored until he was proved white. He once paid the way of a negro student through Yale University, explaining "that he was doing it as his part of the reparation due from every white to every black man."[3] There is many a fine passage in the story of Nigger Jim, but the profoundest touch in all Mark Twain's writing on the race question will be found in the passage where Huck tells Aunt Sally about the steamboat accident:

" 'Good gracious! anybody hurt?'
" 'No'm. Killed a nigger.'
" 'Well, it's lucky; because sometimes people do get hurt.' "

Was there anything more to be said about slavery after that?[4]
Diverse opinions have been entertained concerning Mark Twain's courage as a reformer. Van Wyck Brooks is again the devil's advocate, viewing Mark Twain as the slave of his environment, unwilling ever to take a stand in behalf of an unpopular cause. It was because of this cowardice that he gave up the opportunity to become the great American satirist, donning

instead the cap and bells of the popular entertainer. Ashamed of his own record in this particular, he found his favorite authors among those like Suetonius, Lecky, Pepys, and Saint-Simon— outspoken all, as he had never dared to be—and as time went on he became more and more pessimistic about himself and the world.[5] At the other end of the scale is Mr. DeVoto who declares that "research can find few elements of the age that Mark Twain did not burlesque, satirize, or deride," and cites many instances to prove his argument.[6] The truth lies, I think, somewhere between the two. Mr. DeVoto's facts are facts, but the Gorky incident is a fact also. It is a fact that Mark Twain deliberately withheld from publication many articles of the tenor of the powerful "War Prayer," that he failed publicly to express his convictions on the Boer War, even going so far as to withdraw an article that he had intended for publication, that he deliberately deceived the public with regard to his opinions concerning the conflict between Russia and Japan.[7]

It is a very dangerous thing for a man to write for publication the things that he does not believe, and it is more dangerous, not less, when he tries to spread the compost on the weeds by writing another version of his letter for private consumption. Mark Twain was almost obsessed with the idea that the force of public opinion was irresistible. "If I had lived in the beginning of things," he declared, "I should have looked around the township to see what popular opinion thought of the murder of Abel before I openly condemned Cain. I should have had my private opinion, of course, but I shouldn't have expressed it until I had felt the way." More seriously he argues in behalf of the same course in his paper on "Corn Pone Opinions." He defends Twichell for flattering the prejudices of his congregation by always, after his one early apostasy, voting the Republican ticket. "I have never found any real fault with him . . . for the reason that, situated as he was, with a large family to support, his first duty was not to his political conscience, but to his family conscience. . . . He sacrificed his political independence, and saved his family by it. In the circumstances, this was the highest loyalty, and the best. If he had been a Henry Ward Beecher it would not have been his privilege to sacrifice his political conscience, because in case of dismissal a thousand pulpits would have been open to him, and his family's bread secure." As a piece of reasoning, it is not indefensible, but there is no hint in it of the stuff of which martyrs are made.

He himself was "a Henry Ward Beecher," or something more, yet it is clear that in many ways he was tied up with the established order, and this alliance served as a deterring influence often when he wished to speak out. There was, for example, his friendship with H. H. Rogers. "How Mark Twain can accept favors from him," wrote John Burroughs, after the seventieth birthday celebration, "is a mystery." A friend offers Webster and Company a book arraigning Standard Oil. "I wanted to say," writes Mark Twain, "the only man I care for in the world, the only man I would give a d—n for, the only man who is lavishing his sweat and blood to save me and mine from starvation is a Standard Oil magnate. If you know me, you know whether I want the book or not." Under the circumstances, what else could he say? But he was never in any danger of starvation, however great Rogers' services to him may have been, and it is clear enough that what he takes here is not the social but the personal view.

II

—In his later years, Mark Twain loved to think of himself as a philosopher, and in his own opinion by far the most important aspect of his Testament was, as we have seen, the idea of mechanistic determinism that he called his "Gospel." This has been expounded so carefully in *What Is Man?*—or, more succinctly, in "The Turning Point of My Life"—and so picturesquely illustrated in *The Mysterious Stranger* that no more than the briefest summary need be attempted here. As he put it to Mr. Paine in 1906: "When the first living atom found itself afloat on the great Laurentian sea, the first act of that first atom led to the *second* act of that first atom, and so on down through the succeeding ages of all life, until, if the steps could be traced, it would be shown that the first act of the first atom has led inevitably to the act of my standing here in my dressing-gown at this instant talking to you."

From this presupposition it follows inevitably that man is a machine, an impersonal engine. "Whatsoever the man is, is due to his *make,* and to the *influences* brought to bear upon it by his heredities, his habitat, his associations. He is moved, directed, COMMANDED by *exterior* influences—*solely*. He originates nothing, not even a thought." Mark Twain varies the force he assigns to temperament and training, but he never allows more than an infinitesimal leeway to the will of the individual. "When you come to think of it," he told Kipling, "neither religion, training, nor education avails anything against the force of circumstances that drive a man. Suppose we took the next four-and-twenty years of Tom Sawyer's life, and gave a little joggle to the circumstances that controlled him. He would, logically and according to the joggle, turn out a rip or an angel." Kipling asked: "Do you believe that, then?" And Mark Twain replied: "I think so. Isn't it what you call Kismet?"

Logically, the point of view destroys all personal responsibility for conduct. No merit attaches to the brave man, no blame to the coward. "There are gold men, and tin men, and copper men, and steel men, and so on—and each has the limitations of his nature, his heredities, his training, and his environment." Moreover, he will not allow the possibility of any unselfish action. *"From his cradle to his grave a man never does a single thing which has any* FIRST AND FOREMOST *object but one— to secure peace of mind, spiritual comfort, for* HIMSELF." This does not mean that all men are forever exploiting their fellows. In the development of life from the primordial seed it has fortunately come about that some men can find satisfaction only through doing good. "A man performs but *one* duty—the duty of contenting his spirit, the duty of making himself agreeable to himself. If he can most satisfactorily perform this sole and only duty by *helping* his neighbor, he will do it; if he can most satisfyingly perform it by *swindling* his neighbor, he will do that."

It does not fall within my province to attempt a critical estimate of Mark Twain's philosophy as such. I am interested only
to determine why he adopted it, which of his own needs it satisfied, and what the effect it had upon him may have been, and I
have already anticipated some of the considerations that fall under this head in what I have written concerning his pessimism.
That the system is the product of a brilliant but essentially untrained mind is evident upon the face of it. A keen eye has been
at work, observing certain of the facts of human life; a keen
and fearless mind has made a remorseless analysis of them and
has not shrunk from drawing some very unpalatable conclusions. But there is a good deal, too, that has been overlooked.[8]

That his system did not satisfy all his own needs, we have already seen, and he is far from consistent in his employment of
it. If Mark Twain is anything he is a moralist, yet there is no
room for morality in his philosophy of life. He tries hard to
bring about a *rapprochement* between his mind and his moral
judgments. There is a noble passage in *A Connecticut Yankee*,
where, anticipating his later full-grown determinism, he writes:
"All that is original in us, and therefore fairly creditable or dis-
creditable to us, can be covered up and hidden by the point of a
cambric needle, all the rest being atoms contributed by, and inherited from, a procession of ancestors that stretches back a billion years to the Adam-clan or grasshopper or monkey from
whom our race has been so tediously and ostentatiously and un-
profitably developed. And as for me," he goes on, "all that I
think about in this plodding sad pilgrimage, this pathetic drift
between the eternities, is to look out and humbly live a pure and
high and blameless life, and save that one microscopic atom in
me that is truly *me:* the rest may land in Sheol and welcome for
all I care." The "Gospel" itself has one important passage that
accords as ill with the main line of his determinism: "Diligently
train your ideals *upward* and *still upward* toward a summit
where you will find your chiefest pleasure in conduct which,
while contenting you, will be sure to confer benefits upon your
neighbor and the community." The advice is admirable. Only,

as Paine, who himself accepted Mark Twain's philosophy, remarked truly: "Once admit the postulate that existence is
merely a sequence of cause and effect beginning with the pri-
mal atom, and we have a theory that must stand or fall as a
whole. We cannot say that man is a creature of circumstance
and then leave him to select his circumstance, even in the minutest fractional degree."

Once, with bitter irony, Mark Twain employed the determin-
istic philosophy itself to damn his victim far more thoroughly
than he could ever have been damned on any other basis. He
wrote, it will be recalled, "A Defence of General Funston" for
his treacherous capture of Aguinaldo. Funston, he urged, was
not to blame for what he did: he was only following the natural
bent of his nature, even as George Washington did. "In each
case, the basis or moral skeleton of the man was inborn disposition—a thing which is as permanent as rock, and never under-
goes any actual or genuine change between cradle and grave."
We are told of Funston further that "his It took as naturally to
moral slag as Washington's took to moral gold, but only It was
to blame, not Funston." It would be as unfair to blame him for
this "as it would be to blame him because his conscience leaked
out through one of his pores when he was little—a thing which
he could not help, and he couldn't have raised it, anyway." In
its specific application to Funston, all this is magnificent. But it
hardly solves the logical dilemma.

Since, then, determinism did not satisfy Mark Twain's needs,
since, as we have already seen, it came so far short of satisfying
them as to contribute to the development of the pessimism that
ultimately engrossed him, why did he adopt this philosophy of
life? why did he contend so doughtily in its behalf? The influence of Lecky is unquestionable; Miss Brashear has made it
seem likely that Thomas Paine, Hobbes, Mandeville, Locke,
Hume, and Newton may—any or all of them—have made some
contribution. And there was his friend Macfarlane, who unfortunately seems to have got hold of him at a particularly impres-
sionable moment. But we are in search of more fundamental

causes. Was there anything in Mark Twain's own temperament, in addition to what we have already studied, that made determinism an attractive philosophy to him?

Mr. Brooks, of course, connects the whole thing, once more, with Mark Twain's betrayal of his artistic ideals in the interest of the Gilded Age. He knew that he had sinned against the light. He comforted himself with the reflection that man—including, that is, Samuel L. Clemens—was not responsible for his deeds.

I think it is not necessary to go so far as this, not with that "trained Presbyterian conscience" that Mark Twain possessed, that pernickety, unenlightened conscience that damned him almost as vigorously when he was wholly innocent as it did when he was guilty. Huck complains justly of the clumsy functioning of this instrument. "But that's always the way, it don't make no difference whether you do right or wrong, a person's conscience ain't got no sense, and just goes for him *anyway*. If I had a yaller dog that didn't know no more than a person's conscience does I would pison him. It takes up more room than all the rest of a person's insides, and yet ain't no good, nohow." That this is an accurate description of what went on in Mark Twain himself, there can be no doubt whatever. We have already observed it in his family life. His severest critics will not find him lacking here. Indeed it is likely to be a part of their argument that he sacrificed his artistic integrity to his family devotion. Yet if you were to listen to him, you must conclude that he was the worst husband and father on record, a selfish, heartless, tyrannical blatherskite. One does not need to be a psychoanalyst to realize that a man with such a temperament would inevitably derive a certain comfort from throwing his responsibilities back in the face of the universe.

> Oh, Thou, who Man of baser Earth didst make
> And ev'n with Paradise devise the Snake:
>   For all the Sin wherewith the Face of Man
>   Is blackened—Man's Forgiveness give—and take!

Perhaps such a man, up to a point, needs determinism. If he succeeded in deriving any comfort from it, let us be glad for his sake: there certainly were discomforts and disadvantages in plenty. And what man save one enormously conscientious could make a part of his very "Gospel" of selfishness the principle that mankind's ruling motive is to secure "peace of mind, spiritual comfort" for itself! It is truly an hypothesis which does undeserved honor to the moral aspirations of mankind.

One need not claim for Mark Twain that his self-reproaches were never just; there are times when, being human, he does fail in his responsibilities. The final word in this connection may be given to Mrs. Lucy Lockwood Hazard, who writes in her stimulating study of *The Frontier in American Literature* these words, which I accept without reservation:

"Mark Twain finds himself confronted by the spectacle of a world where the strong use their strength in brutal and unscrupulous domination, where the shrewd achieve their purposes by contemptible trickery, where the weak struggle in vain. He is too intelligent to join in the blind adulation of the successful, he is too tenderhearted to join in the superior scorn of the unsuccessful, he is too deeply involved in the hazards and triumphs of the Gilded Age to extricate himself from it and launch such an unqualified invective as was poured forth a generation later by the muckrakers. He takes refuge in a philosophy of fatalism which transfers the responsibility from the individual to the universal."

III

THE contemporary nudist movement lends a timely interest to the subject of Mark Twain's attitude toward nakedness. Born and reared as he was in a community dominated by Puritan ideals, there was, of course, a considerable distance between young Sam Clemens and a good many modern children, who have never been taught to be ashamed of their bodies, and who, consequently, are no more particularly concerned about their sexual organs than they would be about their great toes. The idea of permitting boys and girls to play naked together had not occurred to many persons as possible or desirable in that day, and so young Sam Clemens recounts the delightful story of his embarrassment when, after rehearsing a bear act for an amateur play in a state of complete nudity, he suddenly discovered that three pairs of feminine eyes were watching him curiously from behind a screen. But when boys were off by themselves, such empty superstitions as modesty and shame did not trouble them, and they accepted as their motto the words of Huck Finn: "Clothes is well enough in school, and in towns, and at balls, too, but they ain't no sense in them where there ain't no civilization nor other kinds of bothers and fussiness around." Huck and Jim wear no clothes on the raft: "we was always naked, day and night, whenever the mosquitoes would let us— the new clothes Buck's folks made for me was too good to be comfortable, and besides I didn't go much on clothes, nohow." The book has never been either filmed or illustrated correctly, from this point of view.

It is not merely that clothes are uncomfortable however: Tom Sawyer and his comrades clearly recognize the play function of nakedness. "After breakfast they went whooping and prancing out on the bar, and chased each other round and round, shedding clothes as they went, until they were naked, and then continued the frolic far away up the shoal water of the bar, against the stiff current, which later tripped their legs from under them from time to time and greatly increased the fun. . . . When they were well exhausted, they would run out and sprawl on the hot, dry sand. . . . Finally it occurred to them that their naked skin represented flesh-colored 'tights' very fairly; so they drew a ring in the sand and had a circus. . . ." Another day, they decided to play Indian; "so it was not long before they were stripped, and striped from head to heel with black mud, like so many zebras—all of them chiefs, of course—and then they went tearing through the woods to attack an English settlement."

We may hope, for his sake, that Mark Twain, in his boyhood,

neglected no opportunity to participate in these shameless
frolics, as they came his way, but years and responsibility took
the blessed privilege away from him; he lived in an upholstered
age. He could denounce the uncomfortableness of men's clothing; he could refuse to wear the fashionable pajamas, because in
them he "missed the refreshing and luxurious sense, induced by
the nightgown, of being undressed, emancipated, set free from
restraints and trammels." As he got older, he could extend this
refreshing and luxurious ease into the day by doing as much of
his work in bed as possible. Even, when as an old man he moved
out to Stormfield, where there were no near neighbors, he could
run about the house, if he chose, in his nightgown and slippers,
and he could write an account of it to his friend Mrs. Rogers, as
if he felt he had been a thoroughly bad boy and had hugely enjoyed it. In his time, a few bare legs were beginning timidly—
his contemporaries would have said brazenly—to appear on our
beaches. "I suppose we can all remember the first time we saw
bare-armed, bare-legged young ladies paddling in the surf, and
how confounded and affronted we were by that gross exhibition
of indecency. But we can stand it now, can't we? Certainly—
and like it, too." When he met a woman like Mrs. Karl Ger-
hardt, who posed nude for her husband's sculpture, and talked
about it frankly, and was absolutely unself-conscious about it, he
marveled—and admired.

That was about all adult America could give him in the way
of nakedness—that and the privilege of denouncing heartily the
inanity of placing fig leaves over the genital organs of works of
sculpture. ("The statue that advertises its modesty with a fig-
leaf really brings its modesty under suspicion.") But fortunately
he traveled, and his travels carried him sometimes into very be-
nighted countries, where the simple natives had never learned
that God is indecent. This strange point of view he encountered
in the Sandwich Islands, where the children ran about as God
made them and intended them to be, "clothed in nothing but
sunshine—a very neat fitting and picturesque apparel indeed,"
and where even grown men and women could bathe naked to-

gether, with no thought of shame. On the astonished eyes of the "Innocents," similar sights often burst: "A girl apparently thirteen years of age came along the great thoroughfare dressed like Eve before the fall"—and it was by no means uncommon to come upon men bathing "stark-naked," in full view of the road, and "making no attempt at concealment." But "an hour's acquaintance with this cheerful custom reconciled the pilgrims to it, and then it ceased to occasion remark." In Germany, even in the days of his "tramp" there, naked children were often encountered, and he enjoyed the sight of their fresh young bodies. In Colombo, much later, when he was "following the equator," he comments particularly on one little boy who "had nothing on but a twine string round his waist, but in my memory the frank honesty of his costume still stands out in pleasant contrast with the odious flummery in which the little Sunday School dowdies were masquerading."

Mark Twain was never a nudist in the sense in which Whitman and Benjamin Franklin were nudists, but this is by no means the only occasion when he places the seal of his approval on nakedness. In a public address toward the close of his life, he declared that "the finest clothing made is a person's own skin," and adds that the best-dressed man he ever knew was a native of the Sandwich Islands who, when he wished to be particularly fine in honor of some public occasion would sometimes put on a pair of spectacles, but who otherwise went as he had been born. Finally, among his private memoranda there are two notes which go far as any nudist could ask:

MODESTY ANTEDATES CLOTHES
& will be resumed when clothes are no more.

MODESTY DIED
when clothes were born.

IV

MARK TWAIN was not a "joiner." It was never his habit to delegate his right to make decisions to others; instead he found "spiritual comfort" and "peace of mind" in standing firmly on his own feet and being responsible to nobody. So it was very natural that he should have no faith in party government, and should pass at will from one political party to another, finding it impossible to give his vote to other than what he considered the best man, regardless of his party affiliation. In 1884, he was vitally interested in the election of Cleveland. At one time, he proposed to solve the American problem by organizing what he called a "casting vote party," which was to consist of a body of independent voters, nominating no candidate of their own, but throwing their support to the best man nominated by the established parties. Such an organization, he believed, must hold the balance of power in any election, and thus compel Republicans and Democrats alike to put their best candidates forward.

His lack of interest in the machinery of government does not mean, however, that he was not interested in the democratic experiment. His political democracy rested on the soundest possible foundation, the one foundation without which political democracy can never be notably successful—I mean his social democracy. "There are no common people," he declares, "except in the highest spheres of society"—which is, perhaps, an inverted form of social snobbery after all, and he generously acknowledged that in the last analysis civilization must ultimately rest upon the hewers of wood and the drawers of water.

Such a man was not likely to have much sympathy with kings. "There never was a throne which did not represent a crime." It sounds a little hysterical today, now that kings are no longer a serious menace and seem to have been succeeded by so much worse evils. Remember that he came out of Hannibal, where the ideals of Jeffersonian democracy were still taken seriously, where the generous dreams of Jean Jacques Rousseau had power over the minds of men. "Another throne has gone down, and I swim in oceans of satisfaction. I wish I might live fifty years longer; I believe I should see the thrones of Europe selling at auction for old iron." He goes to Bayreuth, and the town is so full of royalty that he has difficulty in getting accommodations at the hotel. "The damned Royalty gets ahead of me every time! They get ahead of everything!" And with the charming inconsistency that is so characteristic of him—and of the human race—it must be this man who is singled out for special attention on the part of royalty, who sooner or later meets all the royalty of his time, and who, for all his boasted democracy, finds himself pleased by the attention of these criminals, and as grateful for their favors as any good monarchist could be!

But alas! democracy calls for much more than merely getting rid of kings, and if he did not know it at the outset, he came to realize it bitterly before the end. The Yankee declares that brutal laws are impossible in a democracy, but there were times when Mark Twain was not so sure. He hits the stupidity of Congress as early as the *Innocents,* and there has never been a much more appalling picture of governmental corruption than is presented in *The Gilded Age.* Colonel Sellers is genuinely hurt when Washington suggests that he ought to be in Congress—"I don't think there has ever been anything in my conduct that should make you feel justified in saying a thing like that." When Stormfield was broken into, he warned the burglars that if they persisted in their evil ways, they might expect at last to find themselves in the Senate. His final judgment is summed up in one of the *Equator* aphorisms, and it is devastating: "It could probably be shown by facts and figures that there is no distinctly native American criminal class except Congress."

One admits, of course, considerable exaggeration here for humorous effect: but it was not all exaggeration. And the problem of democratic government in America was a bigger question than that of the criminal impulses of Congressmen. The plain truth of the matter was that the hopes of the fathers had not been fulfilled. America had escaped the exploitation of royal houses, only to fall into the hands of other exploiters instead. Even universal suffrage, that foolproof safety valve, was proving far from infallible in practice. In all too many cases, it meant government by the incompetent, by the ignorant, by

those whose votes could be bought or unfairly controlled. Once
he proposed extra votes for property and learning. But not even
learning quite solved the problem. "There is one thing that always puzzles me: as inheritors of the mentality of our reptile
ancestors we have improved the inheritance by a thousand
grades; but in the matter of the morals which they left us we
have gone backward as many grades." And so, in his old age, he
saw America becoming a monarchy. The battle had been
fought on this side of the Atlantic, and it had been lost.

Of all the problems of government, there is only one, however, on which it is worth while, at this date, to study his views
in any detail, and this is the problem of international peace.
This may best be approached as we view him in connection
with the several national emergencies that he faced in the course
of his life.

The Mexican War was relatively unimportant. He was too
young to be greatly affected by it, nor could he develop a critical
attitude. He was pleased by the rhythm of marching feet, and
he wished he were old enough to march away himself, but this
was impossible. According to his own account in *Life on the
Mississippi,* he was, during his St. Louis days, on one occasion, a
member of a body of young men under military command, organized for the purpose of quelling a mob, but the account is so
plainly "doctored" for burlesque purposes that it is difficult to
make any definite assertion about it.

Similar difficulties confront us when we try to interpret his
Civil War experiences. "The Private History of a Campaign
That Failed" is obviously not an accurate account; Mr. Paine
asserts that the account of the killing of the soldier is pure fiction. Goodpasture dissents from Paine's own interpretation of
this episode, complaining that the biographer sees it in terms of
a Tom Sawyer lark. Mark Twain was no boy at the time, he reminds us. He was twenty-six years old, "a man of wide information and unusual experience of the world," even if he was "a
creature of enthusiasms, which followed one after another, the
latest obliterating all the rest." Goodpasture conjectures that the

real reason for his giving up fighting when he did was Orion's
appointment as Secretary of Nevada Territory, a circumstance
which Mark may first have heard of "while he was invalided
for some weeks, confined to his bed in a private home, with a
sprained ankle."⁹ Miss Brashear inclines to prefer to the "Private History" the reference to this period in the 1891 letter
which I quoted at length in Chapter I. But there is no more reason for regarding this as gospel truth than there is for so accepting the "Private History" itself. Exactly what happened at this
time is probably beyond recovery, but it is clear enough that
when the War began, the dapper young pilot we know as Sam
Clemens was supremely uninterested in the great problems involved, and that though, after the River was closed to naviga-
tion, he did permit himself to be inducted into a Hannibal company, he found the life little to his liking, and shortly took
French leave.¹⁰

Such conduct was by no means so unusual at the time as it
might seem to the modern reader. The West was so far from
the seat of hostilities, and military affairs out there were in such
a chaotic state, that the sense of detachment young Sam Clemens felt was at least as well justified as the same feeling on the
part of the average American when war broke out in Europe in
1914. Absence of purpose stands out clearly nevertheless: Mark
Twain has done no coherent or consecutive thinking either
about war in general or about this war in particular. He was
never very clear about the Civil War, not even as he considered
it retrospectively in later years. Goodpasture notes the significant fact that Susy's biography of her father omits his military
experiences altogether, taking him directly from the River to
Nevada Territory. "Evidently Mark had never talked about his
army life in her presence." But this does not mean necessarily
that he was ashamed of it, for Goodpasture himself quotes from
the speech he made introducing Henry Watterson, at a Lincoln's birthday celebration, in 1901, in Carnegie Hall: "I was
born and reared in a slave state, my father was a slave owner;
and in the Civil War I was a second lieutenant in the Confed-

erate service." This was a rather euphemistic way of putting it. In later years, to be sure, his sympathies were all with the North, Lincoln and Grant were among his great heroes, and he had the time of his life at the Grand Army reunion in Chicago in 1879. The only hint we get from him of any consciousness on his part that all this extravagant admiration conflicts in any way with the ideas he is gradually developing on the subject of war itself comes in one remark about Grant: "I did not admire him so much for winning the war as for *ending* the war."

The Spanish-American War was a very different matter. At the beginning, indeed, he was taken in by it. His chivalry, his sentimentalism, his hatred of monarchy betrayed him. "I have never enjoyed a war—even in written history—as I am enjoying this one. For this is the worthiest one that was ever fought, so far as my knowledge goes. It is a worthy thing to fight for one's freedom; it is another sight finer to fight for another man's. And I think this is the first time it has been done." He was writing from Vienna. He could not be expected to understand the real importance of Cuban sugar in the American market, nor did he know how effectively a race for newspaper circulation may help to stir up a war. He is jocose in his letter to Pond, but there is no doubt where he stands. "Old as I am, I want to go to the war myself. And I should do it, too, if it were not for the danger."

Then certain things happened. The theater of war shifted to the Pacific Ocean. Funston captured Aguinaldo "by methods which would disgrace the lowest blatherskite that is doing time in any penitentiary." An Iowa newspaper printed a letter sent by an American soldier to his mother in which the conduct of our brave troops in battle was accurately described: "We never left one alive. If any one was wounded, we would run our bayonets through him." The idealistic motives we had professed went completely by the board, and we seized the Philippines. To Clemens, as to William Vaughn Moody and Carl Schurz, it seemed a base betrayal of everything worth fighting for, of everything worth living for, in America; and the jester grew overnight into the stature of a major prophet when, in May, 1902, the *North American Review* carried his "Defense of General Funston." No sterner piece of excoriation ever came from the pen of an eighteenth-century satirist. For once his tendency to exaggeration did not betray him; not even his imagination could surpass the horrible truth. There had been times in the past when his denunciations had seemed slightly hysterical, as if he were a man of generous impulses with an imperfect control over his temper; at last he had found a subject that was worthy of him. In 1900, he refused to go to the polls. He would not vote for Bryan on account of his financial heresy, and he could not vote for McKinley, "the man who sends our boys as volunteers out into the Philippines to get shot down under a polluted flag." He was coming to feel that we needed a new flag anyway, one that would more accurately reflect our true aspirations: "we can have . . . the white stripes painted black and the stars replaced by the skull and crossbones."

Other events of the period continued his political education. His visit to South Africa had prepared him for the Boer War, and in 1897, when he wrote his "Letters to Satan," he informed that plenipotentiary that it was quite unnecessary "to grease Mr. Cecil Rhodes's palm any further, for I think he would serve you just for the love of it. . . ." Introducing Winston Churchill at a dinner in New York in 1900, he held forth on the kinship between England and America, concluding with the observation that now that the two nations were "kin in sin," the bond ought to be closer than ever. Privately he told Churchill in no uncertain terms what he thought of his country's conduct, and Churchill fell back on the old bromide, "My country, right or wrong." "Ah," said Mark Twain, "when the poor country is fighting for its life, I agree. But this was not your case." And in the book he gave Churchill he wrote one of his favorite mottoes: "To do good is noble; to teach others to do good is nobler; and no trouble."

Being prepared, he had no need, this time, as in the case of the Spanish-American War, to wait for the course of hostilities

themselves to open his eyes. At the moment the British ultimatum expired, he wrote in his Diary: "Without a doubt the
first shot in the war is being fired to-day in South Africa *at this
moment. Some* man had to be the first to fall; he has fallen.
Whose heart is broken by this murder? For, be he Boer or be
he Briton, it is murder, & England committed it by the hand of
Chamberlain & the Cabinet, the lackeys of Cecil Rhodes & his
Forty Thieves, the South Africa Company." Yet he would not
speak out, as he wished to speak: "Every day I write (in my
head) bitter magazine articles about it, but I have to stop with
that. For England must not fall; it would mean an inundation
of Russian and German political degradations which would envelop the globe and steep it in a sort of Middle-Age night and
slavery which would last till Christ comes again. Even wrong
—and she is wrong—England must be upheld. He is an enemy
of the human race who shall speak against her now."

It was an amazing conclusion, a plain *non sequitur,* and we
shall not be surprised if we find that the principles he deduced
from his war experiences were not altogether consistent. As late
as 1901, in the speech introducing Henry Watterson, which has
already been referred to, he espouses patriotism. "We of the
South were not ashamed, for, like the men of the North, we
were fighting for flags we loved; and when men fight for these
things, and under these convictions, with nothing sordid to tarnish their cause, that cause is holy, the blood spilt for it is sacred, the life that is laid down for it is consecrated." When he is
writing of foreigners, the tone is the same, as in the extraordinary passage from *Following the Equator:* "Patriotism is Patriotism. Calling it Fanaticism cannot degrade it; nothing can degrade it. Even though it be a political mistake, and a thousand
times a political mistake, that does not affect it; it is honorable
—always honorable, always noble—and privileged to hold its
head up and look the nations in the face." And China: "I am
with the Boxers every time. The Boxer is a patriot. He loves his
country better than he does the countries of other people. I wish
him success."

He can go even further than this. He had a childish sort of admiration for West Point, and West Point is one of the institutions with which the Connecticut Yankee blesses Arthurian England. As an "Innocent," he seems to approve Spain's "big stick" policy against the Moors, and his defense of the Jews seems to assume that if a man is to be a good citizen, he must be ready, in time of war, to fight for his country. Once he speaks fearfully of the Yellow Peril. In *Following the Equator,* he goes out of his way to plead for a great merchant marine which shall make it possible for the United States "to assert and maintain her rightful place as one of the Great Maritime Powers of the Planet."

There are times, however, when he will disclaim patriotism altogether. Macfarlane's influence was helpful here, for one of the ideas on which the Scotchman laid special stress was this—that man is "the sole animal in whom was fully developed the base instinct called *patriotism."* Mrs. Fields gathered that Mark was not a patriot: "He is so unhappy and discontented with our government that he says he is not conscious of the least emotion of patriotism in himself. He is overwhelmed with shame and confusion and wishes he were not an American." He feared that patriotism, as commonly taught to children, would make a worse, not a better, country for us in the end: "We teach the boys to atrophy their independence. We teach them to take their patriotism at second-hand; to shout with the largest crowd without examining into the right or wrong of the matter—exactly as boys under monarchies are taught and have always been taught."

It would be pretty difficult to reconcile such sentiments with those expressed in the preceding paragraphs, but consistency was never Mark Twain's strong point. On one subject, however, he is consistent, and this happens to be a subject which has been much in the public mind during recent years. When the Supreme Court of the United States refused to grant citizenship to Professor Douglas Clyde Macintosh, of the Yale Divinity School, because he would not swear to take part in any and all future wars in which the United States might see fit to engage, regardless of whether the quarrel in question were approved by his own conscience or not; when on similar grounds the application of Madame Rosika Schwimmer was refused, the state virtually claimed supreme control over the private conscience of the individual. On this issue, Mark Twain is perfectly clear. "I believe you said something about the country and the party. Certainly allegiance to these is well, but certainly a man's first duty is to his own conscience and honor; the party and country come second to that, and never first." He will not give up his right of private judgment. "I would not voluntarily march under this country's flag, or any other, when it was my private judgment that the country was in the wrong. If the country *obliged* me to shoulder the musket, I could not help myself, but I would never volunteer. . . . The unanimous vote of the sixty millions could not make me a traitor. I should still be a patriot, and, in my opinion, the only one in the whole country." The Connecticut Yankee perceives clearly that what the "country right or wrong" people are preaching is not patriotism but treason, for true loyalty is "loyalty to one's country, not to its institutions or its office-holders."

His instinctive, personal reaction to war is one of intense aversion always. Huck Finn turns physically sick at the sight of the feud, disgusted by the slaughter and killing practiced by the damned human race. The brutality of war comes out even in the Joan of Arc story, and Joan, like General Grant, is praised not so much for winning the war as for ending it. When he heard that the notorious General Blucher had received an honorary degree from Oxford, he was shocked, and the luster of his own honor was dimmed in his eyes. "Blucher a doctor like myself! And people like that, who delight in murder and rapine, receive honorary degrees!" He was shocked by the piling up of armaments, and never for a moment was he deceived by the fatuous lie that the way to avoid war is to be ready for it. "Tolstoy was right," he exclaims, "in calling army life 'a school for murder,'" and he speaks elsewhere of "that enslaver of nations, the standing army." In the light of what has been happening in America during recent years, as we have seen our government shooting up the figures for military expenditures to ridiculous heights—probably for the purpose of proving to the rest of the nations that we believe in our own Kellogg Pact—while our schools and colleges, all over the country, operate on drastically reduced budgets, and while, for many months, the teachers of the second largest city in the United States received not one penny in the way of salary, there is a statement in one of Mark Twain's speeches that one can hardly read today without approaching its irony. "When I read the Russian despatch further," he says, "my dream of world peace vanished. It said that the vast expense of maintaining the army had made it necessary to retrench, and so the Government had decided that to support the army it would be necessary to withdraw the appropriation from the public schools. This is a monstrous idea to us. We believe that out of the public school grows the greatness of a nation." Well, if we do, we have a curious way of showing it.

As a matter of fact, imperialism was already upon us—"It seems curious now that I should have been dreaming dreams of a future monarchy and never suspect that the monarchy was already present and the Republic a thing of the past"—and though Mark Twain may not have thought through the problem of war per se, he never had the slightest doubts concerning imperialism. The myth of white superiority made no appeal to him—though he was not an educated man, he could have "spotted" Spengler and Madison Grant for the silly charlatans that they are—and, like Shailer Mathews, he knew that the white man's burden is composed principally of loot. As for enlarging one's sphere of influence, "That is a courteous phrase which means robbing your neighbor. . . ." I am afraid Mark Twain had a very simple mind. It never occurred to him that the Christian virtues apply only to individuals, while nations are wholly exempt from their requirements; he could not grasp the sublime truth that while murder on a retail scale is always

murder, murder on a wholesale scale is sometimes a sacred
duty.

It was under the influence of his hatred of imperialism that
Mark Twain came, then, to write the caustic commentaries that
make it possible for us to claim him today, at his best, as a
prophet of the modern peace movement. "All Christendom is
a soldier camp," he cried. "The poor have been taxed in some
nations to the starvation point to support the giant armaments
which Christian governments have built up, each to protect itself from the rest of the Christian brotherhood, and incidentally
to snatch any scrap of real estate left exposed by a wealthy
owner." With such ideas in mind, he wrote his "War Prayer"
and prepared his fearful pageant of progress.[11] From this point
of view also he wrote his magnificent "Greeting from the Nineteenth to the Twentieth Century": "I bring you the stately nation named Christendom, returning, bedraggled, besmirched,
and dishonored, from pirate raids in Kiao-Chou, Manchuria,
South Africa, and the Philippines, with her soul full of meanness, her pocket full of boodle, and her mouth full of pious
hypocrisies. Give her soap and a towel, but hide the looking-
glass."

But, for all his indignation, he does not perceive the connection between imperialism, militarism, and the economic system.
He felt a warm sympathy for the poor, and he contended for
the right of labor to organize—a right not always granted very
gracefully in his day—but that was as far as he got. Howells is
perfectly just when he writes: "No one can read *The Connecticut Yankee* and not be aware of the length and breadth of his
sympathies with poverty, but apparently he had not thought out
any scheme for righting the economic wrongs we abound in."
It was the old story! He hated the sufferings, the injustices, the
inequalities that capitalism produces, but he never went so far
as to doubt the capitalist view of society as such.

There are times, too, when Mark Twain's very liberalism be-
clouds the peace issue for him, just as it does for the Commu-

nists of today. So thoroughly was he committed to the cause of
political democracy that it was very difficult for him not to feel
that violence was righteous if it resulted in overthrowing an unjust or a tyrannical government. He seems to have developed
this point of view under the influence of his enthusiasm for the
French Revolution. Of this he derived his impressions largely
from Carlyle and Dickens, though his enthusiasm surpasses that
of either one. "When I finished Carlyle's French Revolution in
1871," he writes Howells in 1887, "I was a Girondin; every time
I have read it since, I have read it differently—being influenced
and changed, little by little, by life and environment (and
Taine and St. Simon): and now I lay the book down once
more, and recognize that I am a Sansculotte!—And not a pale,
characterless Sansculotte, but a Marat. Carlyle teaches no such
gospel: so the change is in me—in my vision of the evidences."
Two years later, he speaks of the Revolution as, "next to the 4th
of July and its results . . . the noblest and holiest thing and the
most precious that ever happened in this earth."

Some persons could reason thus concerning the French Revolution—way off, so safe, a hundred years in the past—and still
shrink from applying the same reasoning to the problems of
their own time. Not so Mark Twain, not with the toiling,
sweating millions of Russia groaning and dying before his eyes.
"What is the Czar of Russia but a house afire in the midst of a
city of eighty millions of inhabitants?" If redress cannot come
in any other way, he is even ready to go so far as to sanction a
private revolution: "Of course I know that the properest way to
demolish the Russian throne would be by revolution. But it is
not possible to get up a revolution there; so the only thing left
to do, apparently, is to keep the throne vacant by dynamite
until a day when candidates shall decline with thanks." Emma
Goldman could not expect him to go further. In "The Czar's
Soliloquy," published in 1905, in the *North American Review,*
and not yet included in his collected works, this question is considered in some detail, and the Czar is made to say that the
moralists protect his family from the just reward of their crimes

by teaching that assassination is a crime, while the truth of the matter is that the Romanoffs, having made themselves independent of the law, must be regarded as outlaws, and "outlaws are a proper mark for anyone's bullet." When Theodore Roosevelt put an end to the Russo-Japanese War, Mark Twain's love of peace came into conflict with his desire to see a real revolution in Russia, and it was the latter that proved stronger. Had the war been allowed to go on, Japan, he believed, must thoroughly have trounced Russia, and the chains of Russian political enslavement would have been cut then and there. He can find nothing harsh enough to say, privately, of those who were so obtuse as to prevent this consummation and, as he believed, to postpone indefinitely the day of Russian freedom.

There can be no doubt, then, concerning the conclusions that he drew, not only as they affected Russia, but in general. The Yankee declares categorically that "all gentle cant and philosophizing to the contrary notwithstanding, no people in the world ever did achieve their freedom by goody-goody talk and moral suasion; it being immutable law that all revolutions that will succeed, must *begin* in blood, whatever may answer afterward." In his own person, he is quite as clear: "Do these liberation-parties think that they can succeed in a project which has been attempted a million times in the history of the world and has never in one single instance been successful—the 'modification' of a despotism by other means than bloodshed?" Is it Mark Twain, or is it Reinhold Niebuhr, writing *Moral Man and Immoral Society* in the bitter disillusionment of 1933?

In truth, all these problems are a good deal more compelling today than they were in Mark Twain's time; in feeling as he did about imperialism and about war, he was, in many ways, ahead of his time. Can we, then, claim for him a prophetic function? Mr. Brooks does not think that we can. "In all the years of his travelling to and fro through Europe," he writes, "he divined hardly one of the social tendencies that had so spectacular a dénouement within four years of his death." In Austria, for example, he was greatly impressed by the assassination of the empress, but he failed completely to understand the meaning of the clash between the Czech and the German deputies in the Reichsrath. But Mr. Paine assures me Mark Twain did know the War was coming and spoke of it specifically during a walk at Stormfield in 1909.

There are times when, as it were in spite of himself, Mark Twain glimpses the future—and recoils before it with something of the shocked humanity of the heroine of *Berkeley Square*. Like his younger contemporary, H. G. Wells, he had long appreciated the increasing futility and hopelessness of the armament race. He had observed, too, the fact that armaments were changing, that if war were to survive as an institution, its character must be radically changed. As men of the past had known it, war was doomed—he could see that—and he was wise enough to draw the conclusion to which Lord Bryce gave probably the classical expression when he remarked shortly before his death: "If we do not find some way to destroy war, war will destroy us."

Mark Twain's aging eyes were clouded as he peered into the future, clouded with anxiety and fear. There was science. He had never understood it very well, but he had believed in it. It was lifting the curse of backbreaking labor from mankind, making it possible for men to devote their energies to the business of developing a really beautiful human life. It was, too, demolishing ancient superstitions, so that man's soul, as well as his body, might stand upright, so that at last he might come to feel at home in this world where he must live. And now it seemed as if, in the end, science had prostituted itself. Man's moral and spiritual development had not kept pace with his mechanical development. It was Caliban, not Prospero, that ruled the world, and the very thing that had been counted upon to redeem humanity might turn out to be the thing that would destroy it altogether. He had had his doubts and fears for a long time. At the end of *A Connecticut Yankee,* he had shown how it might come. His readers had taken it there as mere burlesque, but he himself knew it might some day come to be enacted on the stage of the world in bitter earnest. Not even the torpedo, filled "with Greek fire and poisonous and deadly missiles," by the aid of which, when it was attached to a balloon, Colonel Sellers hoped to be able to capture the city of St. Louis was quite so ridiculous as people had taken it to be.[12] The Colonel never completed his torpedo because he was never able to get hold of his Greek fire. Some day men would get it—or something worse—and what must happen then? One day the Kaiser spoke of sending his U-boats to invade England, and Mark, his imagination set to work, got busy and developed a Wellsian kind of defense. But it was always easier to destroy than it was to defend—he knew that—and the defenses somehow did not seem to keep pace.

In *The Mysterious Stranger* he passed the ages in review. What did progress amount to except building ever deadlier and deadlier weapons? And what had Christianity, for all its boasted lip service of peace, ever done to arrest this development? Satan himself was shocked as he contemplated it: "In five or six thousand years five or six high civilizations have risen, flourished, commanded the wonder of the world, then faded out and disappeared; and not one of them except the latest ever invented any sweeping and adequate way to kill people. They all did their best—to kill being the chiefest ambition of the human race and the earliest incident in its history—but only the Christian civilization has scored a triumph to be proud of. Two or three centuries from now it will be recognized that all the competent killers are Christians; then the pagan world will go to school to the Christian—not to acquire his religion, but his guns. The Turk and the Chinaman will buy those to kill missionaries and converts with." Sometimes it even seemed to him, in his despair, that there was no use grieving over such things; a race capable of such stupidity and cruelty deserves nothing better than to be destroyed.

At the close of his *Education,* Henry Adams speculates on the possibility that "perhaps some day—say 1938, their centenary—" he and his two closest friends might be permitted to return to this earth for a holiday, "to see the mistakes of their own lives made clear in the light of the mistakes of their successors; and perhaps then," he continues, "for the first time since man began his education among the carnivores, they would find a world that sensitive and timid natures could regard without a shudder." Mark Twain's centenary is here; if he could come back, what would he have to say to us? He called us fools in 1910. I think he would be disposed now to take that back. The old adage tells us that experience keeps a dear school, but fools will learn in no other. The plain implication would be that even fools do learn in the school of experience. But we have lived through four years of hell in the longest and bitterest and most futile war that mankind has ever experienced. And here we are in 1935 with huge armies and navies and an American Legion approach to international problems. No, I think he could not call us fools.

Mark Twain had no peace program. He was not a statesman; he was ignorant of political economy. There are times when he plays into the hands of the enemy; there are times, too, when he comes perilously close to anticipating recent developments, as when, in his letter to W. T. Stead, he developed the idea of securing peace by compulsion, through a concert of the great powers.[13] But let us not forget that he has been dead for twenty-five years. "As far as I can make out," wrote Stuart Sherman, "he grew in sympathy, insight, bitterness, courage, and passion to the end. . . . Some of us had to wait for the sad years of the Great War, some of us for the sadder years after the war and some of us are still waiting, for the vision which came to him sharply in the last decade of the nineteenth century from observation of misery in India, in the atrocities of history, from personal sorrow, from the Spanish War and the Boer War and the pacification of the Philippines." He would have gone on growing could he have remained with us during these latter years when his passion and his insight have been so desperately needed, and if he were alive today, he would be in the very foremost rank of the peace movement. It would be something to hear him damn the imperialists and the big navy men and the munitions-makers and the patrioteers, burning them up in the white fury of his anger and consigning them to a thousandfold more terrible hell than ever Dante knew. Thanks to science and mechanical invention, mankind has come now, for the first time in the history of the world, to a place where it actually would be possible to build a paradise upon this earth. Nobody need ever go hungry any more; nobody need break his back with toil. And because we are too lethargic to intrust the operation of our political and economic machinery to those who have the brains and the conscience to take advantage of these circumstances for us, it must be at this very moment that we face the imminent possibility of such terror and destruction as mankind has never known, the possibility, indeed, of a return to chaos, which would undo everything that all the builders have achieved since life crawled out of the primeval slime. That would be the thing that would sadden Mark Twain most if he could come back on this, his centenary. But I think he would be glad that we connect him with our hopes as well as with our despairs. As late as 1932, an American presidential candidate, a successful candidate moreover, took from his pages the slogan and the battle cry of the "New Deal."[14] He would be in favor of a "New Deal" and yet a newer "New Deal" among the sons of men, and if the day ever comes when we have a warless world, then, at last, the boy from Hannibal will take his place among the prophets.

NOTES

Notes

BOOK I: MARK TWAIN

CHAPTER I: THE MATRIX

1. For further comments on the art of Dickens along the lines here indicated, *see* Edward Wagenknecht, *The Man Charles Dickens* (Boston, Houghton Mifflin Co., 1929), pp. 35–37. Among recent writers, the same type of experience is beautifully exemplified in Katherine Mansfield; *see* her *Letters* (New York, Alfred A. Knopf, 1929), October 11, 1917, February 10–11, 1918, November 3, 1920.

2. Paine, I, 26—chap. 7.

3. All this material is now conveniently summarized in Miss Brashear's *Mark Twain, Son of Missouri* (*see* Bibliography), the most important contribution to our knowledge of Mark Twain since Paine's biography itself. My facts concerning Hannibal, hereinafter, derive directly from Miss Brashear.

4. *Mark Twain, Son of Missouri*, pp. 85 ff.

5. In emphasizing the value for Mark Twain of the varied experiences through which life led him, one must not lose sight of the sound common sense in these words of Professor William Lyon Phelps: "And because Mark Twain was brought up on wider and more primitive scenes, it does not follow that he knew more about 'life' than Emerson, Hawthorne, Longfellow, Lowell, and Holmes. This is the boyish error of supposing that a man in a flannel shirt with his trousers tucked into his boots is more masculine than a man in evening clothes. Holmes was a physician; Hawthorne, Lowell, Longfellow lived for years in Europe; Emerson, the Yankee villager, made an estimate of Napoleon, the man of action, so shrewd and penetrating that no historian has ever been able to improve on it. Furthermore, these men were familiar with the Bible, Chaucer, Shakespeare, wherein they learned more about human nature than most cowboys will ever know. Radclyffe Hall cannot shock anyone who remembers the first chapter of St. Paul's epistle to the Romans. Mark Twain was fortunate in having certain experiences to use as material; but the reason he is a greater writer than Holmes is not because he knew more about 'life,' but because he was a man of genius." (*Scribner's Magazine*, XCIII [1933], 183.)

CHAPTER II: THE WORLD WITHIN

1. *Following the Equator* (Uniform Edition), II, 256 ff., chap. 23.

2. *Iowa Journal of History and Politics*, XXVII, 454.

3. E. W. Kemble, in *The Colophon*, Pt. I.

4. Cf. Gamaliel Bradford, *D. L. Moody, A Worker in Souls* (New York, George H. Doran & Co., 1927), chap. 4, sect. 7.

5. Professor Olin H. Moore's was the pioneering article in the study of Mark Twain's reading; since then both Mr. Pochmann and Miss Brashear have done a great deal in this field. (*See* Bibliography.) The basic references I had already collected for myself before consulting their work. Since then, however, I have derived great benefit from them, and all three have been very kind to me personally. I have made an effort to indicate specific indebtedness wherever possible.

6. Will Clemens was not a relative, and Mark Twain never had any use for him

or for his book. As a reporter he is inaccurate and must be used with caution, but in this instance the quoted passage seems to fit the known facts.

7. Professor Moore points out that Tom Sawyer evidences knowledge of the stories of Robin Hood, Friar Tuck, Guy of Gisborne, Much the Miller's son, and the Sheriff of Nottingham. He has some acquaintance with American history, especially the colonial period, and there are touches which seem to come from Lecky. In *Huckleberry Finn*, Tom knows also *Don Quixote*, *The Lady of the Lake*, *The Arabian Nights*, *The Count of Monte Cristo*, and the lives of Cellini, Casanova, Baron Trenck, and the Vicomte de Bragelonne. He is familiar with heraldry and knows about Henry of Navarre and the attempted flight of Louis XVI. Even Huck instructs Jim concerning Solomon, Louis XVI, and others. Moore declares further that at this point Tom is no faithful portrait of the boy Sam Clemens, for Sam was no lover of books. I think it likely that Sam read more than Moore gives him credit for, though I do not deny that some material with which Mark Twain became familiar only after he had left Hannibal enters the picture at this point.

8. When *Is Shakespeare Dead?* was published, the *Independent* suggested that it might be a skit to "hoist the Baconians with their own petard—an exquisite parody." Miss Brashear (pp. 217–218 n.) accepts this view, and quotes a passage from *Midstream* in which Helen Keller records having told Mark Twain a friend had found evidence that Bacon wrote Shakespeare's plays, only to have Mark ridicule it heartily. This evidence, however, seems to me a mere drop in the scales against what is recorded in Paine, to say nothing of *Is Shakespeare Dead?* itself.

9. On *The Gilded Age* question, I am less interested in the question of specific features imitated—as the alleged resemblances between Sellers and Micawber—than I am in the question of style. Sellers' description of the clock in chap. 7 seems to me extremely Dickensian, and Senator Dilworthy's speech in chap. 53 (or chap. 22 of vol. II) might have been modeled directly on the remarks of the Reverend Mr. Chadband, in *Bleak House*, chapter 19. *See*, further, on the Dickens matters, M. M. Brashear, *Mark Twain, Son of Missouri*, pp. 211–212.

10. On November 16, 1886, Mark Twain writes to Mrs. A. W. Fairbanks: "It is very enjoyable work: only it takes three days to prepare an hour's reading. It takes me much longer to learn how to read a page of Browning than a page of Shakespeare. And mind you, I'm on the ABC only—his *easy* poems. The other day I took a glance at one of his mature pieces, to see how I am likely to fare when I get along over there. It was absolutely opaque!" MS., Huntington Library. For another amusing comment, see Mark Twain's letter to Mary Hallock Foote (Hartford, Dec. 2, 1887), in De Casseres, *When Huck Finn Went Highbrow*.

11. "I have written a new play by myself since we came to the farm, but I think I will let it lie & ripen under correction some months yet before producing it. I have a vast opinion of the chief character in it. I want to play it myself in New York or London but the madam won't allow it. She puts her 2½ down with considerable weight on a good many of my projects."—From a letter to Mollie Fairbanks, August 6, 1877. MS., Huntington Library.

12. In the essay, "About Play Acting," in *The Man That Corrupted Hadleyburg*.

13. From a letter to Mrs. Fairbanks, October 31, 1877. MS., Huntington Library.

14. *Letters*, II, 737–738 (May 4, 1903).

15. Cf. Chauncey W. Wells, "Thackeray and the Victorian Compromise," *University of California Publications in English*, I, 184: "If ever a literary movement might be called revolutionary the earlier romanticism deserved to be. But after Waterloo reaction gained the ascendancy, and the vogue of the Waverley novels was perhaps less a tribute to the genius of their author than a witness to a social ideal. In them

The World Within 271

an aristocratic society saw itself as in a flattering mirror, a vista of repeating mirrors, wherein even defects seemed often beautiful in picturesque distances."

16. A good many nonliterary works come in for special mention, including J. Howard Moore's *The Universal Kinship*, Andrew D. White's *History of the Warfare of Science with Theology*, and *The Religion of a Democrat* by Charles Zueblin. There is much quoted matter in Mark Twain's writings from informational books. Miss Brashear counts 9,000 words quoted in *The Innocents Abroad*, nearly 11,000 in *Roughing It* and the same amount in *Life on the Mississippi*, while *Following the Equator* has 25,000, or 1/25 of the whole.

17. Professor Moore's own summary of his article follows: "The influence of Cervantes, apparent already in *The Innocents Abroad*, is very manifest in *Life on the Mississippi*, where Mark Twain chooses Cervantes as a sort of standard bearer against the romantic Walter Scott. In *Tom Sawyer*, and especially in *Huckleberry Finn*, Mark Twain parallels closely the masterpiece of Cervantes. He alters the character of Tom Sawyer so that, like Don Quixote, he is an omnivorous reader of romance, and desires to act out the rôles of his favorite heroes. He alters also the character of Huckleberry Finn, transforming him from a very imaginative character to a prosaic Sancho Panza, a foil to the brilliant Tom Sawyer. For the romances of chivalry which turned the brain of Don Quixote, Mark Twain substitutes more modern romances, such as the Life of Baron Trenck, and *Monte Cristo*, which inspire the wild fancies of Tom Sawyer. In attempting the rôles of his favorite heroes, Tom Sawyer falls into frequent altercations with Huckleberry Finn which resemble closely the arguments between Don Quixote and Sancho Panza. One or two episodes from Don Quixote are imitated directly in Huckleberry Finn, with acknowledgment by the author. The *Connecticut Yankee in King Arthur's Court*, which contains numerous reminiscences of *Huckleberry Finn*, is essentially another imitation of *Don Quixote*, because of its satire upon chivalry and chivalric romances. Alisande ('Sandy'), speaking the language of Malory, or a modified version of Lecky, is the author's Don Quixote. The scoffing Yankee is his glorified Sancho Panza. One or two episodes in the *Connecticut Yankee* are apparently imitated directly from *Don Quixote*, and the author's style of humor is often strikingly similar to that of Cervantes." (*PMLA*, XXXVII, 345–346.) Schönemann (*Mark Twain als literarische Persönlichkeit*, p. 46) feels that Don Quixote influenced Colonel Sellers also.

18. *See* Charles Honce, *ed.*, *Adventures of Thomas Jefferson Snodgrass*, in Bibliography, I, B.

19. Schönemann's parallels concern not only *Gulliver* and *A Tale of a Tub*, but also "A Modest Defense of the Proceedings of the Rabble in All Ages," "A Critical Essay upon the Art of Canting," "A Discourse Concerning the Mechanical Operation of the Spirit," "A Critical Essay upon the Faculties of the Mind," and "Digression on the Nature, Usefulness, and Necessity of Wars and Quarrels." *Op. cit.*, pp. 42–43.

20. Originally published in *The Galaxy*, this paper is now available in *The Curious Republic of Gondour, and Other Whimsical Sketches* (New York, 1919). Schönemann (pp. 97–98) finds the influence of Goldsmith in such varied pieces as "A True Story" and "Riley—Newspaper Correspondent" (both character sketches); "Journalism in Tennessee," "Disgraceful Persecution of a Boy," "Lionizing Murderers," etc. (social and political essays); and numerous fables, dreams, anecdotes, etc. More specifically, he would have us compare *Citizen of the World*, 45–46, with "A Fable," *C.W.*, 12, with "The Undertaker's Chat," *C.W.*, 15 and 69, with "A Dog's Tale" (p. 90).

21. There is an amazing passage in a letter to Mollie Fairbanks, August 6, 1877—MS., Huntington Library—in which Mark Twain follows his introductory statement that he hasn't been reading anything of late with a long and varied list of books that he has read. Mr. Paine would take this and other letters to the Fairbankses "with

salt." "He was a great hand to 'show off,' especially to Mrs. Fairbanks, and others who understood him, and would take it in the half-mocking way he intended it."

22. Moore shows clearly the influence of both Malory and Lecky in *A Connecticut Yankee*. Cf. *PMLA*, XXVII, 340 ff.

23. Schönemann, *op. cit.*, pp. 74–75.

CHAPTER III: THE DIVINE AMATEUR

1. Constance Rourke (p. 214) cites Mark Twain's remarks, in *Life on the Mississippi*, on the nutritiousness of Mississippi water, and remarks thereupon: "That grotesque naturalism which had often approached ancient myth lived again briefly in such glimpses, here recalling—as in caricature—the legend of the buried Osiris, from whose body sprang the growing stalk of the corn."

Mr. West (*see* Bibliography) has made a careful study not only of the Mississippi Valley folklore in *Tom Sawyer* and *Huckleberry Finn,* but also of Mark Twain's interest in the folklore of other lands that he visited on his travels, and of his use of Continental folklore in *Joan of Arc*. His conclusion is that though Mark Twain was at times guilty of some confusion, as in his account of the Cardiff Giant, or when he makes Eve fear a ghost, still his interest in the subject was "almost scientific," and "he would have been an avid student of folklore," had the opportunity come his way.

2. From a letter to Mrs. A. W. Fairbanks, February 20, 1868. MS., Huntington Library.

3. Other influences have sometimes been adduced in this connection. The average reader thinks, first of all, of Mark Twain's platform work. His platform work undoubtedly accentuated his tendency to improvisation, but it did not cause it; in other words, he turned to the platform because the natural bent of his genius already lay in this direction. Mr. DeVoto is right when he tells us that, in order to understand Mark Twain, it is necessary to go back of the lyceum: we need to see him "in crossroads stores, on sunny wharves along the river, in the saloons and pilot houses of steamboats making downstream voyages by daylight above no bottom." (*Mark Twain's America*, p. 243.) Howells suggests still another influence: "In other words, Mr. Clemens uses in work on the larger scale the method of the elder essayists, and you know no more where you are going to bring up in *The Innocents Abroad* or *Following the Equator* than in an essay of Montaigne." Mark Twain, as we have seen, knew "the elder essayists" fairly well, but I am inclined to look upon the frontier background as the thing basically determinative.

4. Will M. Clemens tells this story (pp. 54–55). It is a great pity that we of these latter days can no longer hear Mark Twain's voice. No mere sentimental interest impels us, but rather the conviction that, Clemens being what he was, we shall never be able fully to understand him otherwise. Mr. Paine tells me that Mark Twain made a record of his seventieth birthday speech, but his secretary stored the wax cylinders in a warm attic and they were ruined. I am told further that the Fox Film Company made a reel of motion pictures showing Mark Twain at Stormfield; I hope Mark Twain museums, libraries, memorial associations, etc. will secure prints of these and preserve them for the future before it may be too late.

5. Cf. Dickens: "So real are my characters to me that on one occasion I had fixed upon the course which one of them was to pursue. The character, however, got hold of me and made me do exactly the opposite to what I had intended; but I was so sure that he was right and I was wrong that I let him have his own way." And, again: "My notion always is, that when I have made the people to play out the play,

it is, as it were, their business to do it, and not mine." *See* my *Man Charles Dickens,* pp. 21–22.

6. Mr. Brooks makes much of these limitations of Mark Twain, reinforcing his own theory that the man was at war with his environment, fundamentally out of sympathy with the kind of book he was trying to create. I cannot help remembering Chaucer, a writer who was securely at peace with his environment. Chaucer has, indeed, no difficulty in getting unity of tone. But of all his more elaborate undertakings, he brought only one—the *Troilus and Criseyde*—to completion.

7. John Macy writes (*The Spirit of American Literature,* p. 259): "To maintain Huck's idiom and through it to describe a storm on the Mississippi with intense vividness; through the same dialect to narrate the tragic feud between the Grangerfords and the Shepherdsons; to hint profound social facts through the mouth of a boy and not violate his point of view—this is the work of a very great imagination." I cannot agree that the mask is never laid aside. The achievement is, nevertheless, a great one.

8. To the article, "A Simplified Alphabet," included in the *What Is Man?* volume, Mr. Paine prefixes the note: "This article, written during the autumn of 1899, was about the last writing done by Mark Twain on any impersonal subject."

9. From a letter to Mrs. A. W. Fairbanks, April(?) 26, 1871. MS., Huntington Library.

10. From a letter to Mrs. A. W. Fairbanks, June 3, 1876, MS., Huntington Library.

11. Julian Hawthorne writes (*Overland Monthly,* LXXXVII, 111): "When a literary club to which we both belonged began to accept members on other grounds than that they should have 'produced works proper to literature,' he handed in his resignation; he wasn't paying his dues for the sake of consorting with office boys and millionaires."

12. Told in a letter to me from Professor Thomas Ollive Mabbott.

13. Howells, *My Mark Twain,* p. 49. The "certain author" is not therein further identified, but a letter from Howells in his daughter Mildred's collection (II, 281) makes it practically certain that it was Will N. Harben. "You seem to require a novelist to be true to the facts," writes Howells, "and if the facts are not pleasant to be pleasant himself. That seems rather difficult."

14. Swift, it will be remembered, defined style as the perfect word in the perfect place, and Emerson also laid considerable stress on this factor. Schönemann may be right in suggesting here the possible influence of Emerson on Mark Twain. (*Op. cit.,* p. 117.)

15. Told in a letter to Mrs. A. W. Fairbanks, February 25, 1874. MS., Huntington Library.

16. *Letters,* I, 230. To W. D. Howells, 1874.

BOOK II: MR. SAMUEL L. CLEMENS

CHAPTER I: PARADOXES

1. There is an asinine interpretation of this incident in terms of the Freudian "death-wish" in the notoriously ridiculous study of Mark Twain included in *The American Mind in Action,* by Harvey O'Higgins and Edward H. Reede. These gentlemen have apparently had very little experience with nervous children.

2. Madame Gabrilowitsch (*My Father Mark Twain,* pp. 84–85) tells of only one instance when his anger was directed against her, and this occurred when she held

up the traffic in Paris, making him and herself the cynosure of all eyes, by interfering with a brute who was beating his horse. His reaction is rather difficult to sense here, for nobody was ever more tender toward animals, and he certainly never objects, on other occasions, to being the center of men's attention. It may be, however, that he felt his daughter's conduct was not "ladylike." He would have been quite capable of it in one of his "respectable" moods.

3. My friend, Professor O. B. Sperlin heard Major tell the story at a reception in Shelbyville, Indiana, in 1904.

4. Mr. Paine has described how, in dictating his *Autobiography*, Mark Twain would waver between anger and pity. Once, after a denunciation, he added: "However, he's dead, and I forgive him." Then: "No, strike that last sentence out. . . . We can't forgive him—yet." (*Collier's*, LXXV [January 3, 1925], 6.)

5. Mr. DeVoto is much impressed by this incident, remarking absurdly that very few of the men who have attempted to write American literature have ever felt any such strong emotion as the passion to kill. He is answered for all time by Mr. Mumford, who points out that the attempt to solve a problem or to get rid of an unwelcome person by killing him is precisely the mark of the undeveloped mind.

6. As in the case of E. P. Hingston. Cf. Paine, I, 464, chap. 86.

7. From a letter to Mrs. A. W. Fairbanks, December 12, 1867. MS., Huntington Library.

8. Paine, I, 440, chap. 82.

9. John Burroughs, "Waiting."

10. Cf. her *New Methods for the Study of Literature* (University of Chicago Press, 1927).

11. The most impure suggestion in Mark Twain's canonical writings comes in an 1874 speech on "Cats and Candy" (*Speeches*, p. 262), where, telling the story of Jim Wolfe, he remarks, "He and I slept together—virtuously." In the last chapter of *A Tramp Abroad,* already referred to, he discusses literature and pornography, complaining how unfair it is that while art still possesses her liberties, literature should have lost hers. Inasmuch as he has just been in a tempest of righteous indignation over Titian's abuse of these privileges, it is hardly likely, however, that he meant this to be taken seriously.

12. *Iowa Journal of History and Politics*, XXVII, 538.

13. He had himself anticipated it, a decade before, in an inconspicuous passage in *Life on the Mississippi*, p. 239, chap. 31.

14. For the telephone, cf. "The Loves of Alonzo Fitz-Clarence and Rosannah Ethelton," in *Tom Sawyer Abroad.* For the radio, cf. Paine, III, 1364, chap. 253; Clara Clemens, *My Father Mark Twain*, p. 264. For motion pictures, cf. Paine, II, 871–872, chap. 167. For television, cf. "From the 'London Times' of 1904," in *The Man That Corrupted Hadleyburg.*

15. For the letter, cf. Lewis Mumford, *The Golden Day*, pp. 173–175.

16. For the juvenile literature, cf. Roades in Bibliography. George Wharton James (*Pacific Monthly*, XXIV, 126) shows clearly that in its own time *The Innocents Abroad* was not regarded as something new under the sun. Californians ranked it with John F. Swift's *Going to Jericho* and the travel books of Ross Browne.

17. Cf. Edward Wagenknecht, *A Guide to Bernard Shaw* (New York, D. Appleton & Co., 1929).

CHAPTER II: GOD'S FOOL

1. Professor Thomas Ollive Mabbott, who told me this incident, had it from his father, Dr. J. Milton Mabbott.

2. From a letter to Charles Fairbanks, June 25, 1890. MS., Huntington Library.

3. From a letter to Mrs. A. W. Fairbanks, February 9, 1868. MS., Huntington Library.

4. From a letter to Mrs. A. W. Fairbanks, March 13, 1869. MS., Huntington Library.

5. Cf. Paine, I, 195, chap. 35.

6. In an interesting essay on Mark Twain in *The Tocsin of Revolt,* Brander Matthews tells (pp. 289–290) the amusing story of how the humorist conducted himself during the academic procession at New Haven when he received a degree from Yale. Seven distinguished authors marched with him—Howells, Aldrich, Cable, Gilder, Thomas Nelson Page, Woodrow Wilson, and Matthews himself. But so far as the crowd along the street was concerned, Mark Twain was the only one, and he graciously received their homage as his royal due. His intimates in the procession accepted all this as a matter of course and enjoyed it, but Matthews wondered how those less closely associated with him must feel.

CHAPTER III: THE DAMNED HUMAN RACE

1. *See,* in this connection, the remarkable postscript to a letter to Rev. Joseph H. Twichell, November 4, 1904 (*Letters,* II, 763–764). "I wish I could learn to remember that it is unjust and dishonorable to put blame upon the human race for any of its acts." The passage should be read in full.

2. *See, also,* for satire on women: *Sketches of the Sixties,* pp. 188–190; remarks on the ugliness of French women (*Innocents Abroad,* I, 147, chap. 15) and of Mormon women (*Roughing It,* I, 121, chap. 14); *Speeches,* p. 317; *Life on the Mississippi,* chap. 45.

3. M. M. Brashear, *Mark Twain, Son of Missouri,* pp. 258–259, relates Mark Twain's attitude toward women to the background of his youth.

4. Fisher, pp. 78–79.

5. The article "Why Not Abolish It?" in *Harper's Weekly. See* Bibliography.

6. Howe, p. 255.

7. *Missouri Historical Review,* XXIV, 47.

8. I think Mr. Brooks may be amused at the suggestion that he overlooked at this point an argument he might have used. Mark Twain surrendered his freedom; the cat is the one altogether independent domestic animal; therefore Mark Twain admired the cat!

9. I am very much surprised to note that Mr. Pochmann has counted 186 references to dogs in Mark Twain's writings, as compared to only 140 to cats.

10. Cf. the birds in *A Tramp Abroad,* I, 23, chap. 2; the coyote in *Roughing It,* I, 48, chap. 5; the tiger cub in *Following the Equator,* II, 6, chap. 1.

CHAPTER IV: THE ROOT OF EVIL

1. *Iowa Journal of History and Politics,* XXVII, 438.

2. I discount H. W. Fisher's impression (*Abroad with Mark Twain and Eugene Field,* p. 137) that Mrs. Clemens drove her husband, that "she had the commercial spirit that Mark lacked—and God knows he needed prodding once in a while," or that he sometimes feigned rheumatism to avoid working. It does not ring true or harmonize with the known facts.

CHAPTER V: LITERATURE AND LOVE

1. *Missouri Historical Review,* XXIV, 48.

2. The italics are mine. Note the careful qualifications. Such statements can be accepted at face value.

3. For the cut, *see* Caroline Ticknor's *Bookman* article. Cf. Bibliography.

4. *See* Mark Twain's letter to Mrs. Fairbanks (January 6, 1870), in which he describes the changes Livy has effected in him and concludes: "These reforms were calculated to make a man fractious and irritable, but bless you she has a way of instituting them that swindles one into the belief that she is doing him a *favor* instead of curtailing his freedom & doing him a fatal damage." MS., Huntington Library.

5. From a letter to Mrs. A. W. Fairbanks, April 23, 1875. MS., Huntington Library.

6. Mr. William R. Langfeld has an undated letter to Osgood, of which he has kindly sent me a copy: "Mrs. Clemens informs me that I am going to the Papyrus orgie. A remark of that sort, emanating from that quarter, has this resemblance to the moving of the previous question: it is not debatable."

7. From a letter to Mrs. A. W. Fairbanks, February 9, 1868. MS., Huntington Library.

8. Mr. Paine comments: "Not now, but you would have resented it 50 years ago, I think." Howells, of course, not Mrs. Clemens, was fundamentally responsible for this change.

9. Mr. Paine's fitting comment: "It would have been the worst possible taste to put them into one volume."

BOOK III: THE SAGE OF REDDING

CHAPTER I: CHARTS OF SALVATION

1. John Quarles was, indeed, given to untrammeled speculation on the problems of human destiny in a manner faintly prophetic of Mark Twain himself. *See* T. V. Bodine's article in Bibliography.

2. *My Mark Twain,* Pt. I, chap. 8.

3. *See* the testimony of Dr. C. C. Rice, in *Mentor,* XII (May, 1924), 48.

4. *Overland Monthly,* LXXXVII, 105.

5. Paine, III, 1407–1409, chap. 260.

CHAPTER II: HYMN TO DEATH

1. Mr. Paine writes the following comments on this paragraph: "It takes an optimist to be a speculator. Mark Twain, within ten days of his death, wanted to buy some stocks, for the rise which he believed would come." "He was really an optimist one day (or moment) and a pessimist the next." "One might say that he was impulsively an optimist and reflectively a pessimist."

2. Compare a more direct expression of this idea in a letter to Mrs. A. W. Fairbanks, June 3, 1876 (MS., Huntington Library):

"I received the Herald containing the news. What a curious thing life is. We delve away, through years of hard-ship, wasting toil, despondency; then comes a little butterfly season of wealth, ease, & clustering honors. Presto! the wife dies, a daughter marries a spendthrift villain, the heir & hope of the house commits suicide the laurels fade & fall away.

"Grand result of a hard-fought, successful career & a blameless life: Piles of money, tottering age, & a broken heart.

"My, how the disasters pour when they once begin! It does seem as if Mr. Benedict's case is about the ordinary experience, & must be fairly expected by everybody. And yet there are people who would try to save a baby's life & plenty of people who cry when a baby dies. In fact, all of us cry, but some are conscious of a deeper feeling of content, at the same time—*I* am at any rate."

3. Cf. Albert Schweitzer's autobiography, *Out of My Life and Thought* (New York, Henry Holt & Co., 1933).

CHAPTER III: TESTAMENT

1. Paine, I, 228–231, ch. 41.

2. Cf. *Following the Equator,* I, 247–248, chap. 27; II, 50–52, chap. 5.

3. Howells, p. 35.

4. Mark Twain's tendency to champion the underdog would seem to have failed him, however, in connection with the Goshoot Indians, whom he came in contact with in Nevada, and whom he denounced as "scum o' the earth," and of whom he declared that to exterminate them would be a charity "to the Creator's worthier insects and reptiles." He denounces as sentimentalists those who sympathize with the Indians and rejoices that "the inquiry has always got to come *after* the good officer has administered his little admonition." But it is clear that he hates the Indian for his cruelties to women and children. Cf. *Galaxy,* X (1870), 426–429; *Missouri Historical Review,* XXV (1930), 29.

5. Under these conditions, a writer *might*, of course, be attracted by those who had done what he failed to do; he might also be repelled by them and stay as far away from them as possible. Pepys was not outspoken in his own time; he confided his daring observations to his own system of shorthand.

6. *Mark Twain's America,* pp. 267–268.

7. Cf. *Letters,* II, 776.

8. Cf. Ludwig Lewisohn's interesting comments in this connection (*Expression in America,* pp. 225–226): "He sat down to develop out of his own head, like an adolescent, like a child, a theory to fit the facts as he seemed to see them, and the only influence discernible in his theory is that of Robert Ingersoll." "Mark Twain had no suspicion, apparently, of the existence of either anthropology or psychology, or any knowledge of the growth and function of *mores* and their connection with the totality of human development. He sought to solve problems which he did not know enough to state."

9. *Tennessee Historical Magazine,* ser. II, vol. I (July, 1931), 257–258.

10. In view of these facts, his slur at Samuel J. Tilden's Civil War record, when the latter was a candidate for the presidency, seems hardly in the best of taste. Cf. Paine, II, 581, chap. 108.

11. "The War Prayer" is included in *Europe and Elsewhere.* For the pageant, *see* Paine, III, 1149–1150, chap. 218.

12. *Gilded Age,* I, 180, chap. 18. This chapter, however, was written by Charles Dudley Warner.

13. *Letters,* II, 672.

14. Cyril Clemens, *Mark Twain and Mussolini,* p. 51.

BIBLIOGRAPHY

Bibliography

I. PRIMARY SOURCES

A. Bibliographies

Johnson, Merle. A Bibliography of the Work of Mark Twain. New York, Harper & Brothers, 1910.

Edwards, Mrs. Frances M., *ed.* Twainiana Notes from the Annotations of Walter Bliss. Hartford, Conn., The Hobby Shop, 1930.

Potter, John K. Samuel L. Clemens, First Editions and Values. Chicago, Black Archer Press, 1932.

Brownell, George Hiram. Mark Twain's First Published Literary Effort. *American Book Collector*, III (1933), 92–95.

Brownell, George Hiram. Mark Twainiana. *American Book Collector*, III (1933), 172–177, 207–212.

B. Writings of Mark Twain

1. The Uniform Trade Edition of the Writings of Mark Twain consists of the following volumes, published by Harper & Brothers, New York, under various imprints:

a. The Innocents Abroad.
b. Roughing It.
c. The Gilded Age (with Charles Dudley Warner).
d. Sketches New and Old.
e. The Adventures of Tom Sawyer.
f. A Tramp Abroad.
g. The Prince and the Pauper.
h. Life on the Mississippi.
i. The Adventures of Huckleberry Finn.
j. A Connecticut Yankee in King Arthur's Court.
k. Pudd'nhead Wilson *and* Those Extraordinary Twins.
l. Personal Recollections of Joan of Arc.
m. Tom Sawyer Abroad, Tom Sawyer Detective, and Other Stories.
n. Following the Equator.
o. In Defense of Harriet Shelley and Other Essays.
p. The Man That Corrupted Hadleyburg and Other Stories and Essays.
q. The $30,000 Bequest and Other Stories.
r. Christian Science.
s. What Is Man? and Other Essays.
t. The Mysterious Stranger and Other Stories.
u. Europe and Elsewhere.

2. The following volumes contain material not included in the Uniform Trade Edition:

The Curious Republic of Gondour, and Other Whimsical Sketches. New York, Boni & Liveright, 1919.

Sketches of the Sixties. By Bret Harte and Mark Twain. Being forgotten material now collected for the first time from *The Californian, 1864–1867*. San Francisco, John Howell, 1926.

The £1,000,000 Bank Note. New York, Harper & Brothers, 1917.

Fireside Conversation in 1601 at Ye Time of Queen Elizabeth. Being Number One of the Airedale Series. Privately published, 1925.

Slovenly Peter (Der Struwwelpeter). Translated into English Jingles from the Original German of Dr. Heinrich Hoffman by Mark Twain. New York, The Limited Editions Club, 1935.

The Choice Humorous Works of Mark Twain [etc.]. London, Chatto & Windus, 1912.

HONCE, CHARLES, *ed*. Adventures of Thomas Jefferson Snodgrass. With Foreword by Vincent Starrett and a Note on "A Celebrated Village Idiot," by James O'Donnell Bennett. New York, Covici Friede, 1928.

3. The following magazine articles have not been taken up into any collection:

Capable Humorist, A. *Harper's Weekly*, LIII (Feb. 20, 1909), 13.

Carl Schurz, Pilot. *Harper's Weekly*, L (1906), 727.

Carnegie Spelling Reform, The. *Harper's Weekly*, L (1906), 488.

Concerning Copyright. *North American Review*, CLXXX (1905), 1–18.

Czar's Soliloquy, The. *North American Review*, CLXXX (1905), 321–326.

Defence of General Funston, A. *North American Review*, CLXXIV (1902), 613–624.

Forty-Three Days in an Open Boat. *Harper's Magazine*, XXIV (1866), 104–113.

"From My Unpublished Autobiography." *Harper's Weekly*, XLIX (1905), 391. (The introductory letter was not reprinted in the book publication.)

Gift from India, A. *Critic*, XXVIII (1896), 285–286.

How I Secured a Berth. *Galaxy*, XI (1871), 285–286.

James Hammond Trumbull. *Century*, LV (1897), 154–155.

John Hay and the Ballads. *Harper's Weekly*, XLIX (1905), 1530.

Memoranda. *Galaxy*, IX (1870), 717–726, 858–867; X (1870), 133–141, 286–287, 424–432, 567–576, 726–735, 876–885; XI (1871), 150–159, 312–321.

Mrs. Eddy in Error. *North American Review*, CLXXVI (1903), 505–517.

Simplified Spelling. *Putnam's*, I (1906), 219–220.

Unbiased Art Criticism, An. *Californian*, March 18, 1865.

Wanted—a Universal Tinker. *Century*, N.S. IX (1885), 318. (Open Letter, signed X.Y.Z.)

Why Not Abolish It? *Harper's Weekly*, XLVII (1903), 732.

C. Autobiography

Mark Twain's Autobiography. With an Introduction by Albert Bigelow Paine. 2 vols. New York, Harper & Brothers, 1924.

D. Letters

Mark Twain's Letters. Arranged with Comment by Albert Bigelow Paine. 2 vols. New York, Harper & Brothers, 1917.

Mark Twain for Jerome. *Harper's Weekly*, LXIX (1905), 1238.

Letter to Samuel Hopkins Adams on Quackery. *Collier's*, XXXVII (Sept. 22, 1906), 16–17.

Letter about the Japanese Schoolboy. *Collier's*, XLI (August 8, 1908), 22.

Letter to George Harvey congratulating *Harper's Weekly* on its editorials concerning the inauguration of President Taft. *Harper's Weekly,* L (March 27, 1909), 6.

Letter to the editor of the *Spectator* concerning John C. Hotten. *Bookman* (New York), XXXIII (1911), 114–115.

Letters Young Mark Twain Wrote in 1857. *Kansas City Star Magazine,* March 21, 1926. (Letters to Annie Taylor.)

Some Unpublished Letters by Mark Twain. *Overland Monthly,* LXXXVII (1929), 115, 122, 124.

DE CASSERES, BENJAMIN. When Huck Finn Went Highbrow. New York, Thomas F. Madigan, Inc., 1934.

Letters to Mrs. A. W. Fairbanks and others. MS. Henry E. Huntington Library, San Marino, California.

E. Speeches

Mark Twain's Speeches. With an Introduction by William Dean Howells. New York, Harper & Brothers, 1910.

F. The Authorized Biography

PAINE, ALBERT BIGELOW. Mark Twain: A Biography. The Personal and Literary Life of Samuel Langhorne Clemens. 3 vols. New York, Harper & Brothers, 1912.

II. SUPPLEMENTARY SOURCES

ABBOTT, KEENE. Tom Sawyer's Town. *Harper's Weekly,* LVII (August 9, 1913), 16–17.

ADE, GEORGE. Mark Twain as Our Emissary. *Century,* LXXXI (1910), 204–206.

ALDRICH, MRS. THOMAS BAILEY. Crowding Memories. Boston, Houghton Mifflin Co., 1920.

American Academy of Arts and Letters. Public Meeting under the Auspices of the Academy and the National Institute of Arts and Letters Held at Carnegie Hall, New York, November 3, 1910, in Memory of S. L. Clemens. New York, The Academy, 1922.

ARMSTRONG, C. J. Mark Twain's Early Writings Discovered. *Missouri Historical Review,* XXIV (1930), 485–501.

BARR, ROBERT. Samuel L. Clemens, "Mark Twain," A Character Sketch. *McClure's Magazine,* X (1898), 246–251.

BARRUS, CLARA. The Life and Letters of John Burroughs. Vol. II. Boston, Houghton Mifflin Co., 1925.

BAY, J. CHRISTIAN. Tom Sawyer Detective: The Origin of the Plot. In: Essays Offered to Herbert Putnam by His Colleagues and Friends on His Thirtieth Anniversary as Librarian of Congress, 5 April, 1929. New Haven, Yale University Press, 1929.

BEARD, DAN. Mark Twain as a Neighbor. *American Review of Reviews,* XLI (1910), 705–709.

BLANKENSHIP, RUSSELL. American Literature as an Expression of the National Mind. New York, Henry Holt & Company, 1931.

BODINE, T. V. A Journey to the Home of Mark Twain. *Kansas City Star Magazine,* May 19, 1912.

Bok, Edward. The Americanization of Edward Bok. New York, Charles Scribner's Sons, 1920.

Bookman, The. (New York.) Mark Twain number. Vol. XXXI (June, 1910).

Bradford, Gamaliel. American Portraits, 1875–1900. Boston, Houghton Mifflin Co., 1922.

Brashear, Minnie M. Formative Influences in the Mind and Writings of Mark Twain. Thesis, Ph.D., University of North Carolina, 1930.

—— Mark Twain Juvenilia. American Literature, II (1930), 25–53.

—— Mark Twain, Son of Missouri. Chapel Hill, University of North Carolina Press, 1934.

Brooks, Sidney. Mark Twain in England. Harper's Weekly, LI (1907), 1053–1054.

—— England's Ovation to Mark Twain. Harper's Weekly, LI (1907), 1086–1089.

Brooks, Van Wyck. The Ordeal of Mark Twain. New York, E. P. Dutton & Co., 1920 and London, J. M. Dent, Ltd.

Buxbaum, Katherine. Mark Twain and American Dialect. American Speech, II (1927), 233–236.

Canby, Henry Seidel. Mark Twain. Literary Review, IV (1923), 201–202.

Carnegie, Andrew. The Autobiography of Andrew Carnegie. Boston, Houghton Mifflin Co., 1920.

Chapman, John W. The Germ of a Book: A Footnote on Mark Twain. Atlantic Monthly, CL (1932), 720–721.

Cheiro. Fate in the Making. Revelations of a Lifetime. New York, Harper & Brothers, 1931.

Churchill, Winston S. A Roving Commission. My Early Life. New York, Charles Scribner's Sons, 1930.

Clark, Champ. My Quarter Century of American Politics. Vol. II. New York, Harper & Brothers, 1920.

Clemens, Clara. My Father Mark Twain. New York, Harper & Brothers, 1931.

Clemens, Cyril. Mark Twain and Mussolini. Webster Groves, Missouri, International Mark Twain Society, 1934.

—— Mark Twain Anecdotes. Webster Groves, Missouri, Mark Twain Society, 1929.

—— Mark Twain the Letter Writer. Boston, Meador Publishing Co., 1932.

—— The True Character of Mark Twain's Wife. Missouri Historical Review, XXIV (1929), 40–49.

Clemens, J. R. Some Reminiscences of Mark Twain. Overland Monthly, LXXXVII (1929), 102.

Clemens, Mildred Leo. Trailing Mark Twain Through Hawaii. Sunset, XXXVIII (May, 1917), 7–9, 95–98.

Clemens, Will M. Mark Twain: His Life and Work. San Francisco, The Clemens Publishing Co., 1892.

Compton, Charles H. Who Reads Mark Twain? American Mercury, XXXI (1934), 465–471.

Conway, Moncure D. Autobiography, Memories, and Experiences of Moncure Daniel Conway. Vol. II. Boston, Houghton Mifflin & Co., 1904.

Cooper, Lane. Mark Twain's Lilacs and Laburnums. Modern Language Notes, XLVII (1932), 85–87.

Corey, William Alfred. Memories of Mark Twain. Overland Monthly, LXVI (1915), 263–265.

Cortissoz, Royal. The Life of Whitelaw Reid. 2 vols. New York, Charles Scribner's Sons, 1921.

Cournos, John. A Modern Plutarch. Indianapolis, The Bobbs-Merrill Co., 1928.

CROTHERS, SAMUEL McCHORD. The Hibernation of Genius. In: The Dame School of Experience and Other Papers. Boston, Houghton Mifflin Co., 1920.

DALY, JOSEPH FRANCIS. The Life of Augustin Daly. New York, The Macmillan Co., 1917.

DAM, HENRY J. W. A Morning with Bret Harte. *McClure's Magazine,* IV (1894), 38–50.

DEPEW, CHAUNCEY M. My Memories of Eighty Years. New York, Charles Scribner's Sons, 1922.

DeQUILLE, DAN. Reporting with Mark Twain. *Californian Illustrated Magazine,* IV (1893), 170–178.

DEVOTO, BERNARD. Mark Twain's America. Boston, Little, Brown & Co., 1932.

DONOVAN, M. M. Custodian of a Famous Cabin. *Sunset,* LVII (September, 1926), 47.

DREW, JOHN. My Years on the Stage. New York, E. P. Dutton & Co., 1922.

EGGLESTON, GEORGE CARY. Recollections of a Varied Life. New York, Henry Holt & Co., 1910.

ELLSWORTH, WILLIAM WEBSTER. A Golden Age of Authors. Boston, Houghton Mifflin Co., 1919.

FAIRBANKS, MARY MASON. The Cruise of the "Quaker City." With Chance Recollections of Mark Twain. *Chautauquan,* XIV (1892), 429–432.

FEDERICO, P. J. Mark Twain as an Inventor. *Journal of the Patent Office Society,* VIII (1925), 75–79.

FIELDER, ELIZABETH DAVIS. Familiar Haunts of Mark Twain. *Harper's Weekly,* XLIII (1898), 1258–1259.

FISHER, HENRY W. Abroad with Mark Twain and Eugene Field. Tales They Told to a Fellow-Correspondent. New York, Nicholas L. Brown, 1922.

FRANK, WALDO. Our America. New York, Boni & Liveright, 1919.

GARLAND, HAMLIN. Companions on the Trail. A Literary Chronicle. New York, The Macmillan Co., 1931.

—— Roadside Meetings of a Literary Nomad. *Bookman* (New York), LXXI (1930), 423–434.

GILLIS, WILLIAM R. Gold Rush Days with Mark Twain. New York, Albert and Charles Boni, 1930.

—— Memories of Mark Twain and Steve Gillis. Sonora, California, The Banner, 1924. (Contents practically identical with Gold Rush Days with Mark Twain.)

GODDARD, HENRY P. Anecdotes of Mark Twain. *Harper's Weekly,* L (1906), 280.

GOODPASTURE, A. V. Mark Twain, Southerner. *Tennessee Historical Magazine,* Ser. II, Vol. I (July, 1931), 253–260.

GOODWIN, C. C. As I Remember Them. Salt Lake City, Salt Lake Commercial Club, 1913.

GRATTAN, C. HARTLEY. Mark Twain. In: American Writers on American Literature, *ed.* by John Macy. New York, Horace Liveright, Inc., 1931.

GREENSLET, FERRIS. The Life of Thomas Bailey Aldrich. Boston, Houghton Mifflin Co., 1908.

HAPGOOD, NORMAN. The Changing Years. New York, Farrar & Rinehart, 1930.

HARPER, J. HENRY. I Remember. New York, Harper & Brothers, 1934.

HARRIS, FRANK. Contemporary Portraits. 4th ser. New York, Brentano's, 1923.

HARRIS, JULIA COLLIER. The Life and Letters of Joel Chandler Harris. Boston, Houghton Mifflin Co., 1918.

HAWEIS, H. R. American Humorists. 3d ed. London, Chatto & Windus, 1890.

HAWTHORNE, JULIAN. Mark Twain as I Knew Him. *Overland Monthly,* LXXXVII (1929), 111, 128.

HAZARD, LUCY LOCKWOOD. The Frontier in American Literature. New York, Thomas Y. Crowell Co., 1927.

HENDERSON, ARCHIBALD. Mark Twain. London, Duckworth & Co., 1911.

HEWLETT, MAURICE. Mark on Sir Walter. *Sewanee Review*, XXIX (1921), 130–133.

HIGGINSON, MARY THACHER. Letters and Journals of Thomas Wentworth Higginson, 1846–1906. Boston, Houghton Mifflin Co., 1921.

HOLLISTER, WILFRED R., and NORMAN, HARRY. Five Famous Missourians. Kansas City, Missouri, Hudson-Kimberly Publishing Co., 1900.

HOLMES, RALPH. Mark Twain and Music. *Century*, CIV (1922), 844–850.

HOLT, HENRY. Garrulities of an Octogenarian Editor. Boston, Houghton Mifflin Co., 1923.

HOPPE, WILLIE. Thirty Years of Billiards. New York, G. P. Putnam's Sons, 1925.

HOWE, M. A. DEWOLFE. Memories of a Hostess. Boston, The Atlantic Monthly Press, 1922.

HOWELLS, MILDRED, *ed.* Life in Letters of William Dean Howells. 2 vols. Garden City, Doubleday, Doran & Co., Inc., 1928.

—— HOWELLS, WILLIAM DEAN. My Mark Twain. Reminiscences and Criticisms. New York, Harper & Brothers, 1911.

HUGHES, ROBERT M. A Deserter's Tale. *Virginia Magazine of History and Biography*, XXXIX (1931), 21–28.

HUTTON, LAURENCE. Talks in a Library. New York, G. P. Putnam's Sons, 1905.

HYSLOP, JAMES H. Contact with the Other World. New York, The Century Co., 1919.

JAMES, GEORGE WHARTON. Mark Twain and the Pacific Coast. *Pacific Monthly*, XXIV (1910), 115–134.

JAMES, HENRY, *ed.* The Letters of William James. 2 vols. Boston, The Atlantic Monthly Press, 1920.

JOHNSON, ROBERT UNDERWOOD. Remembered Yesterdays. Boston, Little, Brown & Co., 1923.

JOSEPHSON, MATTHEW. Portrait of the Artist as American. New York, Harcourt, Brace & Co., 1930.

KELLER, HELEN. Midstream, My Later Life. Garden City, Doubleday, Doran & Co., Inc., 1929.

—— The Story of My Life. New York, Doubleday, Page & Co., 1903.

KEMBLE, E. W. Illustrating Huckleberry Finn. *The Colophon*, Pt. I, 1930.

KING, GRACE. Memories of a Southern Woman of Letters. New York, The Macmillan Co., 1932.

KIPLING, RUDYARD. From Sea to Sea, Letters of Travel, Pt. II. (The Writings in Prose and Verse of Rudyard Kipling, Vol. XIV.) New York, Charles Scribner's Sons, 1925.

KITTON, FREDERIC G. Charles Dickens by Pen and Pencil. London, Frank T. Sabin and John F. Dexter, 1889.

KITTREDGE, HERMAN E. Ingersoll, A Biographical Appreciation. New York, The Dresden Publishing Co., 1911.

LAROM, WALTER H. Mark Twain in the Adirondacks. *Bookman* (New York), LVIII (1924), 536–538.

LAWTON, MARY. A Lifetime with Mark Twain. The Memories of Katy Leary, for Thirty Years his Faithful and Devoted Servant. New York, Harcourt, Brace & Co., 1925.

LEACOCK, STEPHEN. Mark Twain. New York, D. Appleton & Co., 1933.

—— Mark Twain and Canada. *Queen's Quarterly*, XLII (1935), 68–81.

—— Two Humorists: Charles Dickens and Mark Twain. *Yale Review*, XXIV (1934), 118–129.

LEWIS, OSCAR. The Origin of the Celebrated Jumping Frog of Calaveras County. San Francisco, The Book Club of California, 1931.

LEWISOHN, LUDWIG. Expression in America. New York, Harper & Brothers, 1932.

LORCH, FRED W. Lecture Trips and Visits of Mark Twain in Iowa. *Iowa Journal of History and Politics*, XXVII (1929), 507–547.

—— Mark Twain in Iowa. *Iowa Journal of History and Politics*, XXVII (1929), 408–456.

—— A Mark Twain Letter. *Iowa Journal of History and Politics*, XXVIII (1930), 268–276.

—— A Source for Mark Twain's "The Dandy Frightening the Squatter." *American Literature*, III (1931), 309–313.

—— The Tradition, Molly Clemens's Note Book, Literary Apprenticeship, Adrift for Heresy, The Closing Years. *The Palimpsest*, X (1929), 353–386.

LYMAN, GEORGE D. The Saga of the Comstock Lode. New York, Charles Scribner's Sons, 1934.

LYNCH, DENIS TILDEN. Grover Cleveland, A Man Four-Square. New York, Horace Liveright, Inc., 1932.

MABBOTT, T. O. Mark Twain's Artillery, A Mark Twain Legend. *Missouri Historical Review*, XXV (1930), 23–69.

MACARTHUR, JAMES. Books and Bookmen. *Harper's Weekly*, XLVIII (1904), 753.

McCALL, SAMUEL W. The Life of Thomas Brackett Reed. Boston, Houghton Mifflin Co., 1914.

MACY, JOHN. The Spirit of American Literature. Garden City, Doubleday, Page & Co., 1913.

MASON, LAURENS D. Real People in Mark Twain's Stories. *Overland Monthly*, LXXXIX (1931), 12–13, 27.

MATTHEWS, BRANDER. Memories of Mark Twain. In: The Tocsin of Revolt and Other Essays. New York, Charles Scribner's Sons, 1922.

Mentor, The. Mark Twain number. Vol. XII, no. 4 (May, 1924).

MERRILL, W. H. When Mark Twain Lectured. *Harper's Weekly*, L (1906), 199, 209.

MEYER, HAROLD. Mark Twain on the Comstock. *Southwest Review*, XII (1927), 197–207.

MIEROW, HUBERT EDWARD. Cicero and Mark Twain. *Classical Journal*, XX (1924–25), 167–169.

MILLARD, BAILEY. When They Were Twenty-One. *Bookman* (New York), XXXVII (1913), 296–304.

Millicent Library. Mark Twain and Fairhaven. Fairhaven, Mass., Millicent Library, 1913.

MOORE, OLIN HARRIS. Mark Twain and Don Quixote. *Publications of the Modern Language Association*, XXXVII (1922), 324–346.

MUMFORD, LEWIS. The Golden Day. New York, Boni & Liveright, 1926.

—— "Prophet, Pedant, and Pioneer." *Saturday Review of Literature*, IX (1933), 573–575.

O'HIGGINS, HARVEY, and REEDE, EDWARD H. The American Mind in Action. New York, Harper & Brothers, 1924.

PAINE, ALBERT BIGELOW. The Boys' Life of Mark Twain. New York, Harper & Brothers, 1916.

—— Innocents at Home. *Collier's*, LXXV (January 3, 1925), 5–6, 45.

—— Mark Twain at Stormfield. *Harper's Weekly*, CXVIII (1909), 955–958.

—— A Short Life of Mark Twain. New York, Harper & Brothers, 1920.

—— Th. Nast, His Period and His Pictures. New York, The Macmillan Co., 1904.

PARRINGTON, VERNON LOUIS. Main Currents in American Thought. Vol. III. New York, Harcourt, Brace & Co., 1930.

PARTINGTON, WILFRED. Mark Twain—in Love, in Anger, and in Bibliography. *Bookman* (New York), LXXVI (1933), 313–324, III–IV.

PATTEE, FRED LEWIS. Mark Twain (Samuel Langhorne Clemens). Representative Selections, with Introduction and Bibliography. ("American Writers Series.") New York, American Book Co., 1935.

—— On the Rating of Mark Twain. *American Mercury*, XIV (1928), 183–191.

PECKHAM, H. HOUSTON. The Literary Status of Mark Twain, 1877–1890. *South Atlantic Quarterly*, XIX (1920), 332–340.

PEMBERTON, T. EDGAR. Life of Bret Harte. London, C. Arthur Pearson, 1903.

PENNELL, ELIZABETH ROBINS. Charles Godfrey Leland: A Biography. Vol. II. Boston, Houghton Mifflin & Co., 1906.

PHELPS, WILLIAM LYON. Essays on Books. New York, The Macmillan Co., 1914.

—— Essays on Modern Novelists. New York, The Macmillan Co., 1910.

—— ed. Letters of James Whitcomb Riley. Indianapolis, The Bobbs-Merrill Co., 1930.

—— The Real Mark Twain. *Scribner's Magazine*, XCIII (1933), 182–183.

PHILLIPS, MICHAEL J. Mark Twain's Partner. *Saturday Evening Post*, CXCII (September 11, 1920), 22–23, 69–70, 73–74.

POCHMANN, HENRY A. The Mind of Mark Twain. Thesis, M.A., University of Texas, 1924.

POND, J. B. Eccentricities of Genius. Memories of Famous Men and Women of the Platform and Stage. New York, G. W. Dillingham Co., 1900.

RASCOE, BURTON. Titans of Literature, from Homer to the Present Day. New York, G. P. Putnam's Sons, 1932.

RIDEING, WILLIAM H. Many Celebrities and a Few Others. Garden City, Doubleday, Page & Co., 1912.

—— Mark Twain in Clubland. *Bookman* (New York), XXXI (1910), 379–382.

ROADES, SISTER MARY TERESA. Cervantes and Mark Twain. Thesis, M.A., University of Kansas, 1926.

ROSEWATER, VICTOR. How a Boy Secured a Unique Autograph of Mark Twain. *St. Nicholas*, XLIII (1916), 415.

ROURKE, CONSTANCE M. American Humour. New York, Harcourt, Brace & Co., 1931.

SCHÖNEMANN, FRIEDRICH. Mark Twain als literarische Persönlichkeit. Jena, Verlag der Frommanschen Buchhandlung (Walter Biedermann), 1925.

—— Mark Twain and Adolf Wilbrandt. *Modern Language Notes*, XXXIV (1919), 372–374.

—— Mark Twain's Weltanschauung. *Englische Studien*, LV (1921), 53–84.

—— Mr. Samuel Langhorne Clemens. *Archiv*, CXLIV (1923), 184–213.

SCOTT, HAROLD P. Mark Twain's Theory of Humor: An Analysis of the Laughable in Literature. Thesis, Ph.D., University of Michigan, n.d.

SEDGWICK, HENRY DWIGHT. The New American Type. Boston, Houghton Mifflin Co., 1908.

SHERMAN, STUART. The Main Stream. New York, Charles Scribner's Sons, 1927.

—— Mark Twain. In: The Cambridge History of American Literature. Vol. III. New York, G. P. Putnam's Sons, 1921.

—— Mark Twain. *Nation*, XC (1910), 477–480.

—— On Contemporary Literature. New York, Henry Holt & Co., 1917.

SHUSTER, GEORGE NAUMAN. The Tragedy of Mark Twain. *Catholic World*, CIV (1917), 731–737.

SIMBOLI, RAFFAELE. Mark Twain from an Italian Point of View. *Critic*, XLIV (1904), 518–524.

SMITH, ANNELLA. Mark Twain—Occultist. *Rosicrucian Magazine*, XXVI (1934), 65–68.

SOSEY, FRANK H. Palmyra and Its Historical Environment. *Missouri Historical Review*, XXIII (1929), 361–379.

STEDMAN, LUCY, and GOULD, GEORGE M. Life and Letters of Edmund Clarence Stedman. 2 vols. New York, Moffat, Yard & Co., 1910.

STEWART, GEORGE R., JR. Bret Harte, Argonaut and Exile. Boston, Houghton Mifflin Co., 1931.

STEWART, WILLIAM M. Reminiscences of Senator William M. Stewart of Nevada. *Ed.* by George Rothwell Brown. The Neale Publishing Co., 1908.

STOCKTON, FRANK R. Mark Twain and His Recent Works. *Forum*, XV (1893), 673–679.

STODDARD, C. W. Exits and Entrances. Boston, Lothrop Publishing Co., 1903.

—— In Old Bohemia, II. The "Overland" and the Overlanders. *Pacific Monthly*, XIX (1908), 261–273.

STODDART, ALEXANDER McD. "Twainiana." *Independent*, LXVIII (1910), 960–963.

STRATE, JESSIE B. Mark Twain and Geography. *Journal of Geography*, XXIII (1924), 81–92.

TICKNOR, CAROLINE. Mark Twain's Missing Chapter. *Bookman* (New York), XXXIX (1914), 298–309.

TRENT, W. P. Mark Twain as an Historical Novelist. *Bookman* (New York), III (1896), 207–210.

TWICHELL, JOSEPH H. Mark Twain. *Harper's Magazine*, XCII (1896), 817–827.

UNDERHILL, IRVING S. Diamonds in the Rough. Being the Story of Another Book that Mark Twain Never Wrote. *The Colophon*, Pt. XIII (1923).

VALE, CHARLES. Mark Twain as an Orator. *Forum*, XLIV (1910), 1–13.

VAN DOREN, CARL. The American Novel. New York, The Macmillan Co., 1921.

—— Mark Twain and Bernard Shaw. *Century*, CIX (1925), 705–710.

WALLACE, ELIZABETH. Mark Twain and the Happy Island. Chicago, A. C. McClurg & Co., 1913.

WATTERSON, HENRY. Marse Henry. An Autobiography. Vol. I. New York, George H. Doran, 1919.

WEBSTER, DORIS and SAMUEL. Whitewashing Jane Clemens. *Bookman* (New York), LXI (1925), 531–535.

WELLS, CAROLYN. "An Item of Interest." *New York American* (Sept. 19, 1933).

WEST, VICTOR ROYCE. Folklore in the Works of Mark Twain. *University of Nebraska Studies in Language, Literature, and Criticism*, No. 10, 1930.

WHARTON, HENRY M. The Boyhood Home of Mark Twain. *Century*, LXIV (1902), 675–677.

WHEELER, CANDACE. Yesterdays in a Busy Life. New York, Harper & Brothers, 1918.

WHITE, EDGAR. Mark Twain's Printer Days. *Overland Monthly*, N.S., LXX (1917), 573–576.

WHITE, FRANK MARSHALL. Mark Twain as a Newspaper Reporter. *Outlook*, XCVI (1910), 961–967.

WHITMAN, SIDNEY. Things I Remember. London, Cassell & Co., Ltd., 1916.

WIGGIN, KATE DOUGLAS. My Garden of Memory. Boston, Houghton Mifflin Co., 1923.

WILDMAN, EDWIN. Mark Twain's Pets. *St. Nicholas*, XXVI (1899), 185–188.

WILSON, FRANCIS. Francis Wilson's Life of Himself. Boston, Houghton Mifflin Co., 1924.

WINTERICH, JOHN T. The Life and Works of Bloodgood Haviland Cutter. *The Colophon*, Pt. II (1930).

WOODBRIDGE, HOMER E. Mark Twain and the "Gesta Romanorum." *Nation*, CVIII (1919), 424–425.

WOOLF, S. J. Painting the Portrait of Mark Twain. *Collier's*, XLV (May 14, 1910), 42–44.

YATES, EDMUND. Celebrities at Home. 3d ser. London, Office of "The World," 1879.

Unsigned Articles

The Anecdotal Side of Mark Twain. *Ladies' Home Journal*, XV (October, 1898), 5–6.

Further Anecdotes of Mark Twain. *Harper's Weekly*, L (1906), 421.

In School with Becky Thatcher and Tom Sawyer. *Literary Digest*, C (March 9, 1929), 60, 62, 63, 64.

Mark Twain as a Reader. (M.B.C.). *Harper's Weekly*, LV (1911), 6.

Mark Twain's Childhood Sweetheart Recalls Their Romance. *Literary Digest*, LVI (March 23, 1918), 70, 73–75.

Mark Twain's Investments. *Collier's*, XLVI (November 12, 1910), 32.

Mark Twain's New Deal. *Saturday Review of Literature*, X (1933), 352.

Mark Twain's Private Girls' Club. *Ladies' Home Journal*, XXIX (February, 1912), 23, 54.

Mark Twain's Seventieth Birthday—Souvenir of Its Celebration. *Harper's Weekly*, XLIX (1905), 1883–1914.

One Who Didn't Like Mark Twain. *Literary Digest*, XLV (1912), 1014–1015.

The Originals of Some of Mark Twain's Characters. *American Review of Reviews*, XLII (1910), 228–230.

Stormfield, Mark Twain's New Country Home. *Country Life in America*, XV (1909), 607–611, 650, 652.

Two Etymologies. *Word-Study*, IX (November, 1933), 5–6.

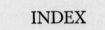

INDEX

Index

those which draw upon memories of his early life, 61–62. His hesitant approach to the writer's life, 63; his attitude toward himself as a man of letters, 63–64; his inability to judge his own work, 64–65; on *Tom Sawyer* and *Huckleberry Finn,* 65–66; on *Joan of Arc,* 66. Yet he has faith in his work, 66–68; his love of praise, 68; not always true to his art but fundamentally a man of letters, 68–69. Van Wyck Brooks on *M.T.'s* humor, 69–70; his humor interwoven with the very quality of his mind, 70–71; but he is not merely a humorist, 71–72; element of perversity in his attitude toward humor, 72; recognition of its power, 72; always feels need of improvement, 72–73. Never developed a critical theory, 73–74; disliked naturalism, 74; did not write for cultivated classes, 74; interested in technical aspects of style, 74–76. As poet and dramatist, 76–77. Habits as an author, 78; relations with publishers, illustrators, etc., 178–180.

His personal appearance, 83–87; his clothes, 87–88. His physical health, 88–89; his nervousness, 89; his abnormal sensitiveness to sound, 90–91. His food and drink, 91–93; his use of tobacco, 93–94. His essential youthfulness, 94–97. His temper, 97–100; his profanity, 100–102; his anger and resentment, 102–104. His energy, 104–108. His ambition, 108–112; his memory, 109; his independence of spirit, 111–112. His faith in education, 112–113; his own learning, in history, 114–115; in science and mathematics, 115–116; in languages, 116–117; his care in documentation, 117; the quality of his thinking, 117–118; his ignorance not necessarily a handicap as a creative writer, 118–120. His bawdry, 120–124. His antiromanticism, 125–126; his modernism, his glorying in material progress, 126–127; some problems and paradoxes suggested by this, 127–130. His attitude toward himself, 131; enjoys being a celebrity, 132; fundamentally modest, 133–134. Always the

king-figure in his group, 134–135; prefers monologue to conversation, 135–136; all this indicates eagerness rather than egoism, 136; absorbed in his own ideas, 136–137; thoughtfulness toward others, 137–138.

His contempt for humanity in the abstract, 139; his tenderness toward individuals, 139–140; his "reverence for life," 140–141. His dependence upon human companionship, 141–142; his social life, 142–143; his indifference to sports, 143–144; his attitude toward indoor amusements, 144–145; his disregard of convention, 145; his occasional sentimentality, 145–146

His attitude toward women, 146–148. His love of children, 148–150. His relations with his servants, 150–151. His love of cats and other animals, 151–154

His attitude toward money, 156–157. Interested in the economic aspects of literature, 157–158. His extravagance, 158–161. His speculations, 161–162; as a business man, 162–163. The visionary quality in his adventures with money, 163–164; his scrupulous honesty, 164–165

His relations with his wife, 166–185

His early religious training, 189; revolt against it, 199–200; his attitude toward the church, 191; charge of irreverence considered, 191–192; his association with clergymen, especially J. H. Twichell, 192–195; formal religious exercises in early married life, 195–196. His superstition, 196–197; his interest in psychic phenomena, 198–204. His conception of God, 204–206; his attitude toward Jesus, 206–207; his interest in Satan, 207–208; his attitude toward prayer, 208–209; as biblical critic, 209; interest in life after death, 209–210; his respect for religious belief he cannot share, 211; his attitude toward Roman Catholic Church, 211–212; rejected Christian theology but not the Christian ethic, 212–213. Unable to throw off inherited Calvinism, 213–216; his determinism an inverted Calvinism, 216–217; influ-